3 ★ All-Star

Linda Lee ★ **Kristin Sherman**

Stephen Sloan ★ **Grace Tanaka** ★ **Shirley Velasco**

McGraw-Hill

All-Star 3 1st Edition

Published by McGraw-Hill ESL/ELT, a business unit of The McGraw-Hill Companies, Inc. 1221 Avenue of the Americas, New York, NY 10020. Copyright © 2005 by The McGraw-Hill Companies, Inc. All rights reserved. No part of this publication may be reproduced or distributed in any form or by any means, or stored in a database or retrieval system, without the prior written consent of The McGraw-Hill Companies, Inc., including, but not limited to, in any network or other electronic storage or transmission, or broadcast for distance learning.

ISBN 978-0-07-284679-9
MHID 0-07-284679-8 (Student Book)
5 6 7 8 9 10   QPD   09 08 07

ISBN 978-0-07-322341-4
MHID 0-07-322341-7 (Student Book with Audio Highlights)
 7 8 9 10   QPD   09 08

ISBN 978-0-07-111545-2
MHID 0-07-111545-5 (International Student Edition)
1 2 3 4 5 6 7 8 9 10   QPD   09 08 07 06 05 04

Editorial director Tina B. Carver
Executive editor Erik Gundersen
Director of sales and marketing Thomas P. Dare
Developmental editors Jennifer Monaghan, Terre Passero
Production manager Juanita Thompson
Interior designer Wee Design Group
Cover designer Wee Design Group
Illustrators Burgundy Beam, Andrew Lange, Rich Stergulz, Carlotta Tormey
Photo Research David Averbach, Tobi Zausner

ACKNOWLEDGEMENTS

The authors and publisher would like to thank the following individuals who reviewed the *All-Star* program at various stages of development and whose comments, reviews, and field-testing were instrumental in helping us shape the series:

Carol Antunano • The English Center; Miami, FL

Feliciano Atienza • YMCA Elesair Project; New York, NY

Nancy Baxer • Lutheran Social Ministries of New Jersey Refugee Resettlement Program; Trenton, NJ

Jeffrey P. Bright • Albany Park Community Center; Chicago, IL

Enzo Caserta • Miami Palmetto Adult Education Center; Miami, FL

Allison Freiman • YMCA Elesair Project; New York, NY

Susan Gaer • Santa Ana College School of Continuing Education; Santa Ana, CA

Toni Galaviz • Reseda Community Adult School; Reseda, CA

Maria Hegarty • SCALE; Somerville, MA

Virginia Hernandez • Miami Palmetto Adult Education Center; Miami, FL

Giang Hoang • Evans Community Adult School; Los Angeles, CA

Edwina Hoffman • Miami-Dade County Adult Schools; Miami, FL

Ionela Istrate • YMCA of Greater Boston International Learning Center; Boston, MA

Janice Jensen • Santa Ana College School of Continuing Education; Santa Ana, CA

Jan Jerrell • San Diego Community College District; San Diego, CA

Margaret Kirkpatrick • Berkeley Adult School; Berkeley, CA

LaRanda Marr • Oakland Unified School District; Office of Adult Education; Oakland, CA

Patricia Mooney-Gonzalez • New York State Department of Education; Albany, NY

Paula Orias • Piper Community School; Broward County Public Schools; Sunrise, FL

Linda O'Roke • City College of San Francisco; San Francisco, CA

Betsy Parrish • Hamline University; St. Paul, MN

Mary Pierce • Xavier Adult School; New York, NY

Marta Pitt • Lindsey Hopkins Technical Education Center; Miami, FL

Donna Price-Machado • San Diego Community College District; San Diego, CA

Sylvia Ramirez • Community Learning Center; MiraCosta College; Oceanside, CA

Inna Reydel • YMCA of Greater Boston International Learning Center; Boston, MA

Leslie Shimazaki • San Diego Community College District; San Diego, CA

Betty Stone • SCALE; Somerville, MA

Theresa Suslov • SCALE; Somerville, MA

Dave VanLew • Simi Valley Adult & Career Institute; Simi Valley, CA

Scope and Sequence

Civics Concepts	Math Skills	CASAS Life Skill Competencies	SCANS Competencies (Workplace)	EFF Content Standards	Literacy Completion Points (LCPs)
		• 0.1.2, 0.1.4, 0.2.1, 0.2.4, 7.2.3, 7.4.6	• Decision making • Sociability • Knowing how to learn	• Communicate so that others understand • Reflect on and reevaluate opinions and ideas	• 56.01, 56.02, 66.01, 66.03
• Identify educational opportunities and research education/training requirements to achieve personal goals • Interact with school system regarding child's education • Identify ways to prepare for citizenship exam • Learn about Pell grants		• **1**: 0.1.2, 0.2.1, 0.2.4, 7.2.4, 7.5.1, 7.5.5 • **2**: 7.1.1, 7.1.2, 7.2.1, 7.3.4, 7.4.2 • **3**: 0.1.6, 7.2.1, 7.4.2 • **4**: 4.1.7, 4.4.1, 4.4.2, 7.1.1, 7.2.1, 7.4.2, 7.5.1 • **5**: 7.2.4 • **6**: 0.2.4, 4.1.9, 7.1.1, 7.5.1 • **7**: 7.1.4, 7.4.7, 7.4.8 • **RS**: 7.4.1 • **WS**: 7.2.6, 7.3.4, 7.4.2, 7.4.8	Emphasized are the following: • Reasoning • See things in the mind's eye • Know how to learn • Organize and maintain information • Problem solving • Self-management • Decision making • Creative thinking	Emphasized are the following: • Participate in group processes and decision making • Create vision of future • Plan and renew career goals • Pursue personal self-improvement • Reflect on and reevaluate opinions and ideas • Develop a sense of self that reflects your values	• **1**: 56.02, 65.02, 66.06, 67.06 • **2**: 52.01, 52.02, 65.01, 66.07, 66.13 • **3**: 52.01, 66.01, 66.02, 66.07 • **4**: 56.02, 66.02, 66.05, 66.06, 66.07 • **5**: 66.05, 67.02 • **6**: 52.01, 56.01, 66.05, 66.07, 68.03 • **7**: 66.01, 66.08, 66.19 • **RS**: 66.12, 66.19 • **WS**: 66.08, 67.06
• Understand how to look for housing • Understand the Fair Housing Act	• Calculate housing costs	• **1**: 0.1.2, 1.4.1, 7.2.3, 7.2.5, 7.2.7, 7.4.2, 7.4.8, 7.5.1 • **2**: 0.1.2, 1.4.1, 1.4.2, 7.2.3, 7.3.4, 7.4.3 • **3**: 0.1.2, 0.1.3, 0.1.6, 1.4.7, 7.2.1, 7.2.6, 7.3.1, 7.3.2, 7.4.2, 8.2.6 • **4**: 1.4.3, 1.4.5, 5.3.1, 7.2.3, 7.3.4, 7.4.1, 7.4.2, 7.4.3 • **5**: 7.2.1, 7.2.3 • **6**: 1.4.5, 2.5.1, 2.7.2, 2.7.4, 5.3.1, 5.3.2, 5.6.2, 6.0.3, 6.0.4, 6.1.1, 6.1.2, 6.1.5, 7.2.5, 7.5.3, 8.3.2 • **7**: 7.1.4, 7.4.7 • **RS**: 7.2.4, 7.2.5, 7.2.6, 7.4.1 • **WS**: 0.1.2, 0.2.3, 1.6.3, 7.2.2, 7.3.2, 7.5.6	Emphasized are the following: • Decision making • Reasoning • Acquire and evaluate information • See things in the mind's eye • Know how to learn • Organize and maintain information • Creative thinking • Integrity and honesty	Emphasized are the following: • Reflect on and reevaluate opinions and ideas • Find and use community resources and services • Recognize and understand your human and legal rights and civic responsibilities • Communicate so that others understand • Participate in group processes and decision making	• **1**: 56.02, 66.07, 66.08 • **2**: 57.01, 66.06, 66.12 • **3**: 56.02, 57.01, 57.02, 62.01, 66.01, 66.02, 66.11 • **4**: 66.02, 66.07, 66.12 • **5**: 66.02, 67.01, 67.04 • **6**: 56.02, 63.02, 66.07, 66.19 • **7**: 66.01, 66.19, 67.02 • **RS**: 66.05, 66.07 • **WS**: 62.02, 66.07, 66.11, 66.13, 66.16, 67.06

CASAS and LCP standards: Numbers in bold indicate lesson numbers. • **RS**: Reading Strategy Spotlight • **WS**: Writing Strategy Spotlight

Scope and Sequence

	Life Skills				
Unit	Listening and Speaking	Reading and Writing	Critical Thinking	Vocabulary	Grammar
3 **Healthy Living** *page 40*	• Talk about healthy and unhealthy behavior • Listen to conversations between patients and doctors • Role-play conversations between patients and doctors • Give opinions about healthy and unhealthy behavior • Give health advice • Share ideas about getting healthy	• Preview the text • Read a health history questionnaire • Write about healthy behaviors • Read a bar graph about top reasons for doctor's visits • Take notes on conversations • Read an advice column • Write about a health problem • Read about hotlines and emergency services • Write a letter asking for advice • Read information in a telephone directory **Spotlight:** Skim and scan; read prescription labels **Spotlight:** Use compound and complex sentences; read a magazine article; write about your own healthy or unhealthy behavior as a child	• Classify • Interpret • Summarize • Evaluate	• Healthy and unhealthy activities • Words used on health forms • Words used on medicine labels • Ways to give suggestions and advice • Hotlines; emergency services • Collocations • Types of diseases	• Present perfect • Simple past and present perfect
4 **Money and Consumer Issues** *page 58*	• Offer polite disagreement • Talk about big purchases • Listen to conversations between customers and car salespeople • Role-play conversations between customers and car salespeople	• Read a vehicle warranty • Take notes on conversations • Read general product warranties • Read a glossary of banking terms • Read an article on teaching children money basics • Write about a purchase you made **Spotlight:** Find the main idea **Spotlight:** Make an outline from a cluster diagram	• Synthesize • Use context • Interpret • Evaluate • Choose the best alternative • Solve problems	• Activities at a car dealership • Words associated with automobiles • Ways to disagree politely • Words used in warranties and guarantees • Banking terms • Money management	• Gerunds

Correlations to National Standards

Civics Concepts	Math Skills	CASAS Life Skill Competencies	SCANS Competencies (Workplace)	EFF Content Standards	Literacy Completion Points (LCPs)
• Understand medical habits in the U.S. • Understand prescription labels • Identify telephone numbers for emergency health services	• Convert units of measurement	• **1:** 0.1.2, 3.4.2, 3.5.8, 3.5.9, 7.2.3, 7.2.5, 7.2.7, 7.4.8, 7.5.1, 7.5.4 • **2:** 0.1.2, 3.2.1, 3.3.2, 3.4.1, 3.5.9 • **3:** 0.1.2, 0.1.3, 1.1.3, 3.1.1, 3.1.3, 3.5.9, 6.7.2, 7.2.2, 7.3.2, 7.4.8, 7.5.6 • **4:** 0.1.2, 0.1.3, 3.1.1, 3.1.3, 3.5.9, 7.3.1, 7.3.2, 7.3.3, 7.3.4, 7.4.2, 8.3.2 • **5:** 0.1.2, 7.4.8 • **6:** 0.1.2, 1.1.2, 1.1.4, 2.1.1, 2.1.2, 2.5.1, 2.5.3, 2.5.9, 3.1.3, 3.4.5, 3.5.7, 4.9.3, 5.6.2, 6.0.4, 6.1.3, 6.2.2, 6.2.3, 6.6.1, 7.3.2, 7.4.4, 7.5.4, 7.5.5, 8.3.2 • **7:** 7.1.4, 7.4.7 • **RS:** 3.3.1, 3.3.2, 3.4.1, 7.4.1, 7.4.7 • **WS:** 3.5.9, 7.5.1	Emphasized are the following: • Decision making • See things in the mind's eye • Self-management • Integrity and honesty • Acquire and evaluate information • Organize and maintain information • Know how to learn • Reasoning • Work well with others • Creative thinking • Problem solving • Use resources wisely	Emphasized are the following: • Provide for physical needs • Participate in group processes and decision making • Establish rules and expectations for children's behavior • Provide a nurturing home environment • Pursue personal self-improvement • Communicate so that others understand • Reflect on and reevaluate opinions and ideas • Find, interpret, and analyze diverse sources of information • Pass on values, ethics, and cultural heritage • Listen to and learn from others' experience and ideas • Direct and motivate others • Give and receive support outside the immediate family • Help self and others • Find and use community resources and services	• **1:** 56.02, 58.01, 63.02, 66.07, 66.19 • **2:** 58.01, 58.04, 67.02 • **3:** 56.02, 58.01, 66.01, 66.02, 66.08 • **4:** 56.02, 58.01, 66.02, 66.07, 66.09. 66.13, 66.16, 66.19 • **5:** 67.02 • **6:** 58.05, 61.02, 63.02, 66.07, 66.13 • **7:** 66.01, 66.08, 66.19 • **RS:** 58.04, 66.06, 66.07 • **WS:** 66.13, 66.15
• Identify financial service options • Understand automobile terms • Distinguish U.S. coins and bills • Teach children to be money savvy	• Compute interest on loans	• **1:** 0.1.2, 1.2.2, 1.5.2, 1.9.5, 7.4.1, 7.4.8, 7.5.1 • **2:** 0.1.2, 0.1.4, 1.2.2, 1.7.1, 1.9.5, 6.5.1, 7.2.3, 7.2.5, 7.2.6, 7.5.6 • **3:** 0.1.2, 1.6.3, 1.7.1, 1.7.5, 1.9.3, 7.2.6, 7.3.1, 7.3.2, 7.3.4 • **4:** 1.3.3, 1.5.2, 1.8.1, 1.8.2, 1.8.4, 1.8.5, 6.0.4, 6.1.1, 6.1.2, 6.2.1 • **5:** 7.2.6 • **6:** 0.1.2, 1.1.6, 1.2.2, 1.5.1, 6.2.1, 6.2.3, 6.2.5, 6.4.3, 7.1.1, 7.2.3, 7.2.4, 7.3.2, 7.5.1 • **7:** 7.1.4, 7.4.7 • **RS:** 7.2.1, 7.2.2, 7.4.1 • **WS:** 7.2.2, 7.2.5, 7.2.6, 7.2.7, 7.4.2, 7.4.8	Emphasized are the following: • Decision making • See things in the mind's eye • Know how to learn • Reasoning • Acquire and evaluate information • Organize and maintain information • Problem solving • Use resources wisely • Understand how systems work • Work within the system • Integrity and honesty • Teach others new skills • Act as leader	Emphasized are the following: • Participate in group processes and decision making • Reflect on and reevaluate opinions and ideas • Communicate so that others understand • Find, interpret, and analyze diverse sources of information • Figure out how systems work • Find and use community resources and services • Serve as a role model for child • Pass on values, ethics, and cultural heritage • Teach children • Establish rules and expectations for children's behavior • Manage resources	• **1:** 56.02, 66.07, 66.12 • **2:** 56.02, 62.04, 66.01, 66.02, 66.08 • **3:** 56.02, 62.02, 62.04, 66.01 • **4:** 56.02, 59.02, 59.03, 59.04, 66.07 • **5:** 66.15, 66.19, 67.06 • **6:** 56.02, 59.04, 66.18, 66.19 • **7:** 66.01, 66.19 • **RS:** 66.09 • **WS:** 56.02, 66.08, 66.13

Scope and Sequence

	Life Skills				
Unit	Listening and Speaking	Reading and Writing	Critical Thinking	Vocabulary	Grammar
5 **Accidents and Emergencies** *page 76*	• Talk about work injuries • Talk about personal injuries • Listen to conversations between employees and employers • Role-play conversations between employees and employers • Talk about safety procedures • Talk about health hazards **Pronunciation Focus:** *Intonation in clauses*	• Fill out accident reports • Take notes on conversations • Read and take notes on a first aid guide • Read about evacuation plans • Read and understand an evacuation plan diagram • Read about safety and rights on the job • Write about job preferences **Spotlight:** Use the SQ3R strategy (survey, question, read, recite, and review) **Spotlight:** Make a Venn diagram; write a paragraph from a Venn diagram	• Interpret • Analyze • Make decisions • Evaluate	• Health hazards • Safety signs • Types of injuries • Types of emergencies • Ways to apologize • Basic first aid terms	• Past continuous • Simple past and past continuous
6 **Community** *page 94*	• Talk about community • Talk about rules in the community • Listen to conversations between citizens and authorities • Role-play conversations between drivers and police officers • Discuss differences in laws in different cultures • Talk about the accomplishments of Cesar Chavez • Accept criticism **Pronunciation Focus:** *Reductions with* to	• Read a newspaper article • Read a biography • Read a crime report • Rewrite a paragraph in your own words • Write a summary of a story **Spotlight:** Paraphrase **Spotlight:** Summarize	• Use context • Classify • Interpret • Analyze • Predict	• Necessary documents • Community issues • Community activities • Community rules and consequences • Ways to accept criticism	• Infinitives

Correlations to National Standards

Civics Concepts	Math Skills	CASAS Life Skill Competencies	SCANS Competencies (Workplace)	EFF Content Standards	Literacy Completion Points (LCPs)
• Identify health hazards • Understand safety signs • Understand basic first aid • Understand safety procedures • Understand safety rights on the job		• **1:** 0.1.2, 4.3.1, 4.3.3, 4.3.4, 4.5.1, 7.2.2, 7.4.1, 7.4.8 • **2:** 0.1.2, 0.1.3, 3.4.2, 3.4.3, 3.5.9, 7.2.6, 7.3.1, 7.3.2, 7.4.1, 7.4.5 • **3:** 0.1.2, 3.4.2, 4.3.3, 4.3.4, 4.4.3, 4.6.1, 4.8.1, 7.2.1, 7.2.2, 7.2.4, 7.5.6 • **4:** 0.1.2, 2.1.2, 2.5.1, 3.4.3, 7.2.2, 7.2.3, 7.2.7, 7.3.2, 7.3.3, 7.4.2 • **5:** 0.1.2 • **6:** 0.1.2, 4.3.2, 4.4.3, 4.6.1, 4.6.3, 4.6.5, 7.2.1, 7.3.2, 7.4.8 • **7:** 7.1.4, 7.4.7 • **RS:** 4.3.2, 4.3.4, 4.9.3, 7.2.1, 7.4.1, 7.4.2 • **WS:** 7.2.3, 7.2.5, 7.2.6, 7.2.7, 7.4.2, 7.4.8	Emphasized are the following: • See things in the mind's eye • Reasoning • Know how to learn • Analyze and communicate information • Creative thinking • Decision making • Acquire and evaluate information • Organize and maintain information • Problem solving	Emphasized are the following: • Participate in group processes and decision making • Provide for physical needs • Identify and monitor problems • Listen to and learn from others' experiences and ideas • Communicate with others inside and outside the organization • Find and use community resources and services • Put ideas and directions into action • Teach children • Establish rules and expectations for children's behavior	• **1:** 53.05, 56.02, 66.19 • **2:** 58.01, 66.02, 66.11, 66.12 • **3:** 53.01, 53.04, 53.05, 56.02, 58.02, 66.01, 66.02, 66.11 • **4:** 56.02, 58.01, 66.02, 66.07 • **5:** 66.07, 66.15, 66.19, 67.02, 67.06 • **6:** 53.05, 64.02, 64.17, 66.02, 66.07, 66.08, 66.17, 68.03 • **7:** 66.01, 66.19, 67.02 • **RS:** 53.05, 66.02, 66.06, 66.07, 66.18 • **WS:** 66.08, 66.13
• Identify common laws and ordinances • Identify a local community need • Interpret and identify legal response to regulations • Identify community issues • Commit to making a difference in your community • Understand community rules • Understand how to interact with law enforcement • Learn how to report a crime		• **1:** 0.1.2, 5.6.1, 7.2.5, 7.5.5 • **2:** 0.1.2, 2.5.4, 2.5.7, 2.6.1, 2.6.3, 2.7.3, 3.4.2, 7.2.3, 7.2.6, 7.4.8 • **3:** 0.1.2, 0.1.4, 2.7.3, 5.3.7, 5.5.6, 7.2.1, 7.2.2, 7.2.3, 7.4.1, 7.4.2, 7.5.3, 7.5.6 • **4:** 0.1.2, 2.7.2, 2.7.3, 4.2.2, 5.6.1, 7.2.1, 7.2.6, 7.3.1, 7.3.2, 7.3.4, 7.4.2 • **5:** 7.2.2, 7.2.5, 7.3.1 • **6:** 0.1.2, 2.1.2, 5.3.1, 5.3.7, 5.5.6, 5.6.1, 7.2.3 • **7:** 7.1.4, 7.4.7, 7.4.8 • **RS:** 7.2.1, 7.4.1, 7.4.3, 7.4.7 • **WS:** 7.2.1, 7.2.2, 7.3.4, 7.4.1, 7.4.2	Emphasized are the following: • Know how to learn • Creative thinking • Analyze and communicate information • Decision making • Responsibility • Integrity and honesty • Self-management • See things in the mind's eye • Organize and maintain information • Problem solving • Work well with others • Use resources wisely • Select the right technology for the task	Emphasized are the following: • Participate in group processes and decision making • Identify and monitor problems, community needs, strengths, and resources • Develop a sense of self that reflects your history, values, beliefs, and roles in the larger community • Reflect on and reevaluate opinions and ideas • Get involved in the community and get others involved • Define common values and goals and resolve conflict • Listen to and learn from others' experiences and ideas • Negotiate differences and build common plans • Use technology • Recognize and understand your human and legal rights and civic responsibilities	• **1:** 56.02, 63.02, 66.07 • **2:** 66.07, 66.11 • **3:** 56.02, 60.06, 66.01, 66.02, 66.11, 66.19 • **4:** 66.02, 66.05, 66.07, 66.11, 66.18 • **5:** 66.19, 67.06 • **6:** 56.02, 61.02, 63.02, 66.03, 66.19, 68.02 • **7:** 66.01, 66.08, 66.19 • **RS:** 66.02, 66.13, 66.19 • **WS:** 66.02, 66.07, 66.09, 66.13

CASAS and LCP standards: Numbers in bold indicate lesson numbers. • **RS:** Reading Strategy Spotlight • **WS:** Writing Strategy Spotlight

Scope and Sequence

	Life Skills				
Unit	**Listening and Speaking**	**Reading and Writing**	**Critical Thinking**	**Vocabulary**	**Grammar**
7 **Work** *page 112*	• Ask questions about a position • Talk about qualities of the workplace • Talk about benefits • Talk about ways to find a job • Listen to conversations between employers and job applicants • Role-play conversations between receptionists and applicants	• Read an article about workplace benefits • Take notes on conversations • Read online job listings • Read two types of résumés • Read a cover letter • Write a cover letter • Write a résumé **Spotlight:** Make inferences **Spotlight:** Revise and proofread résumés	• Make inferences • Apply knowledge • Evaluate • Reason • Classify • Make associations • Analyze	• Qualities of the workplace • Benefits • Ways to ask polite questions • Parts of a résumé • Parts of a cover letter	• Real conditionals
8 **Communication** *page 130*	• Talk about the ways people communicate • Talk about communication skills • Talk about communication at work • Listen to various conversations of people communicating • Role-play conversations • Talk about good listening skills • Practice phone skills: conversations and messages **Pronunciation Focus:** *Word stress patterns in two-syllable words*	• Write a summary of a conversation • Preview the text • Read an article about communication skills • Write a summary of an article • Read sample answering machine messages • Read persuasive paragraphs • Write a persuasive paragraph **Spotlight:** Distinguish fact and opinion **Spotlight:** Give examples; support your ideas	• Interpret • Evaluate • Analyze	• Ways of communicating • Communication skills	• Present unreal conditional statements

Correlations to National Standards

Civics Concepts	Math Skills	CASAS Life Skill Competencies	SCANS Competencies (Workplace)	EFF Content Standards	Literacy Completion Points (LCPs)
• Locate, analyze, and describe job requirements • Identify and access employment and training resources • Compare and contrast the U.S. workplace culture with that of other countries • Understand work benefits • Understand how to look for a job	• Understand payroll deductions	• **1:** 0.1.2, 4.1.9, 4.4.4, 4.4.5, 7.1.1, 7.1.2, 7.2.2, 7.2.3, 7.2.5, 7.2.6, 7.2.7, 7.4.8, 7.5.1 • **2:** 0.1.2, 4.2.1, 7.1.1, 7.2.3, 7.2.4, 7.2.6, 7.4.1, 7.4.2, 7.4.3, 7.4.8, 7.5.1 • **3:** 0.1.2, 2.1.8, 4.1.3, 4.8.3, 7.4.2, 7.5.6 • **4:** 0.1.2, 4.1.2, 7.2.2, 7.2.5, 7.4.1 • **5:** 7.2.4, 7.2.6 • **6:** 4.1.2, 4.1.3, 4.2.1, 6.1.1, 6.1.3, 6.2.1, 6.2.2, 6.2.3, 6.2.5, 7.1.1, 7.5.1 • **7:** 7.1.4, 7.4.7, 7.4.8 • **RS:** 7.2.4, 7.2.5, 7.4.2 • **WS:** 4.1.2, 7.2.7	Emphasized are the following: • Decision making • See things in the mind's eye • Reasoning • Work well with others • Know how to learn • Acquire and evaluate information • Organize and maintain information • Self-management • Creative thinking • Use resources wisely • Self esteem	Emphasized are the following: • Participate in group processes and decision making • Pursue personal self-improvement • Create a vision of the future • Plan and renew career goals • Balance and support work, career, and personal goals • Organize, plan, and prioritize work and use resources • Reflect on and reevaluate opinions and ideas • Find and get a job • Communicate with others inside and outside the organization	• **1:** 52.01, 53.01, 56.02 • **2:** 53.02, 56.02 • **3:** 52.02, 53.04, 57.01, 66.01, 66.02 • **4:** 56.02, 52.03, 66.02, 66.07 • **5:** 66.19 • **6:** 52.02, 53.02, 66.16 • **7:** 66.01, 66.08, 66.19 • **RS:** 66.19 • **WS:** 52.03, 66.14
• Understand how to communicate at work		• **1:** 0.1.1, 0.1.2, 2.7.3, 7.2.4, 7.2.5 • **2:** 0.1.2, 0.1.3, 0.1.4, 4.6.1, 7.2.4, 7.5.3 • **3:** 0.1.2, 0.1.3, 0.1.4, 4.6.1, 4.8.3, 7.2.1, 7.2.4, 7.4.2 • **4:** 0.1.2, 2.7.3, 7.2.1, 7.2.2, 7.4.1, 7.4.2 • **5:** 0.1.3, 7.2.6 • **6:** 0.1.2, 2.1.7, 2.1.8, 7.2.3, 7.2.5, 7.2.6 • **7:** 7.1.4, 7.4.7 • **RS:** 0.1.3, 7.2.4, 7.4.1 • **WS:** 0.1.3, 7.2.1, 7.2.2, 7.2.4, 7.2.5, 7.2.6, 7.5.1	Emphasized are the following: • See things in the mind's eye • Creative thinking • Acquire and evaluate information • Know how to learn • Reasoning • Problem solving • Analyze and communicate information • Organize and maintain information • Understand how systems work	Emphasized are the following: • Participate in group processes and decision making • Communicate so that others understand • Communicate with others inside and outside the organization • Reflect on and reevaluate opinions and ideas • Pursue personal self-improvement • Educate self and others	• **1:** 56.01, 56.02, 56.04 • **2:** 53.04, 56.02, 56.04 • **3:** 53.04, 56.02, 66.01, 66.02, 66.13 • **4:** 56.02, 66.02, 66.05, 66.07, 66.13, 66.18 • **5:** 66.07, 66.19 • **6:** 56.02, 57.01, 66.03, 68.03 • **7:** 66.01, 66.19 • **WS:** 56.02, 66.02, 66.09, 66.13

TO THE TEACHER

All-Star is a four-level, standards-based series for English learners featuring a picture-dictionary approach to vocabulary building. "Big picture" scenes in each unit provide springboards to a wealth of activities developing all of the language skills.

An accessible and predictable sequence of lessons in each unit systematically builds language and math skills around life-skill topics. *All-Star* presents family, work, and community topics in each unit, and provides alternate application lessons in its Workbooks, giving teachers the flexibility to customize the series for a variety of student needs and curricular objectives. *All-Star* is tightly correlated to all of the major national and state standards for adult instruction.

Features

★ **Accessible "big picture" scenes** present life-skills vocabulary, activities, and discussion, and provide engaging contexts for all-skills language development.

★ **Predictable sequence of nine, two-page lessons** in each unit reduces prep time for teachers and helps students get comfortable with the pattern of each lesson type.

★ **Flexible structure** allows teachers to customize each unit to meet a variety of student needs and curricular objectives, with application lessons addressing family, work, and community topics in both the Student Book and Workbook.

★ **Comprehensive coverage of key standards, such as CASAS, SCANS, EFF, and LCPs,** prepares students to master a broad range of critical competencies.

★ **Multiple assessment measures** like CASAS-style tests and performance-based assessment offer a broad range of options for monitoring and assessing learner progress.

★ **Dynamic, Interactive CD-ROM program** in Levels 1 and 2 integrates language, literacy, and numeracy skill building with computer practice.

The Complete *All-Star* Program

★ The **Student Book** features eight, 18-page units, integrating listening, speaking, reading, writing, grammar, math, and pronunciation skills with life-skill topics, critical thinking activities, and civics concepts. As in levels 1 and 2, Student Book 3 addresses the themes central to the lives of adult ESL learners, making it easy to use the *All-Star* series in multi-level classrooms.

★ The **Student Book with Audio Highlights** provides students with audio recordings of all of the conversations and example dialogues in the Student Book.

★ The **Teacher's Edition with Tests** provides:
  • Step-by-step procedural notes for each Student Book activity
  • More than 200 expansion activities for Student Book 3, many of which offer creative tasks tied to the "big picture" scenes in each unit

  • Culture, Grammar, Pronunciation, and Academic Notes
  • Two-page written test for each unit (*Note:* Listening passages for the tests are available on the Student Book Audiocassettes and Audio CDs.)
  • Audio scripts for all audio program materials
  • Answer keys for Student Book, Workbook, and Tests

★ The **Interactive CD-ROM,** included in Levels 1 and 2 incorporates and extends the learning goals of the Student Book by integrating language, literacy, and numeracy skill building with multimedia practice on the computer. A flexible set of activities correlated to each unit builds vocabulary, listening, reading, writing, and test-taking skills.

★ The **Color Overhead Transparencies** encourage teachers to present new vocabulary and concepts in fun and meaningful ways. This component provides a full-color overhead transparency for each of the "big picture" scenes.

★ The **Workbook** includes supplementary practice activities correlated to the Student Book. As a bonus feature, the Workbook also includes alternate application lessons addressing the learner's role as worker, family member, and/or community member. These additional, optional lessons may be used in addition to, or as substitutes for, the application lessons found in Lesson 6 of each Student Book unit.

★ The **Audiocassettes** and **Audio CDs** contain recordings for all listening activities in the Student Book. Listening passages for each unit test are provided at the end of the audio section for that unit.

Overview of the *All-Star* Program

UNIT STRUCTURE

Consult the *Welcome to All-Star* guide on pages xvi–xxi. This guide offers teachers and administrators a visual tour of one Student Book unit.

All-Star is designed to maximize accessibility and flexibility. Each unit contains the following sequence of nine, two-page lessons that develop vocabulary and build language, grammar, and math skills around life-skill topics:

★ Lesson 1: Talk about It

★ Lesson 2: Vocabulary in Context

★ Lesson 3: Listening and Speaking

★ Lesson 4: Reading and Critical Thinking

★ Lesson 5: Grammar

★ Lesson 6: Application

★ Lesson 7: Review and Assessment

★ Spotlight: Reading Strategy

★ Spotlight: Writing Strategy

Each lesson addresses a key adult standard, and these standards are indicated in the upper right-hand corner of each lesson in a yellow bar.

SPECIAL FEATURES OF EACH UNIT

★ *Warm Up.* These activities activate students' background knowledge, access their personal experience, and generate interest in the topic of the lesson. They serve to introduce students to the lesson topic and prompt classroom discussion.

★ *Try This Strategy.* This feature presents students with learning strategies (such as understanding personal learning style), vocabulary strategies (such as learning prefixes and suffixes), and academic learning strategies (such as evaluating texts) towards the beginning of each unit so they can apply them as they proceed through the lessons. These strategies allow students to build skills to continue their lifelong learning.

★ *Communication Strategy.* This feature presents students with communication strategies that will improve their ability to communicate effectively, and help them become more fluid, natural speakers. Communication strategies, such as disagreeing politely, are introduced and then practiced in real-life role-play activities called *Use the Communication Strategy*.

★ *Grammar Lessons.* Grammar is presented and practiced in lesson 5 of each unit. These two-page lessons offer students more in-depth grammar practice than at the lower levels of the series. The essential grammar content is correlated to a variety of national and state standards. A comprehensive *Grammar Reference Guide* at the back of the book summarizes all of the structures and functions presented.

★ *Window on Math.* Learning basic math skills is critically important for success in school, on the job, and at home. As such, national and state standards for adult education mandate instruction in basic math skills. In half of the units, a blue box called *Window on Math* is dedicated to helping students develop the functional numeracy skills they need for basic math work in everyday math applications such as payroll deductions.

★ *Window on Pronunciation.* Improving pronunciation skills can greatly improve students' ability to understand others and to be understood. In half of the units, a blue box called *Window on Pronunciation* is dedicated to helping students achieve two major goals: (1) hearing and producing specific sounds, words, and minimal pairs of words so they become better listeners and speakers; and (2) addressing issues of stress, rhythm, and intonation so that the students' spoken English becomes more comprehensible.

★ *Spotlight: Reading Strategy.* After the *Review and Assessment* lesson in each unit, students and teachers will find a *Spotlight* dedicated to presenting students with academic reading strategies. These are optional, two-page lessons that offer a supplementary focus on reading skill development.

★ *Spotlight: Writing Strategy.* At the end of each unit, students and teachers will find a *Spotlight* dedicated to presenting students with academic and professional writing strategies.

These are optional, two-page lessons that offer a supplementary focus on writing skill development.

TWO-PAGE LESSON FORMAT

The lessons in *All-Star* are designed as two-page spreads. Lessons 5–7 and the Spotlights employ a standard textbook layout, but Lessons 1–4 follow an innovative format with a list of activities on the left-hand page of the spread and rich and textual input visuals supporting these activities on the right-hand page. The textual input includes authentic and adapted newspaper articles, letters, and official forms and applications. The list of activities, entitled *Things To Do*, allows students and teachers to take full advantage of the visuals in each lesson, inviting students to achieve a variety of learning goals, by evaluating, synthesizing, and analyzing.

As in previous levels, Lessons 1-4 provide learners with the input necessary to facilitate comprehension. Student Book 3 includes much of the rich visual input found in Student Books 1 and 2, but also has greater textual input in keeping with the students' more advanced abilities.

"BIG PICTURE" SCENES

Each unit includes one "big picture" scene. In Student Book 3, the "big picture" scene begins each unit in Lesson 1. This scene is the visual centerpiece of the unit and serves as a springboard to a variety of activities provided in the Student Book, Teacher's Edition, and Color Transparencies package. The "big picture" activates background knowledge, accesses students' personal experience, increases their motivation, and serves as a prompt for classroom discussion.

The Teacher's Edition includes a variety of all-skills "Big Picture Expansion" activities that are tied to the Student Book scenes. For each unit, these expansion activities address listening, speaking, reading, writing, *and* grammar skill development, and allow teachers to customize their instruction to meet the language learning needs of each group of students.

In the Color Overhead Transparencies package, teachers will find transparencies of each "big picture" scene, which they can use to introduce the vocabulary and life-skill concepts in each unit. They can also use these transparencies to facilitate the "Big Picture Expansion" activities in the Teacher's Edition.

CIVICS CONCEPTS

Many institutions focus direct attention on the importance of civics instruction for English language learners. Civics instruction encourages students to become active and informed community members. *Application* lessons provide activities that help students develop their roles as workers, parents, and community members. Those lessons targeting the students' role as a community member encourage learners to become more active and informed members of their communities.

CASAS, SCANS, EFF, LCPs, AND OTHER STANDARDS

Teachers and administrators benchmark student progress against national and/or state standards for adult instruction. With this in mind, *All-Star* carefully integrates instructional elements from a wide range of standards including CASAS, SCANS, EFF, and the Literacy Completion Points (LCPs). Unit-by-unit correlations of these standards appear in the scope and sequence on pages iv–xi. Here is a brief overview of our approach to meeting the key national and state standards:

★ **CASAS.** Many U.S. states, including California, tie funding for adult education programs to student performance on the Comprehensive Adult Student Assessment System (CASAS). The CASAS (www.casas.org) competencies identify more than 300 essential skills that adults need in order to succeed in the classroom, workplace, and community. Examples of these skills include identifying or using appropriate non-verbal behavior in a variety of settings, responding appropriately to common personal information questions, and comparing price or quality to determine the best buys. *All-Star* comprehensively integrates all of the CASAS Life Skill Competencies throughout the four levels of the series. Level 3 addresses the CASAS Level B Life Skills test items on CASAS Test Forms 33, 34, 34X, 53, and 54 and begins to bridge students into some of the competencies addressed in Level C.

★ **SCANS.** Developed by the United States Department of Labor, SCANS is an acronym for the Secretary's Commission on Achieving Necessary Skills (wdr.doleta.gov/SCANS/). SCANS competencies are workplace skills that help people compete more effectively in today's global economy. The following are examples of SCANS competencies: works well with others, acquires and evaluates information, and teaches others new skills. A variety of SCANS competencies are threaded throughout the activities in each unit of *All-Star*. The incorporation of these competencies recognizes both the intrinsic importance of teaching workplace skills and the fact that many adult students are already working members of their communities.

★ **EFF.** Equipped for the Future (EFF) is a set of standards for adult literacy and lifelong learning, developed by The National Institute for Literacy (www.nifl.gov). The organizing principle of EFF is that adults assume responsibilities in three major areas of life — as workers, as parents, and as citizens. These three areas of focus are called "role maps" in the EFF documentation. In the parent role map, for example, EFF highlights these and other responsibilities: participating in children's formal education and forming and maintaining supportive family relationships. Each *All-Star* unit addresses all three of the EFF role maps in its *Application* lessons. Lesson 6 in each Student Book unit includes one of the three application lessons for that unit. The remaining two application lessons are found in the corresponding Workbook unit.

★ **LCPs.** Florida and Texas document the advancement of learners in an adult program through their system of Literacy Completion Points (LCPs). Community college and school districts earn an LCP each time an adult student advances to a higher proficiency level or completes a program. *All-Star* Level 3 incorporates into its instruction the vast majority of standards at LCP Level D.

NUMBER OF HOURS OF INSTRUCTION

The *All-Star* program has been designed to accommodate the needs of adult classes with 70–180 hours of classroom instruction. Here are three recommended ways in which various components in the *All-Star* program can be combined to meet student and teacher needs.

★ **70–100 hours.** Teachers are encouraged to work through all of the Student Book materials, incorporating the *Reading* and *Writing Spotlights* as time permits. The Color Transparencies can be used to introduce and/or review materials in each unit. Teachers should also look to the Teacher's Edition for teaching suggestions and testing materials as necessary.

Time per unit: 9–13 hours.

★ **100–140 hours.** In addition to working through all of the Student Book materials, teachers are encouraged to incorporate the Workbook for supplementary practice.

Time per unit: 13–18 hours.

★ **140–180 hours.** Teachers and students working in an intensive instructional setting can take advantage of the wealth of expansion activities threaded through the Teacher's Edition to supplement the Student Book and the Workbook.

Time per unit: 18–22 hours.

ASSESSMENT

The *All-Star* program offers teachers, students, and administrators the following wealth of resources for monitoring and assessing student progress and achievement:

★ **Standardized testing formats.** *All-Star* is correlated to the CASAS competencies and many other national and state standards for adult learning. Students have the opportunity to practice answering CASAS-style listening and reading questions in Lesson 7 of each unit (*What do you know?*) and in Lesson 7 of the Workbook (*Practice Test*). Students practice with the same item types and bubble-in answer sheets they encounter on CASAS and other standardized tests.

★ **Achievement tests.** The *All-Star* Teacher's Edition includes end-of-unit tests. These paper-and-pencil tests help students demonstrate how well they have learned the instructional content of the unit. Adult learners often show incremental increases in learning that are not always measured on the standardized tests. The achievement tests may demonstrate learning even in a short amount of instructional time.

Twenty percent of each test includes questions that encourage students to apply more academic skills such as determining meaning from context, making inferences, and understanding main ideas. Practice with these question types will help prepare students who may want to enroll in academic classes.

★ **Performance-based assessment.** *All-Star* provides several ways to measure students' performance on productive tasks. The Teacher's Edition suggests writing and speaking prompts and rubrics that teachers can use for performance-based assessment. These prompts derive from the "big picture" scene in each unit and provide rich visual input as the basis for the speaking and writing tasks asked of the students.

★ **Portfolio assessment.** A portfolio is a collection of student work that can be used to show progress. Examples of work that the instructor or the student may submit in the portfolio include writing samples, speaking rubrics, audiotapes, videotapes, or projects. The Teacher's Edition identifies activities that require critical thinking and small group project work which may be included, as well as those activities that may be used as documentation for the secondary standards defined by the National Reporting System.

★ **Self-assessment.** Self-assessment is an important part of the overall assessment picture, as it promotes student involvement and commitment to the learning process. When encouraged to assess themselves, students take more control of their learning and are better able to connect the instructional content with their own goals. The Student Book includes *Learning Logs* at the end of each unit, which allow students to check off the vocabulary they have learned and skills and strategies they have acquired. The Workbook provides a *Practice Test Performance Record* where students record their number of correct answers on each practice test, encouraging them to monitor their own progress as they advance through the book.

★ **Other linguistic and non-linguistic outcomes.** Traditional testing often does not account for the progress made by adult learners with limited educational experience or low literacy levels. Such learners tend to take longer to make smaller language gains, so the gains they make in other areas are often more significant. These gains may be in areas such as self-esteem, goal clarification, learning skills, and access to employment, community involvement, and further academic studies. The SCANS and EFF standards identify areas of student growth that are not necessarily language based.

All-Star is correlated with both SCANS and EFF standards. Every unit in the Student Book contains a lesson that focuses on one of the EFF role maps (worker, family member, community member), and the Workbook provides alternate lessons that address the other two role maps. Like the Student Book, the Workbook includes activities that may provide documentation that can be added to a student portfolio.

About the authors and series consultants

Linda Lee is lead author on the *All-Star* series. Linda has taught ESL/ELT in the United States, Iran, and China, and has authored or co-authored a variety of successful textbook series for English learners. As a classroom instructor, Linda's most satisfying teaching experiences have been with adult ESL students at Roxbury Community College in Boston, Massachusetts.

Kristin Sherman is a co-author on *All-Star,* Student Book 3. Kristin has 10 years of teaching experience in both credit and non-credit ESL programs. She has taught general ESL, as well as classes focusing on workplace skills and family literacy. She has authored a number of workbooks and teacher's editions for English learners. Her favorite project was the creation of a reading and writing workbook with her ESL students at the Mecklenburg County Jail.

Stephen Sloan is Title One Coordinator at James Monroe High School in the Los Angeles Unified School District. Steve has more than 25 years of teaching and administrative experience with both high school and adult ESL learners. Steve is also the author of McGraw-Hill's *Rights and Responsibilities: Reading and Communication for Civics.*

Grace Tanaka is professor and coordinator of ESL at the Santa Ana College School of Continuing Education, in Santa Ana, California, which serves more than 20,000 students per year. She is also a textbook co-author and series consultant. Grace has 23 years of teaching experience in both credit and non-credit ESL programs.

Shirley Velasco is assistant principal at Palmetto Adult Education Center in Miami, Florida. She has been a classroom instructor and administrator for the past 24 years. At Palmetto, Shirley has created a large adult ESOL program based on a curriculum she developed to help teachers implement the Florida LCPs (Literacy Completion Points).

Welcome to All-Star

All-Star is a four-level series featuring a "big picture" approach to meeting adult standards that systematically builds language and math skills around life-skill topics.

Accessible, two-page lesson format in Lessons 1–4 follows an innovative layout with a list of activities labeled "Things to Do" on the left and picture-dictionary visuals and readings on the right.

Predictable unit structure includes the same logical sequence of seven two-page lessons and two Spotlight lessons in each unit.

"Big picture" scenes are springboards to a wealth of life-skills vocabulary, activities, and discussions in the Student Book and all-skills expansion activities in the Teacher's Edition.

Warm Up activities activate students' background knowledge and interest in the topic and prompt discussion.

Color overhead transparencies for the "big picture" scenes provide fun and meaningful ways to present new life-skills vocabulary and concepts, and to prompt classroom discussion.

Highlighted life-skills vocabulary is presented through compelling realia, illustrations, and in rich contextual environments. Highlighted vocabulary is defined in the glossary in the appendix.

Comprehensive coverage of key standards such as CASAS, SCANS, EFF, and LCPs prepares students to master critical competencies.

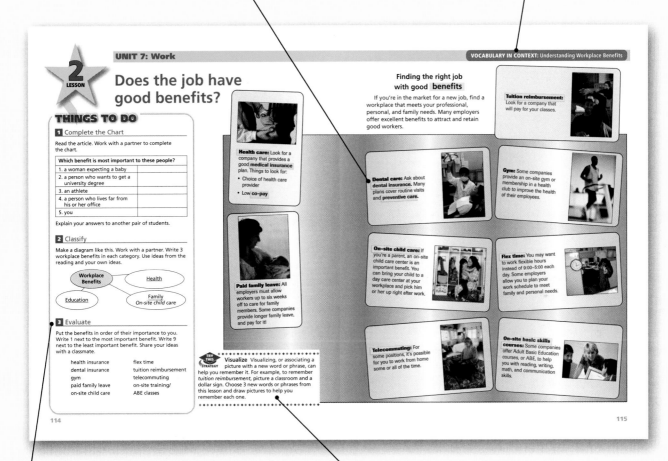

UNIT 7: Work

2 LESSON

Does the job have good benefits?

THINGS TO DO

1 Complete the Chart

Read the article. Work with a partner to complete the chart.

Which benefit is most important to these people?	
1. a woman expecting a baby	
2. a person who wants to get a university degree	
3. an athlete	
4. a person who lives far from his or her office	
5. you	

Explain your answers to another pair of students.

2 Classify

Make a diagram like this. Work with a partner. Write 3 workplace benefits in each category. Use ideas from the reading and your own ideas.

- Workplace Benefits
- Health
- Education
- Family / On-site child care

3 Evaluate

Put the benefits in order of their importance to you. Write 1 next to the most important benefit. Write 9 next to the least important benefit. Share your ideas with a classmate.

health insurance	flex time
dental insurance	tuition reimbursement
gym	telecommuting
paid family leave	on-site training/
on-site child care	ABE classes

Finding the right job with good benefits

If you're in the market for a new job, find a workplace that meets your professional, personal, and family needs. Many employers offer excellent benefits to attract and retain good workers.

Health care: Look for a company that provides a good **medical insurance** plan. Things to look for:
- Choice of health care provider
- Low **co-pay**

Paid family leave: All employers must allow workers up to six weeks off to care for family members. Some companies provide longer family leave, and pay for it!

Tuition reimbursement: Look for a company that will pay for your classes.

Dental care: Ask about **dental insurance.** Many plans cover routine visits and **preventive care.**

Gym: Some companies provide an on-site gym or membership in a health club to improve the health of their employees.

On-site child care: If you're a parent, an on-site child care center is an important benefit. You can bring your child to a day care center at your workplace and pick him or her up right after work.

Flex time: You may want to work flexible hours instead of 9:00–5:00 each day. Some employers allow you to plan your work schedule to meet family and personal needs.

Telecommuting: For some positions, it's possible for you to work from home some or all of the time.

On-site basic skills courses: Some companies offer Adult Basic Education courses, or ABE, to help you with reading, writing, math, and communication skills.

TRY THIS STRATEGY **Visualize** Visualizing, or associating a picture with a new word or phrase, can help you remember it. For example, to remember *tuition reimbursement*, picture a classroom and a dollar sign. Choose 3 new words or phrases from this lesson and draw pictures to help you remember each one.

114

115

Critical thinking activities such as evaluating and classifying, allow students to interact with the content in a meaningful way.

Try This Strategy activities present specific ways to help students learn vocabulary, understand their personal learning style, and approach academic tasks. These are included towards the beginning of each unit.

Listening activities include a rich variety of everyday personal, academic, and workplace conversations. Activities ask students to listen for important details as well as main ideas.

Realia-based readings and narrative selections like advertisements, stories, graphs, and online articles provide the basis for developing reading skills and associating text with listening passages.

UNIT 7: Work

3 LESSON

I'm calling about the ad for a photographer.

LISTENING AND SPEAKING: Calling about a Job

THINGS TO DO

1 Warm Up

Work with your classmates to answer these questions.

1. What are 3–5 things you can do to find a job?
2. How did you or someone you know find out about a job?
3. Read the job listings posted on the website. Which job is most interesting to you? Why?
4. Which job on the website seems the most difficult? Why?

2 Listen and Take Notes

Listen to each conversation and look at the job descriptions on page 117. Write 2 questions each applicant asks. Then write the answers.

Job	Questions	Answers
1. Writer	a. Are you hiring for 1 writer position?	a. No, we're hiring for 2.
	b.	b.
2. Production assistant	a.	a.
	b.	b.
3. Account assistant	a.	a.
	b.	b.

3 Use the Communication Strategy

Work with a partner. Role-play a telephone conversation between a receptionist and a person looking for a job. Replace the underlined words in the example with your own ideas. Try to use the communication strategy.

A: Hi. I'm calling about the ad for a photographer.
B: Yes. How can I help you?
A: Can you tell me a little about the job?
B: Sure. We're looking for an experienced portrait photographer.
A: I've done a lot of portrait photography. Is the job full time?
B: Yes, it is.
A: What should I do if I'm interested in applying?
B: Send 2 copies of your résumé and a cover letter.

Dressed for an interview

COMMUNICATION STRATEGY

Asking Polite Questions

Asking questions directly can sometimes be impolite. Using phrases with models such as *could, can, would,* and *may* to obtain information is more polite.

- Could you tell me . . . ?
- Can you tell me . . . ?
- Would you know . . . ?
- May I ask . . . ?

116

Broadcasting Job Bank

BROADCASTING JOB BANK

BJB

[New Listings]
[Resume Help]
[Apply]
[Announcements]
[What's New]

New Listings:

WBNC, Trenton, NJ
WRITER

Duties: Write news stories, write live updates, contact sources by phone.

Qualifications: College degree preferred. News writing experience preferred. Excellent writing skills, attention to details, good computer skills, ability to gather information quickly, ability to work on a team and meet deadlines.

KNRR, San Jose, CA
PRODUCTION ASSISTANT

Duties: Write, help producer, schedule guests for shows, research story ideas.

Qualifications: College degree, excellent writing skills, good organizational skills, creative, strong computer skills. Must have excellent communication skills and be able to deal with pressure.

WQAP, Tallahassee, FL
ACCOUNT ASSISTANT

Duties: Sell advertising time to advertising agencies and retail businesses. Call on community contacts to develop new business. Develop and maintain business contacts.

Qualifications: Minimum three years sales experience preferred. Ability to meet goals. Excellent oral and written communication skills, strong mathematical ability, Florida driver's license and personal transportation required.

Other Listings:

Meteorologist (4/27)
Account executive (4/20)
Camera operator (4/14)
Sports announcer (4/10)

117

Use the Communication Strategy activities invite students to engage in everyday conversations with their classmates, using the vocabulary, grammar, and communication strategy they have learned.

Communication Strategy boxes present specific strategies that will improve students' ability to communicate effectively, helping them become more fluid, natural speakers.

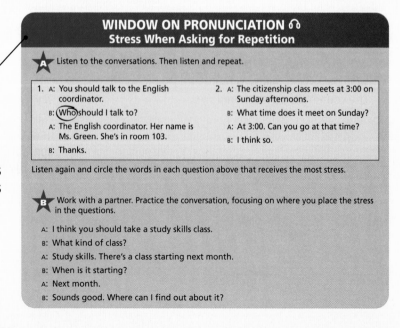

WINDOW ON PRONUNCIATION
Stress When Asking for Repetition

A Listen to the conversations. Then listen and repeat.

1. A: You should talk to the English coordinator.
   B: **Who** should I talk to?
   A: The English coordinator. Her name is Ms. Green. She's in room 103.
   B: Thanks.

2. A: The citizenship class meets at 3:00 on Sunday afternoons.
   B: What time does it meet on Sunday?
   A: At 3:00. Can you go at that time?
   B: I think so.

Listen again and circle the words in each question above that receives the most stress.

B Work with a partner. Practice the conversation, focusing on where you place the stress in the questions.

A: I think you should take a study skills class.
B: What kind of class?
A: Study skills. There's a class starting next month.
B: When is it starting?
A: Next month.
B: Sounds good. Where can I find out about it?

Windows on Pronunciation help students produce difficult sounds in English and address issues of stress, rhythm, and intonation.

A grammar lesson is presented in each unit, offering in-depth grammar practice. The essential grammar content is correlated to a variety of national and state standards.

A grammar box describes the structure of the grammar and offers everyday examples to help students understand usage.

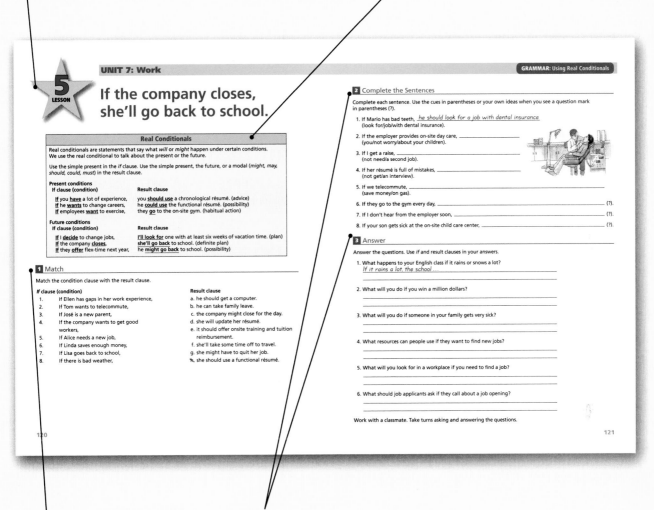

UNIT 7: Work

LESSON 5

GRAMMAR: Using Real Conditionals

If the company closes, she'll go back to school.

Real Conditionals

Real conditionals are statements that say what *will* or *might* happen under certain conditions. We use the real conditional to talk about the present or the future.

Use the simple present in the *if* clause. Use the simple present, the future, or a modal (*might, may, should, could, must*) in the result clause.

Present conditions

If clause (condition)	Result clause
If you **have** a lot of experience,	you **should use** a chronological résumé. (advice)
If he **wants** to change careers,	he **could use** the functional résumé. (possibility)
If employees **want** to exercise,	they **go** to the on-site gym. (habitual action)

Future conditions

If clause (condition)	Result clause
If I **decide** to change jobs,	**I'll look for** one with at least six weeks of vacation time. (plan)
If the company **closes**,	**she'll go back** to school. (definite plan)
If they **offer** flex-time next year,	he **might go back** to school. (possibility)

1 Match

Match the condition clause with the result clause.

If clause (condition)

1. If Ellen has gaps in her work experience,
2. If Tom wants to telecommute,
3. If José is a new parent,
4. If the company wants to get good workers,
5. If Alice needs a new job,
6. If Linda saves enough money,
7. If Lisa goes back to school,
8. If there is bad weather,

Result clause

a. he should get a computer.
b. he can take family leave.
c. the company might close for the day.
d. she will update her résumé.
e. it should offer onsite training and tuition reimbursement.
f. she'll take some time off to travel.
g. she might have to quit her job.
h. she should use a functional résumé.

2 Complete the Sentences

Complete each sentence. Use the cues in parentheses or your own ideas when you see a question mark in parentheses (?).

1. If Mario has bad teeth, *he should look for a job with dental insurance* (look for/job/with dental insurance).

2. If the employer provides on-site day care, _____ (you/not worry/about your children).

3. If I get a raise, _____ (not need/a second job).

4. If her résumé is full of mistakes, _____ (not get/an interview).

5. If we telecommute, _____ (save money/on gas).

6. If they go to the gym every day, _____ (?).

7. If I don't hear from the employer soon, _____ (?).

8. If your son gets sick at the on-site child care center, _____ (?).

3 Answer

Answer the questions. Use *if* and result clauses in your answers.

1. What happens to your English class if it rains or snows a lot?
If it rains a lot, the school ...

2. What will you do if you win a million dollars?

3. What will you do if someone in your family gets very sick?

4. What resources can people use if they want to find new jobs?

5. What will you look for in a workplace if you need to find a job?

6. What should job applicants ask if they call about a job opening?

Work with a classmate. Take turns asking and answering the questions.

120

121

Grammar practice activities guide students through structured and progressively more open-ended ways to use the target grammar.

All-Star
Interactive CD-ROM
LEVEL ☆

Linda Lee ★ Jean Bernard ★ Stephen Sloan
Grace Tanaka ★ Shirley Velasco

Interactive CD-ROM program for **Levels 1 and 2** incorporates and extends the learning goals by integrating language, literacy, and numeracy skill building with computer practice.

Application lessons focus on developing the students' roles in life as workers, parents, and community members.

Real-world documents and situations are highlighted in the *Application* lessons, exposing students to critical concepts they encounter at work, at home, and in the community.

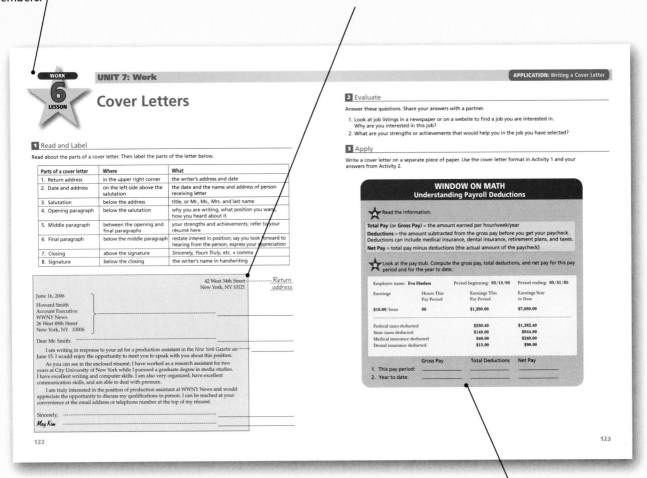

UNIT 7: Work

APPLICATION: Writing a Cover Letter

Cover Letters

1 Read and Label

Read about the parts of a cover letter. Then label the parts of the letter below.

Parts of a cover letter	Where	What
1. Return address	in the upper right corner	the writer's address and date
2. Date and address	on the left side above the salutation	the date and the name and address of person receiving letter
3. Salutation	below the address	title, or Mr., Ms., Mrs. and last name
4. Opening paragraph	below the salutation	why you are writing, what position you want, how you heard about it
5. Middle paragraph	between the opening and final paragraphs	your strengths and achievements; refer to your résumé here
6. Final paragraph	below the middle paragraph	restate interest in position; say you look forward to hearing from the person, express your appreciation
7. Closing	above the signature	*Sincerely, Yours Truly,* etc. + comma
8. Signature	below the closing	the writer's name in handwriting

42 West 34th Street
New York, NY 10121 ···· *Return address*

June 16, 2006
Howard Smith
Account Executive
WWNY News
26 West 49th Street
New York, NY 10006

Dear Mr. Smith:

I am writing in response to your ad for a production assistant in the *New York Gazette* on June 15. I would enjoy the opportunity to meet you to speak with you about this position.

As you can see in the enclosed résumé, I have worked as a research assistant for two years at City University of New York while I pursued a graduate degree in media studies. I have excellent writing and computer skills. I am also very organized, have excellent communication skills, and am able to deal with pressure.

I am truly interested in the position of production assistant at WWNY News and would appreciate the opportunity to discuss my qualifications in person. I can be reached at your convenience at the email address or telephone number at the top of my résumé.

Sincerely,

May Kim

122

2 Evaluate

Answer these questions. Share your answers with a partner.

1. Look at job listings in a newspaper or on a website to find a job you are interested in. Why are you interested in this job?
2. What are your strengths or achievements that would help you in the job you have selected?

3 Apply

Write a cover letter on a separate piece of paper. Use the cover letter format in Activity 1 and your answers from Activity 2.

WINDOW ON MATH
Understanding Payroll Deductions

⭐ Read the information.

Total Pay (or Gross Pay) = the amount earned per hour/week/year

Deductions = the amount subtracted from the gross pay before you get your paycheck. Deductions can include medical insurance, dental insurance, retirement plans, and taxes.

Net Pay = total pay minus deductions (the actual amount of the paycheck)

⭐ Look at the pay stub. Compute the gross pay, total deductions, and net pay for this pay period and for the year to date.

Employee name: **Eva Haslam**   Period beginning: **03/15/05**   Period ending: **03/31/05**

Earnings	Hours This Pay Period	Earnings This Pay Period	Earnings Year to Date
$16.00/hour	80	$1,280.00	$7,680.00

Federal taxes deducted	$250.40	$1,382.40
State taxes deducted	$140.80	$844.80
Medical insurance deducted	$40.00	$240.00
Dental insurance deducted	$15.00	$90.00

	Gross Pay	Total Deductions	Net Pay
1. This pay period:			
2. Year to date:			

123

Windows on Math help students develop functional numeracy skills needed in everyday applications.

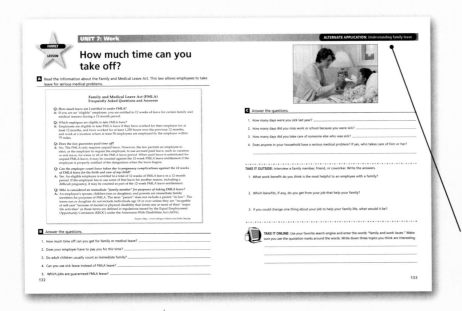

UNIT 7: Work

ALTERNATE APPLICATION: Understanding family leave

How much time can you take off?

A Read the information about the Family and Medical Leave Act. This law allows employees to take leave for serious medical problems.

Family and Medical Leave Act (FMLA)
Frequently Asked Questions and Answers

Q: *How much leave am I entitled to under FMLA?*
A: If you are an "eligible" employee, you are entitled to 12 weeks of leave for certain family and medical reasons during a 12-month period.

Q: *Which employees are eligible to take FMLA leave?*
A: Employees are eligible to take FMLA leave if they have worked for their employer for at least 12 months, and have worked for at least 1,250 hours over the previous 12 months, and work at a location where at least 50 employees are employed by the employer within 75 miles.

Q: *Does the law guarantee paid time off?*
A: No. The FMLA only requires unpaid leave. However, the law permits an employee to elect, or the employer to require the employee, to use accrued paid leave, such as vacation or sick leave, for some or all of the FMLA leave period. When paid leave is substituted for unpaid FMLA leave, it may be counted against the 12-week FMLA leave entitlement if the employee is properly notified of the designation when the leave begins.

Q: *Can the employer count leave taken due to pregnancy complications against the 12 weeks of FMLA leave for the birth and care of my child?*
A: Yes. An eligible employee is entitled to a total of 12 weeks of FMLA leave in a 12-month period. If the employee has to use some of that leave for another reason, including a difficult pregnancy, it may be counted as part of the 12-week FMLA leave entitlement.

Q: *Who is considered an immediate "family member" for purposes of taking FMLA leave?*
A: An employee's spouse, children (son or daughter), and parents are immediate family members for purposes of FMLA. The term "parent" does not include a parent "in-law." The terms son or daughter do not include individuals 18 or over unless they are "incapable of self-care" because of mental or physical disability that limits one or more of their "major life activities" as those terms are defined in regulations issued by the Equal Employment Opportunity Commission (EEOC) under the Americans With Disabilities Act (ADA).

Source: http://www.dol.gov/elaws/esa/fmla/faq.asp

B Answer the questions.

1. How much time off can you get for family or medical leave? _____
2. Does your employer have to pay you for this time? _____
3. Do adult children usually count as immediate family? _____
4. Can you use sick leave instead of FMLA leave? _____
5. Which jobs are guaranteed FMLA leave? _____

132

C Answer the questions.

1. How many days were you sick last year? _____
2. How many days did you miss work or school because you were sick? _____
3. How many days did you take care of someone else who was sick? _____
4. Does anyone in your household have a serious medical problem? If yes, who takes care of him or her? _____

TAKE IT OUTSIDE: Interview a family member, friend, or coworker. Write the answers.

1. What work benefit do you think is the most helpful to an employee with a family? _____
2. Which benefits, if any, do you get from your job that help your family? _____
3. If you could change one thing about your job to help your family life, what would it be? _____

TAKE IT ONLINE: Use your favorite search engine and enter the words "family and work issues." Make sure you use the quotation marks around the words. Write down three topics you think are interesting. _____

133

Alternate application lessons in the Workbook provide a flexible approach to addressing family, work, *and* community topics in each unit.

Listening Reviews help teachers assess listening comprehension, while giving students practice with the item types and answer sheets they encounter on standardized tests.

Vocabulary Reviews provide engaging activities for students to review and assess their knowledge of the vocabulary they learned in each unit.

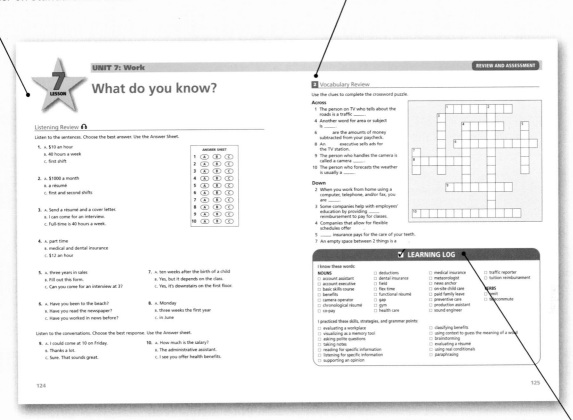

Spotlight: Reading and **Spotlight: Writing** lessons appear at the end of each unit, offering supplementary and targeted reading and writing skill development.

Learning Logs ask students to catalog the vocabulary, grammar, life skills, and strategies they have learned, and determine which areas they need to review.

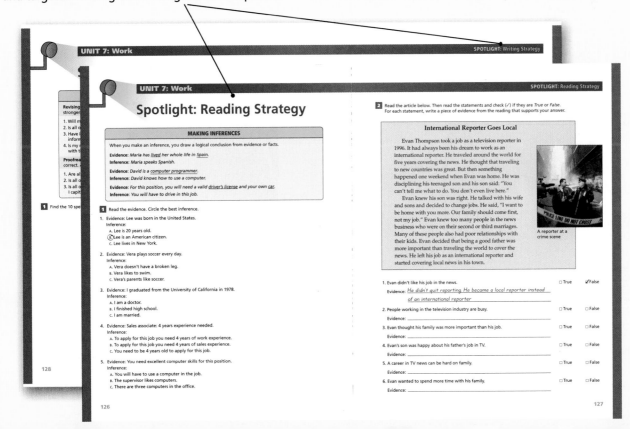

INTRODUCTION

I'd like you to meet my friend.

1 Evaluate

What is the best response to these introductions and greetings? Check (✓) your answers.

1

How do you do? I'm Charles Wilson.

❑ Hi, Charles. I'm Donald.
❑ Nice to meet you, Mr. Wilson. I'm Donald Turner.
❑ Hey, Charles. How are you doing?

2

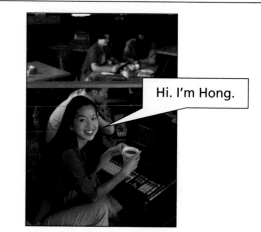

Hi. I'm Hong.

❑ How do you do, Hong? Are you a student here?
❑ Hi. Nice to meet you.
❑ Nice to meet you. My name is Sam. Is this your first class here?

3

Hi. My name is Carmen.

❑ Hi. Are you a student here?
❑ Hi, Carmen. I'm Hector. What do you think of this class?
❑ Hi, I'm Hector.

4

I'd like you to meet my friend Yuko. She's from Japan.

❑ Nice to meet you, Yuko.
❑ Nice to meet you, Yuko. Where in Japan are you from?
❑ Hi, Yuko.

What do you like and dislike about each response? Share ideas with your classmates.

> EXAMPLE: The first response in #1 seems very informal.
> Charles gave his full name, but Donald only gave his first name.

2 Get Together

Introduce yourself to 3 classmates. Then ask 3 questions to learn more about each person. Write their information below.

Sample Questions
- Where are you from?
- When did you move here?
- Does your family live here too?
- What sports do you like?
- What do you do for fun?
-

EXAMPLE:
A: Hello. My name is <u>Nina</u>.
B: Nice to meet you, <u>Nina</u>. I'm <u>Antonio</u>.
A: Nice to meet you, <u>Antonio</u>. Where are you from?
B: I'm from <u>Argentina</u>. How about you?

Classmate #1	**Classmate #2**	**Classmate #3**
Name: _____	Name: _____	Name: _____
Information: _____	Information: _____	Information: _____

Tell the class what you learned about each person.

3 Look It Over

What's in this book? Find each of the things below.

1. The topic of Unit 1 (pages 4–21) is ___*Setting Goals*___.

2. The topic of Unit 5 is _____.

3. You can find the definitions of many words in a glossary on pages _____ to _____.

4. There is a map of _____ on page 189.

5. A _____ begins on page 148.

6. There is a magazine article in Unit 6 on pages _____.

7. There is a business letter in Unit 2 on page _____.

8. There is a job résumé on page _____.

9. There is a picture of a _____ on pages 112 and 113.

10. There is a health questionnaire on page _____.

They have many responsibilities.

LESSON 1

THINGS TO DO

1 Warm Up

Work with your classmates to answer these questions.

1. What are 5 things that are happening in the picture?
2. What do you know about Laura and Ed from the picture? What are some of their responsibilities?
3. What are 10 things that you do every day?

2 Make Inferences

Complete the sentences using information in the picture and your own ideas. Talk with a partner.

1. I think Laura (<u>has</u>/doesn't have) a job because *she is dressed for work and she is wearing a name tag.*
2. I think education (is/isn't) very important to this family because. . .
3. I think the parents (have/don't have) enough time to do everything because. . .
4. I think Laura and Ed (are/aren't) good parents because . . .

3 Find Someone Who

Read the list of household responsibilities in the chart below. Add 3 more. Look at the picture for ideas.

Find someone who has to _____.	Name of classmate with the same responsibility
1. buy food	_____
2. clean the house	_____
3. pay the bills	_____
4. _____	_____
5. _____	_____
6. _____	_____

Talk to your classmates. Find someone who answers yes to your questions about household responsibilities. Write the person's name in the chart.

> A: Do you have to clean the house?
> B: Yes, I do. / No, I don't.

TRY THIS STRATEGY

Preview Before you begin a unit, it's useful to look it over from beginning to end. This helps you set study goals and prepares you for learning. Look over the first 6 lessons in this unit. List the title and the topic of each lesson. Then tell your classmate which lesson looks the most useful to you and why.

UNIT 1: Setting Goals

I have to prioritize.

See page 171 for a glossary of highlighted vocabulary.

THINGS TO DO

1 Complete the Chart

Read about the people and their goals. Complete the chart.

Name	What is the long-term goal?	What is a short-term goal?
Kilim	*get more sleep*	*cut back on telephone calls and TV*
Leila		*fill out an application for financial aid this month*
Sara		
Mauricio	*start own company*	
James		
Tracy	*pay off debts*	
Mike		
David		

Compare your notes with a partner.

2 Read and Match

Match the words with their definitions.

1. tutor
2. focus
3. cut back on
4. prioritize
5. pay off
6. debt
7. financial aid

a. reduce
b. deal with in order of importance
c. amount of money owed
d. teacher who helps students one-on-one
e. center attention on
f. help to pay for education
g. give back money that is owed

3 Write

Write 1 long-term goal. Then write 2–3 short-term goals that will help you reach your long-term goal. Write a paragraph about your goals.

Kilim

I need to get more sleep. I have so many things to do, but I have to **prioritize**. I'm going to spend less time talking on the telephone and watching TV. These are the first things I plan to **cut back on** because they aren't very important.

Mauricio

I want to start my own painting company. This is hard for me because I didn't finish high school. I work as a painter and do a good job, but I can't read very well. I need to take some **continuing education** classes so I can become a better reader. Then I can take some business courses and create a successful company.

TRY THIS STRATEGY ◆ ◆ ◆ ◆ ◆ ◆ ◆ ◆ ◆ ◆ ◆ ◆ ◆ ◆ ◆

Keep a Vocabulary Notebook To remember new words, keep a vocabulary notebook. In your notebook, list the words you want to remember and write sentences using the words. You can also write the definitions. Choose 5 new words from this lesson and start your vocabulary notebook.

◆ ◆ ◆ ◆ ◆ ◆ ◆ ◆ ◆ ◆ ◆ ◆ ◆ ◆ ◆ ◆ ◆ ◆ ◆ ◆

Leila

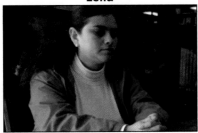

My goal is to attend college. I don't have enough money, and I don't know what to study, so I have to do some research. I'm going to look at the **online job bank** for job listings and fill out an application for **financial aid** this month. I have an appointment with a counselor at the community college tomorrow.

Sara

My husband and I want to buy our own house. I need to talk to a bank officer about getting a **mortgage** . I know we need to save for a **down payment** first.

James

I would like to learn to play the piano, but I never played an instrument as a young man. I have to **focus** and use my time well. I need to **practice** an hour every day. It won't be difficult, because I really enjoy music.

Tracy

I want to **pay off** my **debts** . I plan to save $100 a month by **reducing my expenses** . I'll eat at home more often and buy fewer clothes. I'm also looking for a part-time job.

Mike

I want to be more involved in my children's education. My wife usually goes to the **PTA meetings** and **volunteers** in the classroom. I can't volunteer because I work during the day and on Thursday evenings when they hold the PTA meetings. So this year I am going to change my work schedule so I can go to the **parent-teacher conferences** . I'll also **monitor** the kids' homework in the evenings.

David

I want to become a U.S. citizen. I'm working with a **tutor** twice a week to learn more about American history and government. My tutor is helping me prepare for the interview. I also take English classes 2 nights a week at the community college.

3 LESSON
You should apply for a Pell Grant.

THINGS TO DO

1 Warm Up

Work with your classmates to answer these questions.
1. Where are the people in each picture?
2. What do you think they are saying to each other?
3. What is one of your goals? Who could you go to for advice about reaching that goal?

2 Listen and Take Notes 🎧

Listen to conversation #1 and write the person's long-term goal. Listen again and write the suggested short-term goal. Repeat with conversations #2, #3, and #4.

	What is the person's long-term goal?	What is the suggested short-term goal?
1.	*become a medical technician*	
2.		
3.		
4.		

3 Use the Communication Strategy 🎧

Work with a partner. Role-play a conversation between a student and a counselor. Replace the underlined words with your own ideas. Try to use the communication strategy.

A: Can you tell me how to get money to go back to school?
B: Well, you could apply for a Pell Grant.
A: What could I apply for?
B: A Pell Grant. It's money for school that you don't have to pay back.
A: Sounds great.

COMMUNICATION STRATEGY

Asking for Focused Repetition

When you don't understand a particular word or phrase that someone said, ask for repetition of that word or phrase. You can ask by putting the question word at the beginning or end of the question.

You could apply for a Pell Grant.

I could apply for <u>what</u>?   or   <u>What</u> could I apply for?

You should talk to Ms. Parker in the Financial Aid Office.

I should talk to <u>who</u>?   or   <u>Who</u> should I talk to?

You should go to the Financial Aid Office.

I should go <u>where</u>?   or   <u>Where</u> should I go?

LESSON 4

A Success Story

THINGS TO DO

1 Warm Up

Work with your classmates to answer these questions.

1. What were 2–3 of your goals when you were younger?
2. Did you achieve them? Why or why not?

2 Preview

Read the first 2 sentences and the last 2 sentences in the story. Check (✓) the topic.

- ❏ The AT&T company
- ❏ Homero Acevedo's family
- ❏ A successful businessman named Homero Acevedo

3 Read and Respond

Read the article. Complete the chart.

Paragraph	What was Mr. Acevedo's goal?	How do you think he reached it?
2	to become an outstanding athlete	practiced every day
3		
4		

Compare your answers with a partner. Then retell the story in your own words.

4 Evaluate

Work with several classmates to answer these questions.

1. What do you think Mr. Acevedo means when he says "Anyone can be a success if they are secure with themselves, ready to move, and an achiever"?
2. What is your definition of success? What are the most important qualities needed to achieve success?
3. Describe a successful person you know. Why is he or she successful?

San Antonio, Texas

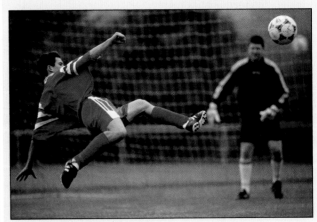
Soccer, one of Acevedo's favorite sports

Person of the Week:
Homero E. Acevedo

1   Homero E. Acevedo is an executive with the American Telephone and Telegraph Company (AT&T). Mr. Acevedo has used his good education and his ability to **communicate** well in English and Spanish to become one of the youngest managers of the AT&T National **Bilingual** Center in San Antonio, Texas. There are lots of things we can learn from Mr. Acevedo.

2   Mr. Acevedo's dad taught him what goals are and helped him achieve some. One of his goals was to become an **outstanding athlete**. He did, and his favorite sports were soccer, baseball, and basketball. At one point, he played semiprofessional soccer. He loves Chicago teams, especially the Bears, Bulls, Cubs, and Blackhawks. Although sports are an important part of Mr. Acevedo's life, they never became his main goal.

3   The most important goal was to get a good education. Mr. Acevedo realized that a good education would open many doors for him in the future. In high school, he studied hard and got excellent grades. He then graduated from the University of Denver. While in college, he had a chance to study in Spain. By being one of the top academic students, he got to meet the king of Spain, Juan Carlos.

4   Mr. Acevedo knew that he needed to be ready to move to different parts of the country to **advance** in his career. He moved to New Jersey for training.

He was **in charge of** testing a new billing system and a new computer system that would take care of eighty million residential customer accounts. This was a great responsibility.

5   After six months of testing the computer system, he was moved to San Antonio, Texas. There he is an operations manager in charge of the International Communications Service Center. Many office managers report to him. There are about 175 people in his department. He makes sure that everything runs smoothly.

6   Mr. Acevedo is able to communicate with people very well. He can speak and write **fluent** English and Spanish. He feels very lucky to know two languages and believes it has helped him be a successful executive. He says, "Anyone can be a success if they are secure with themselves, ready to move, and an achiever."

5 LESSON

When she got home, she made dinner.

Past Time Clauses with *When*	
We use past time clauses with *when* to talk about the relationship between two events in the past. The event in the *when* clause happened before the event in the main clause. The *when* clause can go at the beginning or at the end of the sentence. Use the simple past in the past time clause with *when*.	

Time Clause with *When*	Main Clause
When she got home,	she made dinner.
Main Clause	**Time Clause with *When***
He talked to a counselor	**when** he went to the career center.

1 Complete the Sentences

Complete the sentences. Use the simple past.

1. I bought some fruit when I _____ went _____ to the store. (go)
2. When she _____ , she broke her arm. (fall)
3. They weren't home when I _____. (call)
4. Jack gave her a present when she _____. (graduate)
5. When Laura _____ a promotion, she had a big party. (get)
6. When Kilim _____ on TV, he had more time. (cut back)
7. We bought a house when we _____ enough money. (have)
8. He helped his daughter when she _____ it. (need)
9. They always voted when there _____ an election. (be)
10. When Mauricio first _____ classes, he wasn't very confident. (start)

2 Rewrite

Rewrite the story below. Use the past tense.

My friend Ravi is a student of culinary arts at Brookfield Community College. He wants to become a chef when he finishes school. At BCC, Ravi learns how to prepare menus, and he practices cooking different dishes. Ravi doesn't like his food chemistry class, but he needs it to graduate.

Ravi is busy all the time. When he leaves school, he goes to his full-time job at a restaurant. When he gets home, he helps his wife with the children. Sometimes he doesn't get enough rest and he falls asleep in class.

Future Time Clauses with *When*

We use future time clauses with *when* to talk about the relationship between two events in the future. The event in the *when* clause will happen before the event in the main clause. The *when* clause can go before or after the main clause. Use the simple present in the *when* clause to express the future. Use *will* or *be going to* in the main clause.

Use *will* or *be going to* when talking about future plans or making a prediction about the future.

Time Clause with *When* / Main Clause	Main Clause / Time Clause with *When*
When you're ready, we'll leave.	We're going to leave **when** you're ready.

Use *be going to* when talking about prior plans about the future.

Time Clause with *When* / Main Clause	Main Clause / Time Clause with *When*
When I graduate, I'm going to travel.	I'm going to travel **when** I graduate.

Use *will* when no prior plan has been made and you're deciding to do something while speaking.

Time Clause with *When* / Main Clause	Main Clause / Time Clause with *When*
When we're finished, I'll wash the dishes.	I'll wash the dishes **when** we're finished.

3 Complete the Sentences

Complete the sentences with the verbs in parentheses. Use the simple present in the *when* clause. Use *will* or *be going to* in the main clause.

1. The president *is going to talk* (talk) to the United Nations when he _____*goes*_____ (go) to New York.
2. We _____ (take) a vacation when the store _____ (be) less busy.
3. When Mei _____ (get) a raise, she _____ (buy) a new car.
4. When Sally _____ (improve) her math skills, she _____ (take) the placement test again.
5. When he _____ (find) a babysitter, he _____ (sign up) for classes.
6. Daniela _____ (ask) for help when she _____ (need) it.
7. When you _____ (finish) those chores, we _____ (get) ice cream.
8. I _____ (buy) a motorcycle when I _____ (sell) my car.

4 Write

Write 3 sentences about the picture. Make predictions. Use *will*.

_____

_____

_____

_____

13

Your Dream Job

1 Warm Up

Work with your classmates to answer these questions.

1. What is your dream job?
2. Look at the title of the reading. What do you think it means to get the most from your job?

2 Read and Respond

Read the article. Then read the sentences that follow and check *True* or *False*. Compare your answers with a partner.

How to Get the Most from Your Job

Are you starting a new job soon? Are you looking for a job? Are you recently unemployed, but hope to go back to work? Are you working, but not where you want to be? Whatever your work situation, now is a good time to plan to get the most from your job.

Ask key questions. Think about what you want and ask yourself questions: What do I want to learn? What do I want to earn? Who do I want to work with? What job do I want to have a few years from now? When do I want to leave this job?

Identify goals. Use your answers to the questions above to set your work goals. For example, if you want to earn $10,000 a year more than you do now, you might set a goal to get a raise in the next 6 months.

Prioritize. Look at all the goals you identified. Choose 4 or 5 that are the most important to work on in the next few months.

Make a timeline. For each of the 4 or 5 goals you decided to work on, break the process down into achievable steps. First decide what you can do in the next week, then what can be done in the next few weeks. Finally, review your progress and reset goals every 6 months.

Source: Amy Lindgren, *Saint Paul Pioneer Press*

	True	False
1. Asking key questions can help you decide what you want.	☐	☐
2. Identifying your goals will help you reach them.	☐	☐
3. You should review your progress every 6 months.	☐	☐
4. You should try to work on 5–10 work goals in the next few months.	☐	☐
5. This article is only useful for people who are working.	☐	☐
6. If you want to reach a goal, you should break it down into smaller steps.	☐	☐

3 Apply

Answer the 5 key questions from the reading. Give information about yourself.

Key questions from reading	Your answers
1. What do I want to learn?	
2. What do I want to earn?	
3. Who do I want to work with?	
4. What job do I want to have a few years from now?	
5. When do I want to leave this job?	

Talk about your answers with a partner.

WINDOW ON PRONUNCIATION 🎧
Stress when Asking for Repetition

 Listen to the conversations. Then listen and repeat.

1. A: You should talk to the English coordinator.

   B: (Who) should I talk to?

   A: The English coordinator. Her name is Ms. Green. She's in room 103.

   B: Thanks.

2. A: The citizenship class meets at 3:00 on Sunday afternoons.

   B: What time does it meet on Sundays?

   A: At 3:00. Can you go at that time?

   B: I think so.

Listen again and circle the word in each question above that receives the most stress.

 Work with a partner. Practice the conversation, focusing on where you place the stress in the questions.

A: I think you should take a study skills class.

B: What kind of class?

A: Study skills. There's a class starting next month.

B: When is it starting?

A: Next month.

B: Sounds good. Where can I find out about it?

LESON 7

What do you know?

1 Listening Review 🎧

Listen to the questions and statements. Choose the best answer. Use the Answer Sheet.

1. A. Pick up a mortgage application.
   B. Learn about American history.
   C. Fill out an application.

2. A. Learn about American government.
   B. Take a business class.
   C. Get a loan.

3. A. He should go to bed early.
   B. He can volunteer.
   C. He needs to prioritize.

4. A. Who is it?
   B. Fill out what?
   C. How many are there?

	ANSWER SHEET		
1	Ⓐ	Ⓑ	Ⓒ
2	Ⓐ	Ⓑ	Ⓒ
3	Ⓐ	Ⓑ	Ⓒ
4	Ⓐ	Ⓑ	Ⓒ
5	Ⓐ	Ⓑ	Ⓒ
6	Ⓐ	Ⓑ	Ⓒ
7	Ⓐ	Ⓑ	Ⓒ
8	Ⓐ	Ⓑ	Ⓒ
9	Ⓐ	Ⓑ	Ⓒ
10	Ⓐ	Ⓑ	Ⓒ

Listen to the sentences. Which answer means the same? Use the Answer Sheet.

5. A. Pay back the money you owe.
   B. Borrow the money for the car.
   C. Buy a used car.

6. A. She can get help.
   B. She can decide what is important and do it first.
   C. She gets lots of support from family and friends.

7. A. He is applying for school.
   B. He is applying for a job.
   C. He is applying for a loan.

8. A. You need someone to teach you one-on-one.
   B. You should get a book.
   C. You need to do research in the library.

Listen to the conversations. Then listen to the questions. Choose the correct answer. Use the Answer Sheet.

9. A. a car loan
   B. a mortgage
   C. a student loan

10. A. Pick up a schedule from the office.
    B. Go to school every day.
    C. Attend PTA meetings.

2 Vocabulary Review

Use the clues to complete the crossword puzzle.

Across

2 You should _____ _____ your debts if you want to save money.

3 A teacher who works with a student one-on-one is a _____.

5 When you do things in order of importance, you _____.

7 When people have too much _____ , they can't pay their bills.

8 A synonym for *reduce* is _____ _____.

9 A loan you get to buy a house is a _____.

10 I play the guitar every day. I have to _____ to get better.

Down

1 When people work for free, they _____.

4 Often people buy an expensive item by giving a partial amount or a _____ _____.

6 When a job needs special attention, you should really _____ on it.

✔ LEARNING LOG

I know these words:

NOUNS
- ☐ athlete
- ☐ continuing education
- ☐ debt
- ☐ down payment
- ☐ expenses
- ☐ financial aid
- ☐ long-term goal
- ☐ mortgage
- ☐ online job bank
- ☐ parent-teacher conference
- ☐ PTA meeting

- ☐ short-term goal
- ☐ tutor

VERBS
- ☐ advance
- ☐ communicate
- ☐ cut back (on)
- ☐ focus
- ☐ monitor
- ☐ pay off
- ☐ practice
- ☐ prioritize

- ☐ reduce
- ☐ volunteer

ADJECTIVES
- ☐ bilingual
- ☐ fluent
- ☐ outstanding

OTHER
- ☐ in charge of

I practiced these skills, strategies, and grammar points:

- ☐ previewing the unit
- ☐ setting goals
- ☐ keeping a vocabulary notebook
- ☐ reading for specific information

- ☐ listening for specific information
- ☐ making career plans
- ☐ making inferences
- ☐ asking for focused repetition

- ☐ using future time clauses with *when*
- ☐ using past time clauses with *when*

Spotlight: Reading Strategy

USING CONTEXT TO GUESS MEANING

You can use the words around a new word to understand its meaning. This is called *context.* The context can help in a number of ways. It can provide:

a definition
Homero Acevedo is **bilingual** — he can speak Spanish and English very well.

a description
He is **in charge of** the center. Many office managers report to him. He supervises about 175 people in his department.

a comparison or a contrast
Like parent-teacher conferences, **PTA meetings** are a way to get more involved in your children's education.

cause and effect
I applied for **financial aid**, because I needed to borrow money for school.

an example or examples
One of his goals was to become an outstanding **athlete**. He did, and his favorite sports were soccer, baseball, and basketball.

a series
You can learn new skills if you take a class, study on your own, or work with a **tutor**.

a synonym
If you **cut back on**, or reduce, the amount of TV you watch, you can save time for other things.

---

1 Use context to choose the best definitions for the highlighted words.

1. I **wasted time** playing video games and watching TV.
   a. used time well   b. used time poorly   c. didn't have time

2. To prepare for the citizenship interview, Magda is learning about U.S. presidents, the legal system, and how **Congress** works.
   a. a kind of business   b. English grammar   c. part of the government

3. Like other members of the family, **pets** need food, sleep, and love.
   a. dogs, cats, and other animals   b. beds and chairs   c. books and newspapers

4. Walt is proud of the things he **accomplished** this year. He graduated from college, got married, and got a promotion at work.
   a. started   b. completed   c. continued

2 Read the information. Use context to guess the meaning of new words. Match the terms and definitions below.

Tips for Working Parents

1. Prioritize. Busy parents have too many things to do and not enough time. Prioritizing allows you to choose which tasks are the most important and do those first. For example, if you have to take your children to school, drop clothes at the dry cleaners, get to work by 9 A.M., and call your mother, you may decide to go to the dry cleaners and call your mother after work.

2. Use a support system . As a working parent, you need to develop and use a support system. Find friends and family you can turn to in times of need. If you are sick, maybe a family member can make dinner for the kids.

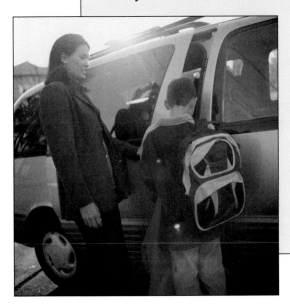

3. Delegate . As you look at your busy schedule, decide if you can delegate. It may be hard to trust others to get jobs done, but sometimes you can't do it all yourself.

4. Set routines . You will use less effort if you make some things routine. If you always do certain tasks in the same way, you won't have to think about them too much.

5. Organize . People often work better when they organize their stuff. Put your things in order with bins, shelves, and folders.

Terms	Definitions
1. _c_ prioritize	a. friends and family who help you
2. _____ support system	b. to ask others to do a job
3. _____ delegate	c̸. to do jobs in order of importance
4. _____ routine	d. to put in order
5. _____ organize	e. a regular, repeated way of doing things

UNIT 1: Setting Goals

Spotlight: Writing Strategy

PREWRITING: BRAINSTORMING

Brainstorming is a good prewriting activity. When you brainstorm:

• write down as many ideas as you can on a given topic.

• don't evaluate the ideas, just think and write quickly.

• set a goal of a certain number — think of 10, 20, or 30 ideas before you stop your list.

EXAMPLE:

Writing topic: *be a good parent*

Brainstorming ideas:

read to children	brush teeth	clean clothes
visit school	regular bedtime	healthy food
eat together	have fun	homework help
spend time together	teach things	sing silly songs

---

1 Choose 1 of the topics below and brainstorm 10 ideas. Write your ideas on the lines.

TOPICS		
be a good community member save money	get in better shape/lose weight start a business	get a better job meet new people

1. _____

2. _____

3. _____

4. _____

5. _____

6. _____

7. _____

8. _____

9. _____

10. _____

Share your ideas with a classmate.

2 Choose 3 or 4 of the ideas you like best and write sentences about the topic.

EXAMPLE: There are many ways to save money. You can eat at home instead of at a restaurant. You can use coupons. You can also buy things when they are on sale.

_____

_____

_____

PREWRITING: MAKING A CLUSTER DIAGRAM

After brainstorming, you can make a cluster diagram. Cluster diagrams can help generate and organize ideas.

- Step 1: Write the topic in the center of your paper and circle it.
- Step 2: Think of related ideas. Write the ideas on the paper around the topic. Circle each new idea and draw a line to connect it to the topic.
- Step 3: Look at the diagram. Add more ideas and connect them to the ideas already on the diagram.

3 Look at the topics again in Activity 1. Choose a different topic. Create a cluster diagram below for your ideas.

4 Write 4 sentences about the topic using your ideas in Activity 3.

_____

_____

_____

_____

LESSON 1

What are the pluses and minuses?

THINGS TO DO

1 Warm Up

Work with your classmates to answer these questions.

1. Would you rather live in a house or an apartment?
2. Who is involved in building and selling a house?
3. What is your opinion of the house in the picture?

2 Identify

Study the picture and the floor plan and check (✓) the things you see. Then compare ideas with a partner.

☐ a porch   ☐ a 2-car garage

☐ a patio   ☐ a family room

☐ a fenced yard   ☐ kitchen appliances

☐ lots of windows   ☐ 4 bedrooms

☐ a deck   ☐ a gas furnace

☐ a chimney   ☐ a pool

☐ a driveway   ☐ _____

3 Evaluate

Work with a partner to evaluate the house in the picture. Identify the pluses (the things you like about the house) and the minuses (the things you don't like).

The Pluses	The Minuses
It has lots of windows.	

Would you buy this house? Why or why not?

Set Learning Goals Below are some things you will do in this unit. Number them in order from most useful to you (1) to least useful (6).

___ read housing ads   ___ identify housing problems

___ learn abbreviations   ___ read a rental agreement

___ listen to phone conversations   ___ write a letter of complaint

Floor Plan

m br
16' x 16'

br 2
14' x 16'

bath

kitchen

2-car
garage
31' x 48'

living room

din rm
25.5' x 16'

BEST ROOFERS

IDA FRANKS
NEW HOUSE
FOR SALE

2 LESSON

It's available immediately.

Duplex

THINGS TO DO

1 Find the Abbreviation

Read the housing ads and find an abbreviation for each word below.

1. **air conditioning** _AC_
2. **utilities** _____
3. **parking** _____
4. **location** _____
5. **electricity** _____
6. **available** _____
7. **immediately** _____
8. **elevator** _____
9. **maintenance** _____
10. **neighborhood** _____
11. **attached** _____
12. **remodeled** _____
13. **security deposit** _____
14. **washer and dryer hookup** _____

What do these words mean? Share ideas with your classmates.

Ranch

2 Use the Vocabulary 🎧

Work with a partner. Take turns role-playing a telephone conversation between a customer and a real estate agent.

A: I'm calling about the apartment for rent .

B: Which one are you interested in?

A: It's the 1-bedroom apartment for $650 a month .

B: The one in the North End ?

A: Yes, that's the one. Could you tell me, is heat included in the rent ?

B: Yes, it is. Would you like to see the place?

A: Yes, I would.

Colonial

1 house for rent / 3-bedroom duplex

for $1,375 a month

is it available immediately

2 house for sale / 2-bedroom house with a pool

for $199,900

is the carport attached to the house

3 apartment for rent / 1-bedroom apartment for $600 a month

on Lake Avenue

is a security deposit required

TRY THIS STRATEGY

Group Words Putting words into groups helps you remember them. Add 5 more words to each group.

Words that describe a house	Parts of a house/apartment
clean	bedroom
modern	garage

CLASSIFIEDS

Apartments — Homes

Unfurnished Apartments

NORTH
2nd flr., 2BR, clean, quiet, heated, prkg., no pets, $800 mo., 555-4556

NO END
2nd flr., 1 bdrm apt, includes ht. Hot water & elec. extra. No smoke/dogs, $650/mo. + sec. 555-4694

WEST SIDE Branch River Apartments. Lg. modern one & two bedroom units, garage & outside parking, AC, balcony, laundry & pool on site, gas ht., 24 hr. maint. $795–$950. Plus utils. Good credit required. Sorry, no dogs. Call 555-4983

LAKE AVE, 14th Floor, 1 BR, $600 + sec. dep., Elev., view. No dogs/utils. 555-4493

EAST, 3rd flr, 2BR, w/d hkup, porch, 1 car prkg, yd. $850/mo htd. Avail. 4/1. 555-9947

Houses for Rent

NORTH END
2 BR home avail immed, 1 car gar., no pets, $1200/mo. 555-4887

BELMONT ST. 3 bdrm. 1.5 ba duplex, gar, lg yard, fm. nghbd, no smoker, pets OK, $1375/mo. 555-9986

SO. END Bright & sunny 3 BR, 1 1/2 ba ranch, 2 car gar., fenced yd, newly remod. $1500 + utils. No pets/smkrs. 555-8897

LAKE AVE
3 bedroom, 1 bath home, W/D hookup, large yd., pets o.k., $900.00 plus utilities, security, references. Call 555-4583

Houses for Sale

WEST SIDE Ranch w/pool in great loc. Many updates including gas furnace, driveway, electrical. 2BR, 1 BA. carport. Price reduced $199,900.

House for Sale

NORTH END 5 rm, 2BR ranch. Eat-in kitchen, master BR w/bath, 2 car att'd gar. $180,000

EAST SIDE New, $210,000. 3 BR, 2 baths, lg patio, nice nghbhrd. Call Ida Franks, 555-2588.

ELIOT LANE
3 bdrm colonial, 1 car garage, new kitchen, all electrical and plumbing updated. Quiet dead end, family neighborhood. $225,000. Call 555-3948

3 LESSON

There seems to be a leak.

THINGS TO DO

1 Warm Up

Work with your classmates to answer these questions.

1. What are some common problems people have with their house or apartment? Which problems do you have to take care of right away?

2. What problems do you think the people in pictures 1, 2, and 3 are having?

2 Listen and Take Notes 🎧

Listen to telephone conversation #1 and write the tenant's problems. Then listen again and write the landlord's response. Repeat with conversations #2 and #3.

In the U.S., tenants can call their landlords to report a problem with their house or apartment. Landlords are responsible for fixing problems like a leaky faucet or a plugged up sink.

	Tenant's problem	Landlord's response
1.		
2.		
3.		

3 Use the Communication Strategy 🎧

Work with a partner. Role-play a telephone conversation between a tenant and landlord. Replace the underlined words in the example with your own ideas. Try to use the communication strategy in your conversation.

A: Hello.

B: Hi. This is your tenant in Apartment <u>16</u>.

A: Yes. What can I do for you?

B: Well, I'm having a problem with the <u>ceiling in the bathroom</u>. <u>There seems to be a leak</u>.

A: Okay. <u>I'll be over as soon as I can</u>.

B: Can you give me a more specific time?

A: It'll probably be <u>somewhere between noon and 3</u>.

B: Great. Thanks.

COMMUNICATION STRATEGY

Asking for a More Specific Time

Here are some ways you can ask for a more **specific time** if someone gives you a general time.

Will that be today?

How soon can you get here?

Can you give me a more specific time?

26

Rental Agreements

THINGS TO DO

1 Warm Up

Work with your classmates to answer these questions.

1. What are a landlord's responsibilities to a tenant?
2. What are a tenant's responsibilities to a landlord?
3. Look at the rental agreement on page 29 and read the sentences that have highlighted words. Use context to guess the meanings of these words.

2 Read and Take Notes

Read the rental agreement on page 29 and take notes in the chart below. Then compare charts with a partner.

Things a landlord **must** do	Things a landlord **can't** do
• provide smoke detectors	
Things a tenant must do	**Things a tenant can't do**
• pay a security deposit	

Signing a rental agreement

Smoke detector

3 Analyze

Work with several classmates to answer these questions. Then share your answers with the class.

1. What utilities must Oscar Mendoza pay for?
2. What is the purpose of a security deposit? Why should a tenant have to pay one?
3. Why do you think the landlord must give 24-hour notice before entering the apartment?
4. Why is it important to have a written rental agreement?

TRY THIS STRATEGY

Learn Word Forms When you learn a new word, look in a dictionary for other forms of the word. This will help you quickly expand your vocabulary. You can keep track of word forms in a chart like this:

Noun Form	Verb Form	Adjective Form
removal	remove	-----
expiration	expire	expired

Make a chart with the words you learned in this lesson.

RENTAL AGREEMENT

1. Parties: The parties to this agreement are ___Sylvia Wang___ hereinafter called *Landlord* and ___Oscar Mendoza___ hereinafter called *Tenant*.

2. **Property**: Landlord hereby **lets** the following property to Tenant for the terms of this Agreement: a) the real property known as ___4453 Meander Ave., Apt 28___ and b) the following furniture and appliances on said property: ___electric stove, refrigerator___.

3. **Term**: The term of this Agreement shall be for ___one year___ beginning on ___May 1, 2005___ and ending on ___April 30, 2006___.

4. Rent: The total rent for said property shall be ___$7,800.00___, to be paid monthly in amounts of ___$650.00___ **due** and payable on the ___first___ day of each month.

5. Utilities: Landlord agrees to **furnish** the following services and/or utilities:

    ☐ electricity   ☑ heat   ☑ water   ☐ hot water
    ☑ trash removal   ☐ gas   ☐ other _____

    Landlord further agrees to provide smoke detectors as required by law.

6. Security Deposit: Tenant shall deposit with the Landlord ___$650.00___ to be held as security deposit. This deposit will be returned **in full**, including any interest acquired, when this lease **expires** if, after inspection by the Landlord, the **premises** are in good condition and Tenant owes no back rent.

7. Tenant shall not **lease** or **sublease** the premises without the written **consent** of the Landlord (but consent of the Landlord shall not be unreasonably withheld).

8. Landlord may enter premises at reasonable times for the purposes of inspection, maintenance, or repair. In all instances, except those of emergency or abandonment, the Landlord shall give 24-hour notice **prior to** such an entry.

9. Tenant agrees not to use the premises in such a **manner** as to **disturb** the peace and quiet of other tenants in the building.

10. Landlord agrees to regularly **maintain** the building and grounds in a clean, **orderly**, and safe manner, including **removal** of ice and snow.

LESSON 5

I'm looking for something bigger.

Comparative and Superlative Adjectives					
Adjectives with One Syllable			**Adjectives with Two or More Syllables**		
Adjective	**Comparative**	**Superlative**	**Adjective**	**Comparative**	**Superlative**
Most adjectives:			**Most adjectives:**		
clean ⟶	cleaner than ⟶	the cleanest	modern ⟶	more modern than ⟶	the most modern
bright⟶	brighter than ⟶	the brightest	unusual ⟶	more unusual than ⟶	the most unusual
Adjectives ending in a single vowel and consonant:			**Adjectives ending in -y:**		
big ⟶	bigger than ⟶	the biggest	sunny ⟶	sunnier than ⟶	the sunniest
thin ⟶	thinner than ⟶	the thinnest	pretty ⟶	prettier than ⟶	the prettiest
Adjectives ending in -e:			**Irregular Adjectives**		
nice ⟶	nicer than ⟶	the nicest	good ⟶	better than ⟶	the best
safe ⟶	safer than ⟶	the safest	bad ⟶	worse than ⟶	the worst

1 Write the Form

Write the comparative and superlative forms of the words below.

	Comparative Form	**Superlative Form**
1. sunny	*sunnier than*	*the sunniest*
2. reasonable		
3. great		
4. uncomfortable		
5. neat		
6. affordable		
7. large		
8. risky		

2 Complete the Sentences

Complete these questions with the correct form of an adjective from the box.
(More than one adjective is possible.) Then ask a partner the questions.

1. Which is ___*bigger*___ —a duplex or a single family home?
2. What is _____ room in your house?
3. Which is _____ —a first floor apartment or a second floor apartment?
4. What is _____ way to heat a house?
5. Which is _____ —a gas stove or an electric stove?
6. Which is _____ —a refrigerator, a stove, or an air conditioner?

Adjectives	
big	good
cheap	nice
comfortable	safe
expensive	sunny

as + adjective + *as*
My new house is **as expensive as** my old house. (They are equally expensive.)
My old house was not **as big as** my new house. (My old house was smaller than my new house.)
An apartment is not **as expensive as** a house. (An apartment is cheaper than a house.)

3 Paraphrase

Rewrite each sentence. Use *not as* + adjective + *as* in your sentence.

1. Your room is cleaner than mine. (dirty)

   Your room is not as dirty as mine.

2. My new apartment is more expensive than my old one. (cheap)

   _____

3. I like my new house because it's bigger than my old house. (small)

   _____

4. A condo is cheaper than a house. (expensive)

   _____

5. The west side of the house is shadier than the east side. (sunny)

   _____

6. In the summer the first floor is cooler than the second floor. (hot)

   _____

4 Match

Match the words in Column A with the phrases in Column B. Then write your own sentences using the phrases in Column B.

Column A	Column B
1. __h__ more expensive than	a. not as big as
2. _____ smaller than	b. not as pretty as
3. _____ dirtier than	c. not as safe as
4. _____ uglier than	d. not as noisy as
5. _____ quieter than	e. not as good as
6. _____ larger than	f. not as tall as
7. _____ newer than	g. not as clean as
8. _____ worse than	h. not as cheap as
9. _____ more dangerous than	i. not as small as
10. _____ shorter than	j. not as old as

The Fair Housing Act

1 Warm Up

Work with your classmates to answer these questions.

1. Did anyone ever treat you unfairly? What did they do? How did you feel?
2. Did anyone ever treat you unfairly because of your nationality or religion?

For each category below, add more examples.

Category	Example
Race	Hispanic, _____
National origin	Canadian, _____
Religion	Catholic, Buddhist, _____
Sex	male, _____
Familial status	married, _____
Disability	blind, _____

2 Read and Respond

Read the information below and answer the questions on page 33.

U.S. Department of Housing and Urban Development (HUD)
Office of Fair Housing and Equal Opportunity

EQUAL HOUSING OPPORTUNITY

Under the Fair Housing Act, it is against the law to:

- Refuse to rent to you or sell you housing
- Tell you housing is unavailable when in fact it is available
- Show you apartments or homes in certain neighborhoods only
- Advertise housing to preferred groups of people only

Based on these factors . . .

- Race or color
- National origin
- Religion
- Sex
- Familial status (including families with children under 18)
- Disability

If you think your rights have been violated, contact the HUD office nearest you to file a complaint.

Source: U.S. Department of Housing and Urban Development

QUESTIONS

1. What is the purpose of the Fair Housing Act?

_____

2. Which agency wrote the Fair Housing Act?

_____

3. What can you do if a landlord refuses to rent to you because of your race or color?

_____

4. What can you do if a landlord refuses to rent to you because of your sex or religion?

_____

3 Apply

Work with one or more classmates. Read each situation below and answer the questions.

1. Jean Davin found the perfect apartment for his wife and two children. He was ready to sign the lease when the owner told him that children were not allowed in the apartment complex. When Jean told him that he had two children, the owner refused to rent him the apartment. Can the landlord refuse to rent Jean the apartment? Why or why not?

2. The house that Frank and Sandra want to rent has a no pets policy. However, Sandra is blind and she has a seeing-eye dog to help her get around. Can the owner of the house refuse to rent to Frank and Sandra?

3. José's tenants just moved out of the apartment on the top floor of his house. José's mother lives with him now and she doesn't speak English very well. José would like to rent the apartment to Spanish speakers so that his mother can talk to them. Can José put a housing ad in the paper that says "Spanish speakers only"? Why or why not?

WINDOW ON MATH
Calculating Housing Costs

When moving into an apartment, it is common practice to pay the first and last month's rent plus a security deposit.

monthly rent	× 2 +	security deposit	=	amount to move in
$700	× 2 +	$700	=	$2,100

1. Pilar found a great apartment to rent. She has to pay the first and last month's rent plus a security deposit of one month's rent. If the rent for the apartment is $600 a month, how much money must she give the landlord prior to moving in? _____

2. Harold has $1,500 in his savings account. The apartment he wants to rent costs $525 a month. In order to rent the apartment, however, he has to pay the first and last month's rent plus a $1,000 security deposit. How much more money does Harold need to rent the apartment? _____

3. When Bruce and Sylvia moved into their rented house in June, they paid the landlord $2,400 for the first and last month's rent and the security deposit. If the monthly rent is $750, how much was the security deposit? _____

⭐7 What do you know?
LESSON

1 Listening Review 🎧

Listen and choose the statement that is closest in meaning to the statement you hear. Use the Answer Sheet.

1. A. You have to pay 3 month's rent in order to rent the apartment.
   B. You have to pay $1,000 to rent the apartment.
   C. A security deposit is not required.

2. A. The landlord can enter the tenant's apartment at any time.
   B. The landlord has to notify the tenant before going into an apartment.
   C. The landlord has to notify the tenant 12 hours before entering the apartment.

3. A. The lease is for six months.
   B. The lease is for one year.
   C. The lease is from January 1, 2007 to January 1, 2008.

4. A. You must pay the rent first.
   B. You must pay the rent before the first day of the month.
   C. You have to pay the rent every fifteen days.

5. A. Electricity is included in the rent.
   B. Only electricity is included in the rent.
   C. Electricity is not included in the rent.

6. A. The apartment on Belmont Street is sunnier than the apartment on Lake Avenue.
   B. The apartment on Belmont Street is not as sunny as the apartment on Lake Avenue.
   C. The apartment on Lake Avenue is not as sunny as the apartment on Belmont Street.

ANSWER SHEET		
1	Ⓐ Ⓑ Ⓒ
2	Ⓐ Ⓑ Ⓒ
3	Ⓐ Ⓑ Ⓒ
4	Ⓐ Ⓑ Ⓒ
5	Ⓐ Ⓑ Ⓒ
6	Ⓐ Ⓑ Ⓒ
7	Ⓐ Ⓑ Ⓒ
8	Ⓐ Ⓑ Ⓒ
9	Ⓐ Ⓑ Ⓒ
10	Ⓐ Ⓑ Ⓒ

Now listen to each conversation and choose the best answer to the question you hear. Use the Answer Sheet.

7. A. She's going to look at a house for sale.
   B. She's going to look at a two-bedroom house for sale.
   C. She's going to look at a three-bedroom house.

8. A. The man wants to look at a house with a garage.
   B. The man wants to look at a house on State Street.
   C. The man wants to look at an apartment on Belmont Street.

9. A. heat and electricity
   B. heat and hot water
   C. heat but not hot water

10. A. The sink is stopped up.
    B. The air conditioning isn't working.
    C. The bathtub won't drain.

2 Vocabulary Review

Write the missing noun or verb form.

NOUN	VERB
1. attachment	*attach*
2.	park
3. reduction	
4. expiration	
5.	consent

NOUN	VERB
6. maintenance	
7.	agree
8. inclusion	
9.	remove
10.	locate

Choose 6 of the words from the charts above and write 6 questions. Then ask your classmates the questions.

EXAMPLE: When does your driver's license expire?

✔ LEARNING LOG

I know these words:

NOUNS
- ☐ air conditioning
- ☐ colonial
- ☐ consent
- ☐ duplex
- ☐ electricity
- ☐ elevator
- ☐ location
- ☐ maintenance
- ☐ manner
- ☐ neighborhood
- ☐ parking
- ☐ premises

- ☐ property
- ☐ ranch
- ☐ removal
- ☐ security deposit
- ☐ term (of an agreement)
- ☐ utilities
- ☐ washer and dryer hookup

VERBS
- ☐ disturb
- ☐ expire
- ☐ furnish

- ☐ lease
- ☐ let
- ☐ maintain
- ☐ sublease

ADJECTIVES
- ☐ attached
- ☐ available
- ☐ due
- ☐ orderly
- ☐ remodeled

ADVERBS
- ☐ immediately

OTHER
- ☐ in full
- ☐ prior to
- ☐ a specific time

I practiced these skills, strategies, and grammar points:

- ☐ setting learning goals
- ☐ grouping words
- ☐ using a dictionary to learn word forms
- ☐ taking notes
- ☐ reading for specific information
- ☐ listening for specific information
- ☐ asking for a more specific time

- ☐ evaluating the pluses and minuses of something
- ☐ paraphrasing information
- ☐ using comparative adjectives
- ☐ using superlative adjectives
- ☐ using *as* + adjective + *as*
- ☐ supporting an opinion

Spotlight: Reading Strategy

PREVIEWING
The word *preview* means to look before. When you preview an article or story, you look over the reading before you read it. Previewing helps you to understand the reading better. Here are ways you can preview a reading: • Look at the title of the article. Make questions from the title. Then predict answers to your questions. • Look at any pictures and ask yourself what is happening in the pictures. • Read the first sentence in each paragraph. Then predict the topic of the reading. • Ask yourself what you already know about the topic of the reading.

1 Look at the title of the article on page 37. Write 2 more questions based on the title. Then predict answers to the questions.

Questions	Possible answers
1. *What is a consumer hero?*	*Maybe it's someone who's a very smart shopper.* *Maybe it's someone who saves other people money.*
2.	
3.	

2 Read the first sentence in each paragraph of the article and check (✓) the predictions you agree with.

Predictions

I think this article is about

☐ an immigrant who had a problem.

☐ someone who didn't have any money.

☐ someone who had a housing problem.

☐ someone who was treated unfairly.

☐ a landlord who had a bad tenant.

☐ someone who couldn't get help.

☐ someone who reported unfair treatment.

3 Read the article quickly and then evaluate the previewing strategies. Answer these questions.

1. Were you able to correctly predict the topic of the article?

2. Which previewing strategy was the most useful to you?

3. Why does it help to preview an article before reading it?

Consumer Hero:
Aslam Ahmed

1 Aslam Ahmed is a Certified General Accountant who now works for Canada Customs and Revenue Agency. His wife, Christina, has worked in the private school system. But none of that mattered 12 years ago when the Ahmeds came to Canada from Bangladesh and settled in Mississauga.

2 The Ahmeds had $25,000 in savings and Christina had a job. But a landlord refused to rent to them because Aslam didn't have a credit rating—he had no history of paying with credit. The **assumption** was that Ahmed was a bad credit risk.

3 "It was terrible. I would not wish it upon my enemy to have a situation like this," Ahmed said. He had no Canadian credit history, because he'd just moved there. And elsewhere, he usually paid cash. "I never **defaulted** on any payments in my life and I couldn't believe it. I mean, why should anybody think I'm a credit risk?"

4 He was so insulted he contacted an immigrant housing authority. With their help he took a risk as a newcomer. Ahmed complained. He argued that no credit shouldn't mean bad credit and that such an assumption was discriminatory.

5 The Ontario Human Rights Commission agreed. Leiloni Farha was Ahmed's lawyer on the case. "What the judgment says is that a landlord cannot use a lack of information as bad information," said Farha. This means that even if you don't have any credit, it doesn't mean that you have bad credit.

Source: Adapted from Canadian Broadcasting Corporation

Spotlight: Writing Strategy

IDENTIFYING A PURPOSE FOR WRITING

People write letters for many different purposes:

to thank	to inform	to get something
to complain	to invite	

---

1 Match each sentence to a purpose for writing.

1. Thank you so much for the beautiful flowers. _to thank_____

2. I called three times last week, but no one returned my call. _____

3. This is to remind you that your appointment in on June 5th. _____

4. It was very kind of you to take my mother to the doctor. _____

5. I'm writing to see if you'd like to have dinner on Friday. _____

6. I am writing to request a copy of your brochure #352 called *Against Discrimination.* _____

2 Read the letter on page 39 and answer these questions.

1. Who wrote the letter? _Rachel Lewis_____

2. When did she write this letter? _____

3. What is the letter writer's apartment number? _____

4. Who is the letter addressed to? _____

5. Who is Ms. Jawkowsky? _____

6. What is the writer's purpose for writing this letter? _____

7. What information does the writer include in her letter? _____

8. Do you think this is an effective letter? Why or why not? _____

3 Write a short letter of complaint. Identify your purpose for writing and use the proper format for a business letter. See the letter on page 39.

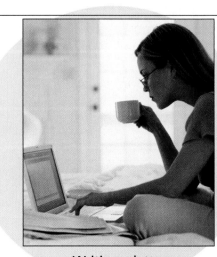

Writing a letter

5532 Bigelow Street
Apartment 125
Chicago, IL 60086

November 12, 2006

Ms. Carol Jawkowsky
Jefferson Point Apartments
5532 Bigelow Street
Chicago, IL 60086

Dear Ms. Jawkowsky:

   I am writing to inform you of a problem I am having in my apartment. I have filed three requests for maintenance to fix a leak in the bathroom. So far, no one has come to take care of this problem. I've had a bucket under my sink for a month now. I would like to call a plumber to fix the leak and deduct the amount of the bill from my next rent check. If you have a problem with this, please contact me as soon as possible.

Yours sincerely,

Rachel Lewis

A worn-out pipe

Are you healthy?

THINGS TO DO

1 Warm Up

Work with your classmates to answer these questions.

1. What do you like to do to relax?
2. What do you do to stay healthy?
3. What do you see people in the picture doing? Which of these things do you do?

2 Classify

Decide if the activities below are healthy or unhealthy. Write *H* (healthy) or *U* (unhealthy).

1. ____ wearing a hat outside
2. ____ sunbathing
3. ____ exercising
4. ____ wearing sunblock when you are outside
5. ____ smoking
6. ____ drinking soda
7. ____ eating junk food
8. ____ sitting in the shade on a sunny day
9. ____ wearing a helmet when you are riding a motorcycle
10. ____ wearing a life vest in a boat
11. ____ relaxing

What other examples of healthy and unhealthy behavior do you see in the picture?

3 Talk about It

Work with your classmates to discuss these questions.

1. Why do people do things that are bad for their health?
2. What else can you do to stay healthy?
3. Where can you get more information about health issues?
4. What can parents do to help their children be healthy?

2 LESSON

Please fill this prescription.

At the dentist's office

THINGS TO DO

1 Talk about It

Study the health history questionnaire on page 43. What do you know about Francisco Lozano? Share ideas with your classmates.

> EXAMPLE: He drinks 5 cups of coffee a day.
> He wears a helmet when he rides his motorcycle.

2 Expand Your Vocabulary

Write the missing word forms. Then complete the questions below.

Noun Form	Verb Form	Adjective Form
a. _____	-----	surgical
b. _____	supplement	-----
c. _____	-----	diabetic
d. _____	prescribe	-----
e. _____	-----	cancerous
f. _____	-----	allergic
g. _____	provide	-----
h. _____	bleed	bloody

1. Did you have ____surgery____ last year?
2. What _____ do you take?
3. What causes _____?
4. Where can you fill a _____?
5. Is there a history of _____ in your family?
6. Are you _____ to cats?
7. What is the name of your health care _____?
8. Does the sight of _____ bother you?

Now work with a partner. Take turns asking the questions.

3 Write

On another sheet of paper, write a paragraph about 5 healthy things that you do.

CARROLL DRUG STORE

Caution: Federal law **prohibits** transfer of this **prescription** drug to any person other than the patient.

RX # 168054
Date Filled 04/12/06
Francisco Lozano

1 TABLET EVERY 4 HOURS IF NEEDED FOR PAIN

HYDROCODONE/APAP 5/500 TABS
DISCARD AFTER 07/23/07

DO NOT DRINK ALCOHOLIC BEVERAGES WHEN TAKING THIS MEDICATION

Dr. LEE, MICHAEL, M.D.

Francisco's prescription

TRY THIS STRATEGY

Learn Collocations When you learn a new noun, it helps to notice any verbs or adjectives that go with it. For example, we often say *fill a prescription* and *see a health provider*. What verbs do we use with the following nouns?

_____ a supplement   _____ surgery

_____ a blood transfusion   _____ a dentist

_____ a check-up   _____ a seatbelt

HEALTH HISTORY QUESTIONNAIRE

Date: _5/2/2006_   Name: _Francisco Lozano_   DOB: _7/4/82_

List all medical problems: List all **surgeries** you have had: List all medication **allergies**:

ear infections food allergies	appendectomy	penicillin

List all medications, vitamins, and **supplements** you are taking now: List all **health care providers** you have seen in the past or are **currently** seeing:

multivitamins	Dr. Benton: Family doctor
calcium	Dr. Wilson: Dentist

Please describe your use of tobacco products.

☑ None   ☐ Cigarettes   ☐ Smokeless Tobacco   ☐ Pipe   ☐ Cigars

How much alcohol do you drink weekly **on average**? _None_
Do you have a problem with **alcohol**?   ☐ Yes   ☑ No

Have you used **illicit** drugs?   ☐ Yes   ☑ No
How much **caffeine** do you drink daily (include coffee, tea, colas)? _5 cups of coffee_
Have you ever had a **blood transfusion**?   ☑ Yes   ☐ No   If yes, what year? _1995_

Please check the behaviors you follow:

☑ Wear seatbelt   ☑ Wear helmet while riding motorcycle
☑ Fire extinguisher in house   ☑ Smoke detector in house
☐ Living will   ☐ Low-fat **diet**
☐ Exercise more than 3 times per week   ☐ Annual **check-ups**

Please check if there is a history of any of the following **diseases** in your family.

☑ Heart Disease   ☑ **Diabetes**   ☐ **Asthma**
☐ Skin **Cancer**   ☑ High **Cholesterol**

Patient Signature _Francisco Lozano_   Date _5/2/2006_

LESSON 3

UNIT 3: Healthy Living

Try to improve your diet.

THINGS TO DO

1 Warm Up

Work with your classmates to answer these questions.

1. When was the last time you went to a doctor? Why did you go?
2. According to the bar graph, what are the 3 most common reasons people visit their doctor?
3. Why do you think the people in the pictures are at the doctor's office?

2 Listen and Take Notes 🎧

Listen to conversation #1 and write the person's reason for visiting the doctor. Then listen again and write the doctor's advice. Repeat with conversation #2.

	Reason for visiting the doctor	Doctor's advice
1.		
2.		

3 Use the Communication Strategy 🎧

Work with a partner. Role-play a conversation between a doctor and patient. Replace the underlined words in the example with your own ideas. Try to use the communication strategy in your conversation.

Doctor: How are you feeling?

Patient: Pretty good. My only complaint is that I feel tired all the time.

Doctor: Are you eating well?

Patient: Probably not. I know I eat too much junk food.

Doctor: Well, I suggest that you try to improve your diet. Why don't you eat some fruit when you feel tired?

Patient: I guess I could try that.

Back pain · · · · ·

Stomach pain · · · · ·

Skin **rash** · · · · ·

Well baby visit · · · · ·

Throat problems · · · · ·

Post Op visit · · · · ·

Cough · · · · ·

Routine prenatal examination · · · · ·

Progress visit · · · · ·

General medical examination · · · · ·

COMMUNICATION STRATEGY

Giving Advice

Here are some common ways that people give suggestions and advice:

- I think that you should . . .
- I suggest that you . . .
- I recommend that you . . .
- Why don't you . . .
- You could . . .
- You'd really better . . .

Top 10 Reasons for Doctors' Office Visits

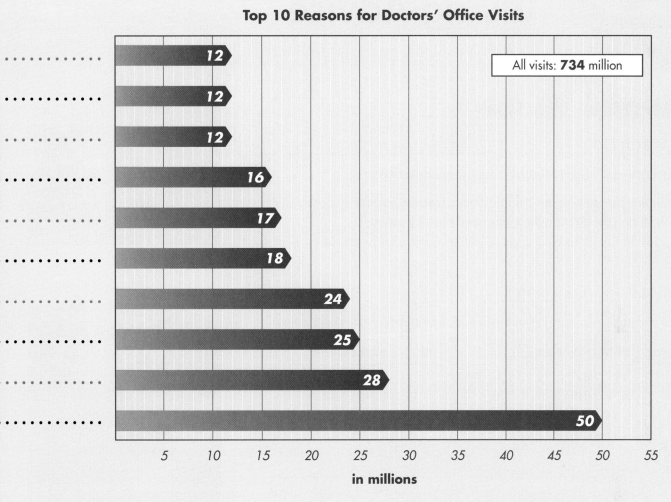

All visits: **734** million

12

12

12

16

17

18

24

25

28

50

| 5 | 10 | 15 | 20 | 25 | 30 | 35 | 40 | 45 | 50 | 55 |

in millions

Source: U.S. Department of Health and Human Services

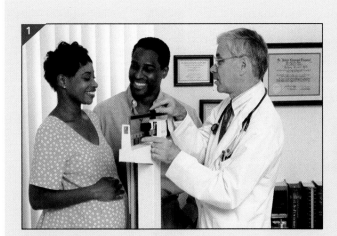

Woman due in 3 weeks

At the doctor's office

LESSON 4

Giving Advice

THINGS TO DO

1 Warm Up

Work with your classmates to answer these questions.

1. Where can you get information about health issues?
2. Who do you talk to when you need medical advice?
3. Look at the picture on page 47. What do you know about this person?

Using the Internet

2 Read and Take Notes

Read the advice column on page 47 and take notes in the chart below.

Writer	Writer's problem	Doctor's advice
1.	Her husband's grandfather won't get a check-up.	
2.		
3.		

Compare notes with a partner. What other advice could you give each writer?

Calling for information

3 Evaluate

Work with 1 or more classmates to answer these questions. Then share your answers with the class.

1. A good friend is having trouble sleeping at night. When she asks you for advice, what do you say?
2. Your friend's 3-week-old baby cries all night. When your friend asks you for advice, what do you say?
3. Your brother hurt his back last week and it's still not better. When he asks you for advice, what do you say?
4. Your coworker is having bad headaches. When she asks you for advice, what do you say?

4 Write

Write a letter to Dr. Sanchez explaining a health problem and asking for advice. Do not use your real name to sign the letter. Exchange letters with a partner and read your partner's letter to the class. Ask your classmates to help you give advice.

Looking for information at the library

Ask Dr. Sanchez

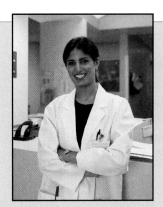

1 Dear Dr. Sanchez,

My husband's elderly grandfather is living with us. He seems to be in very good health, but he doesn't like to go to the doctor for check-ups. He says he can go to the emergency room if he gets sick. I am worried that he might have a sudden serious illness. What should I do?

Worried in New Jersey

Dear Worried,

Make an appointment for your husband's grandfather to get a complete **physical exam** and be **firm** about it. Many times, older people don't want to go to the doctor because they are afraid. They need a lot of encouragement and sometimes a little extra "push" doesn't hurt.

If he or anyone else in your family shows signs of a **life-threatening** illness, call for emergency help right away.

Dr. Sanchez

* * *

2 Dear Dr. Sanchez,

My husband thinks that the best cure for the common cold is fasting. He says three days without food is better than any medicine you can buy. I disagree. What do you think? Is there any truth to this?

Doubtful in New York

Dear Doubtful,

The best advice is to listen to your stomach. If your stomach says "No food," don't worry. Going without food for a short time won't hurt you. But you need to get plenty of fluids, such as water and fruit juice.

Dr. Sanchez

* * *

3 Dear Dr. Sanchez,

I have a regular 9 to 5 office job and I like it pretty much. For the past few months, however, I've started getting really sleepy in the afternoon. I'm afraid that someday my boss is going to come into my office and I'll be asleep at my desk.

Sleepy in Seattle

Dear Sleepy,

You aren't alone. The National Sleep Foundation reports that 1 out of every 4 day workers feels sleepy at work on two or more days each week.

There are a number of things you can do to be more alert. Take some short breaks in the afternoon when you start to feel sleepy. Walk quickly outside for a few minutes if you can. You could also organize your work so that you have easy or interesting tasks to do in the afternoon when you are sleepy.

Dr. Sanchez

5 LESSON

Have you had a check-up this year?

The Present Perfect

We use the present perfect to talk about something that happened (or didn't happen) at an indefinite time before now. To form the present perfect tense, use **have** and the past participle of the verb.

EXAMPLES:
Have you **been** to the doctor this year? → Yes, I **have**. I **have been** to the doctor 3 times.
Has she **ever taken** penicillin? → No, she **has never needed** it.
Has he **been** allergic to cats for a long time? → Yes, he **has**. He's always **been** allergic to cats.

I You We They	**have** **haven't**	**gone** for a check-up this year. **had** a life-threatening illness. **been** sick a number of times this year.
He She It	**has** **hasn't**	

Tip

ever = at any time
never = at no time
yet = before now

• Use "ever" in questions.
• Use "never" in affirmative statements.

Note: Use *yet* in questions and negative statements.
EXAMPLES: Have you eaten **yet**?
I haven't eaten **yet**.

---

1 Complete the Sentences

Complete these sentences with the present perfect tense.
Use the verbs in parentheses.

1. I _haven't been_ sick this year. (not/be)

2. Her brother _____ surgery three times this year. (have)

3. Even though she doesn't feel very well, she _____ a doctor's appointment yet. (not/make)

4. The doctor advised him to stop smoking, but he _____ yet. (not/quit)

5. I _____ to both a dentist and a dermatologist this year. (be)

6. I _____ never _____ a blood transfusion. Have you? (have)

7. The doctors _____ if she should have surgery. (not/decide)

2 Ask Questions

Complete the questions below. Then ask a partner and circle your partner's answer.

1. ___Have___ you ever ___had___ surgery? (have)   Yes, I have.   No, I haven't.

2. _____ you _____ to the doctor this year? (be)   Yes, I have.   No, I haven't.

3. _____ you ever _____ cigarettes? (smoke)   Yes, I have.   No, I haven't.

4. _____ you _____ the dentist this year? (see)   Yes, I have.   No, I haven't.

5. _____ you _____ any caffeine today? (have)   Yes, I have.   No, I haven't.

Simple Past and Present Perfect
Use the simple past to tell about something that happened at a definite time in the past.

EXAMPLES: He **exercised** for an hour <u>yesterday</u>.
            I **had** a fever <u>last night</u>.
            The doctor **gave** me a prescription for penicillin (<u>when I was at his office</u>).

Use the present perfect to tell about something that happened at an indefinite time in the past or that started in the past and continues to the present.

EXAMPLES: I**'ve been** to the dentist <u>many times</u>.
            I**'ve had** a toothache <u>since last Tuesday</u>.
            She **hasn't filled** the prescription <u>yet</u>.

---

3 Read and Identify

Read the paragraph below. Circle the simple past verbs. Underline the present perfect verbs.

My father (learned) the hard way that taking care of your health is important. Last year he had a heart attack. He didn't feel well, so I told him to go to the doctor. But of course he didn't listen. He drank several beers every day, ate a lot of junk food, and never exercised. When he had the heart attack, it really changed his life. Since then he has exercised and eaten better. He tried to quit smoking, but he has smoked a pack a day since he was in his twenties, so it's hard to quit. At least he is smoking less now, which is a good start, and he makes regular visits to the doctor. Even if he hasn't been sick, he makes an appointment with his doctor every 6 months, just to be safe.

4 Write

Complete the paragraph below. Use the simple past or the present perfect of the verb in parentheses.

My older sister is an amazingly healthy person. She _has never been_ (never/be) a patient in a hospital and she_____ (never/have) surgery. Her boss loves her because she hardly ever takes a sick day. Last year she only _____ (miss) two days of work but not because she was sick. She _____ (stay) home from work to take care of her husband because he _____ (be) sick. My older brother is just the opposite of my sister. He _____ (have) surgery twice and last year he _____ (spend) a week in the hospital. It's not that my brother is unhealthy. It's just that he likes to do things that are a little dangerous. He _____ (break) his right arm twice and his left arm once. Two years ago he _____ (break) his right leg when he _____ (fall) off his motorcycle.

Health Hotlines

Poster to prevent drunk driving

1 Warm Up

Work with your classmates to answer these questions.

1. What is a telephone hotline ?
2. What do you think the acronym MADD stands for?
3. What emergency telephone numbers do you know?

2 Read and Respond

Read this information and answer the questions below.

COMMUNITY SERVICES

ABUSE , ASSAULT & DOMESTIC VIOLENCE

National DOMESTIC VIOLENCE Hotline	800-555-3999
Women's Crisis Center	555-1212
Hotline	555-4938

AIDS

AIDS Action Committee	555-9038
Hotline	555-9900
AIDS Hotline	555-4877

ALCOHOL AND DRUG ABUSE

Al-Anon/Alateen	555-6443
Alcohol Abuse & Drug 24 Hour Helpline	555-2900
Alcoholics Anonymous	555-2233
Mothers Against Drunk Driving	555-8805
Narcotics Anonymous	555-3211
Stop Addiction	555-5577

CHILD ABUSE AND/OR NEGLECT

Child at Risk Hotline	800-555-4539
International Child Abuse Network	800-555-3387
National Child Abuse Hotline	800-555-2117
Office of Childcare Services	555-5944
Parental Stress Line	800-555-5499

Telephone book

Volunteer answers call at Domestic Violence Hotline

1. Where can you find this information?
2. What do you think the organization Alcoholics Anonymous might be?
3. Why do you think people would call the parental stress line?
4. What do you think is an example of child abuse?
5. If you wanted to help someone with a drinking problem, what number could you call?

3 Apply

Look in your local telephone directory to find a telephone number for each category below. Write the telephone number next to the category. Then add the name and phone number of 2 more community services.

Alcohol Abuse: _____

Drug Abuse: _____

Domestic Violence: _____

Child Abuse: _____

_____

_____

Talk about the services with a partner. Do you know anyone who has needed any of these services? What happened?

WINDOW ON MATH
Converting Units of Measurement

Use the information in the chart to answer the questions below.

When you know:	You can find:	If you multiply by:
fluid ounces	grams	28
grams	fluid ounces	0.035
pounds	kilograms	0.45
kilograms	pounds	2.2

1. If Franco weighs 70 kilos, how many pounds is that? _____

2. Paula weighs 155 pounds and she is trying to lose 10% of her weight.

   How many pounds is that? _____
   How many kilos is that? _____

3. What is your ideal weight in pounds and kilos? _____

4. Amal takes 2 ounces of a medication every morning. How many grams is that? _____

5. The doctor told Leila to take 3 ounces of a medication. How many grams is that? _____

7 LESSON

What do you know?

1 Listening Review 🎧

Listen and choose the statement that is closest in meaning to the statement you hear. Use the Answer Sheet.

1. A. She doesn't eat a lot of fatty foods.
   B. She doesn't like rich foods.
   C. She wants to gain weight.

2. A. Use 1 drop daily in each ear.
   B. Put 3 drops in each ear every day.
   C. Put 3 drops in each ear three times a day.

3. A. You can get 2 more refills.
   B. You can't refill this prescription for 2 weeks.
   C. You can refill this prescription in 2 weeks.

4. A. She had surgery last week.
   B. She has had surgery several times.
   C. She hasn't had surgery yet.

5. A. He wants to get a check-up.
   B. He has already had a check-up this year.
   C. He needs to get a check-up.

ANSWER SHEET			
1	A	B	C
2	A	B	C
3	A	B	C
4	A	B	C
5	A	B	C
6	A	B	C
7	A	B	C
8	A	B	C
9	A	B	C
10	A	B	C

Now listen to each conversation and choose the best answer to the question you hear. Use the Answer Sheet.

6. A. a health care provider
   B. a new diet
   C. a check-up

7. A. She had surgery.
   B. She had a physical exam.
   C. She had a doctor's appointment.

8. A. a prescription
   B. an illicit drug
   C. a supplement

9. A. penicillin
   B. milk
   C. smoke

10. A. several times a week
    B. once a week
    C. never

2 Vocabulary Review

Use the clues to complete the crossword puzzle.

Across

3 This word means "the action of treating someone badly."

4 An unsigned letter is an _____ letter.

6 Another word for "now" is _____.

7 The opposite of "allow" is _____.

8 Mothers have _____ exams before the birth of their child.

10 A nurse is one type of health care _____.

11 Someone who has lost a lot of blood might need a _____.

Down

1 A pharmacist fills _____.

2 Coffee and chocolate have a lot of this.

4 This medical condition makes breathing difficult.

5 If you cut your hand, it _____.

9 Another word for "strong" is _____.

✔ LEARNING LOG

I know these words:

NOUNS
- ☐ abuse
- ☐ addiction
- ☐ alcohol
- ☐ allergy
- ☐ appendectomy
- ☐ asthma
- ☐ blood transfusion
- ☐ caffeine
- ☐ calcium
- ☐ cancer
- ☐ check-up
- ☐ cholesterol
- ☐ crisis

- ☐ diabetes
- ☐ diet
- ☐ disease
- ☐ domestic violence
- ☐ drug abuse
- ☐ health care provider
- ☐ hotline
- ☐ infection
- ☐ narcotic
- ☐ penicillin
- ☐ physical exam
- ☐ prescription
- ☐ progress
- ☐ rash

- ☐ supplement
- ☐ surgery
- ☐ well baby visit

VERBS
- ☐ bleed
- ☐ infect
- ☐ prescribe
- ☐ prohibit
- ☐ provide
- ☐ supplement

ADJECTIVES
- ☐ allergic
- ☐ anonymous

- ☐ bloody
- ☐ cancerous
- ☐ diabetic
- ☐ firm
- ☐ illicit
- ☐ life-threatening
- ☐ post-op
- ☐ prenatal
- ☐ routine
- ☐ surgical

OTHER
- ☐ currently
- ☐ on average
- ☐ yet

I practiced these skills, strategies, and grammar points:

- ☐ classifying types of activities
- ☐ listening for specific information
- ☐ taking notes
- ☐ reading for specific information
- ☐ reading labels

- ☐ learning word forms
- ☐ giving examples
- ☐ giving advice
- ☐ evaluating
- ☐ converting units of measurements

- ☐ learning collocations
- ☐ interpreting a bar graph
- ☐ using the present perfect
- ☐ using the telephone directory

Spotlight: Reading Strategy

SKIMMING AND SCANNING

Skimming means to look quickly over a piece of writing to find the topic or main idea. When you skim a piece of writing, you look at the title, any pictures, and the first sentence in each paragraph. Then you predict the topic of the piece of writing.

Scanning means to look quickly for specific information. When you scan a piece of writing, you move your eyes quickly across the words to find specific information. You don't read every word.

---

1 Read the questions below. Then scan the prescription label to find the answers.

1. Who wrote the prescription? _____

2. What is the prescription number? _____

3. How often should the patient take the medication? _____

CARROLL DRUG STORE

Caution: Federal law prohibits transfer of this prescription drug to any person other than the patient.

RX # 168054
Date Filled 04/12/06
Rachel Pedula

USE 1 DROP IN EACH EAR
TWICE A DAY

ACETASOL HC EAR DROPS
REFILL 2 TIMES UNTIL 4/12/07

Dr. DeFisher, Lynn, M.D.

2 Skim the reading on page 55 and identify the topic. Then scan it to find the specific information requested below.

Topic

The reading on page 55 is about _____.

Specific information

The source of this reading (where it is from): _____

What you should do if you have unexpected symptoms: _____

An example of a warning on a drug label: _____

How to Get the Best Results from Rx Drugs

Here are some tips to help you use prescription drugs safely and effectively:

- If a drug is not doing what it is supposed to do for you, check with your doctor. You may need a different dosage or a different drug.

- If you have an unexpected symptom—rash, nausea, dizziness, headache—report it to your doctor immediately.

- Don't stop taking your medicine just because you are feeling better. You may prevent the drug from doing its work completely.

- Check drug labels for specific instructions or warnings, such as "do not take on an empty stomach" or "do not take with milk."

- Check the label, or ask the pharmacist, for storing instructions. Some drugs should be refrigerated; others must be protected from light.

- Always keep medicines out of the reach of children. Even though most prescription medicines come in child-proof containers, children sometimes can open these bottles and swallow the contents.

- Never let another person use your medicine. Your symptoms may look the same, but you may be suffering from a different problem.

- Never take medicines without checking the label to make sure you're taking the right one.

- Keep a list of all drugs you are taking to show to your doctor or your pharmacist.

Source: U.S. Food and Drug Administration, *FDA Consumer* Magazine

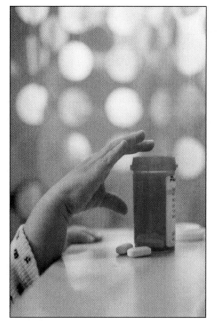

Keep medicine away from children.

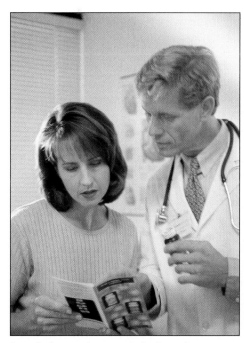

Read about the prescription drugs you take.

Check drug labels for storing instructions.

Spotlight: Writing Strategy

<table>
<tr><td colspan="2" align="center">**USING COMPOUND SENTENCES**</td></tr>
<tr><td colspan="2">A compound sentence is made of 2 or more simple sentences joined together. You can join the simple sentences with a comma (,) and a coordinating conjunction (*and, but, or*), or with a semicolon (;).</td></tr>
</table>

2 Simple Sentences	1 Compound Sentence
I have a regular 9 to 5 job. I like it pretty much.	I have a regular 9 to 5 job, and I like it pretty much.
My grandfather seems to be in good health. He doesn't like to exercise.	My grandfather seems to be in good health, but he doesn't like to exercise.
Make sure you exercise regularly. You will feel better.	Make sure you exercise regularly; you will feel better.

1 Combine each pair of simple sentences to make a compound sentence. Use a comma with *and* or *but*.

1. He always wears a hat outside. He never wears sunblock.

   He always wears a hat outside, but he never wears sunblock.

2. They had a picnic at the park. They played soccer too.

   _____

3. She has diabetes. She has never had asthma.

   _____

4. They have a fire extinguisher in their home. They don't have a smoke alarm.

   _____

5. My brother hurt his back last week. It's still not better.

   _____

6. He eats a low fat-diet. He doesn't drink much caffeine.

   _____

USING COMPLEX SENTENCES

A complex sentence is made of a simple sentence and one or more dependent clauses. A time clause with *when, while, before, after,* or *since* is one type of dependent clause.

(dependent clause)
He had surgery **when** he went into the hospital.

You should get some exercise **before** you go to work.

She has been sick **since** she went on vacation.

When the dependent clause begins the sentence, use a comma at the end of the dependent clause.

When he went into the hospital, he had surgery.

You can make your writing more interesting by using a mix of simple, compound, and complex sentences.

2 Read the story below several times. Then identify each sentence as simple (S), compound (CP), or complex (CX). Write your ideas on the lines to the right.

Mother Said, "No More Chocolate!"
by Xioa Qing Wang

(1) When I was a child, my father was very softhearted. (2) He let me eat anything. (3) My mother was much stricter; she understood nutrition, and she tried to make me eat healthy food. (4) At that age, I loved chocolates with peanuts. (5) Sometimes I ate them as my lunch or breakfast. (6) Of course, that made my mother angry, and she decided to hide them. (7) I wondered why she bought chocolates when she didn't want me to eat them. (8) One day, when she was out, I looked for the chocolates, found them, and ate them quickly. (9) When my mother found out the chocolates were gone, she got very angry. (10) Since that day, she has never bought chocolates again.

1. _CX_
2. _____
3. _____
4. _____
5. _____
6. _____
7. _____
8. _____
9. _____
10. _____

3 Write a paragraph about something healthy or unhealthy that you did as a child. Try to use simple, compound, and complex sentences in your writing.

57

★ LESSON 1

How did you make your decision?

THINGS TO DO

1 Warm Up

Work with your classmates to answer these questions.

1. What was your last big purchase? How did you make your decision?

2. Who is going to buy something in the picture? What do you think is important to him or her?

2 Use Context

Study the picture and read the sentences below. Choose the best meaning for each of the highlighted words.

1. If you don't have enough money to pay for the car, you can get **financing** .
   A. a loan   B. a cheaper car   C. a truck

2. Car dealerships often sell both new and **pre-owned** cars.
   A. expensive   B. special   C. used

3. Most expensive items come with a **warranty** so customers know they will be satisfied.
   A. receipt   B. bill   C. guarantee

4. Some people choose to **lease** a car, and not buy it.
   A. rent   B. take   C. purchase

5. Sometimes customers can make a purchase with **no money down** .
   A. without a loan   B. without paying any cash first   C. without financing

Compare your ideas with a partner.

3 Interview

Work with a partner. Ask and answer these questions.

1. What are 3 things you like to buy new? What are 3 things that are OK to buy used?

2. What products should you have a warranty for?

3. Imagine you are buying a car. What is important to you? Rank these 4 factors from most to least important: color, speed, cost, make.

Ask Specific Questions You can learn more effectively if you relate the lesson's topic to your own needs. Read each lesson title for this unit. For the titles in lessons 1–6, write one question. For example, in Lesson 4, "Banking Needs," you might write, "Where can I get a car loan?"

LESSON 2

This warranty is valid for 6 months.

THINGS TO DO

1 Warm Up

Work with your classmates to answer these questions.

1. What products do you see in each picture?

2. A warranty is a promise that a product is good, and if not, the company will take care of the problem. How important is a warranty to you when you buy a car? A stereo? A cell phone?

2 Use Context

Study the pictures and read the information. Choose the best meaning for each of the highlighted words. Write a word from the box next to each definition below.

defect	workmanship	void
valid	replacement	refund

1. not good or legal anymore: _void_

2. money you get back: _____

3. mistake or problem: _____

4. how well something is made: _____

5. good, legal: _____

6. new product in exchange for the original: _____

3 Use the Vocabulary 🎧

Work with a partner. Take turns role-playing a conversation between a customer and a salesperson.

A: I'd like to return this cell phone .

B: Certainly. Do you have the receipt ?

A: Yes. Here it is.

B: It looks like it's still under warranty . What's the problem?

A: It doesn't ring .

B: Do you want a refund or a replacement ?

A: A replacement, please .

This warranty covers **defects** in materials and **workmanship** of the wireless cellular telephone.

This warranty does not cover **damage** due to scratches, cuts, or accidents.

TRY THIS STRATEGY

◆◆◆◆◆◆◆◆◆◆◆◆◆◆◆◆◆◆◆◆

Notice Suffixes You can expand your vocabulary by adding suffixes. Suffixes are added to the ends of words and they often change the word from one form to another. For example, the suffixes -*ment* and -*ship* usually indicate a noun. Circle the words in this lesson that have these suffixes. Write 2 other words that end in -*ment* and -*ship*.

◆◆◆◆◆◆◆◆◆◆◆◆◆◆◆◆◆◆◆◆

1	2
return this frying pan	get this door fixed
the warranty / the warranty is still valid	your service agreement / it's still under warranty
The coating is coming off.	It doesn't lock.
to make an exchange or get a refund	to leave it or wait while we work on it
A refund, please	I'll leave it

The **period of coverage** of this warranty is for one year from the date of purchase.

Return the product to the store where you bought it for a **refund** or **replacement**.

You can also **make a claim** by calling customer service at

(800) 555-4000.

Improper care and cleaning will make the warranty **void**.

You must present the guarantee certificate and the **original receipt**.

This warranty is **valid** for 6 months from the date of purchase if accompanied by the receipt. The company is not responsible for replacements after 6 months.

LESSON 3

How many miles are on it?

THINGS TO DO

1 Warm Up

Work with your classmates to answer these questions.

1. Who are the people in the pictures? What do you think they are talking about?
2. Look at the vehicle warranty on this page. Is this a good warranty? Why or why not?

2 Listen and Take Notes 🎧

Listen to the 2 conversations. Write the missing information in the chart below.

	Minivan	Pickup truck
What's the **mileage** ? (How many miles are on it?)		
What's the **gas mileage** ? (How many miles does it get per gallon?)		1. *12 mpg* 2.
What year is it?		
What's the price?	*$18,500*	

Listen again and check your answers.

3 Use the Communication Strategy 🎧

Work with a partner. Role-play a conversation between a customer and a salesperson. Replace the underlined words in the example with your own ideas. Try to use the communication strategy.

A: How can I help you today?

B: I'd like to look at <u>a minivan</u>.

A: Sure. How about this one? <u>It has a 3-year warranty, and it's a great price.</u>

B: How much is it?

A: It's only <u>$35,000</u>.

B: <u>I'm afraid that's too expensive</u>.

The mileage is 25,380.

VEHICLE WARRANTY

This chart summarizes the warranty coverage on your new car or truck.

Type of coverage	Years/miles
Car body parts	3/36,000
Rust	3/36,000
Engine	5/50,000
Seat belts	5/50,000

The coverage is for whatever happens first. For example, if you drive 36,000 miles before you reach 3 years, you are covered up to 36,000 miles.

Your dealer will repair or replace any defective parts during the period of coverage.

COMMUNICATION STRATEGY

Disagreeing Politely

In some situations you may want to disagree with someone but not be rude. Try these phrases:

I'm afraid that . . .

I'm sorry, but . . .

Thanks, but . . .

4 LESSON

Banking Needs

THINGS TO DO

1 Warm Up

Work with your classmates to answer these questions.

1. What bank services do you use now?
2. What services would you like to use?
3. Do you know anyone who pays bills online?

2 Read and Respond

Read the glossary of banking terms on page 65. Solve these problems.

1. On May 17th, Alex had $27 in his **checking account**. He wrote a check for $35 to pay for his parking permit. His bank charged him a fee. What was the problem?

2. Katy got a **loan** from her bank of $2,000. She had to pay an annual **interest** rate of 10%. If she repaid the loan one year later, how much would she have to give the bank?

3. Paul had $50 in his checking account. His savings **account balance** was $3,240. He had **overdraft** protection. If he had an overdraft, money would be transferred from his savings account to his checking account. He wrote a check for $460. How much did he have left in savings?

4. Luisa has **direct deposit** of her paycheck. She gets paid on the last day of every month. Her check is $1,754.30. On January 30th, she has $943.00. What does she have in her account the next day?

3 Synthesize

Work with several classmates to answer these questions. Then share your answers with the class.

1. How can you prevent bounced checks?
2. What are 2 ways to pay for a new car?
3. What are some advantages and disadvantages of online banking?

At an ATM

Swiping a credit card

Paying bills online

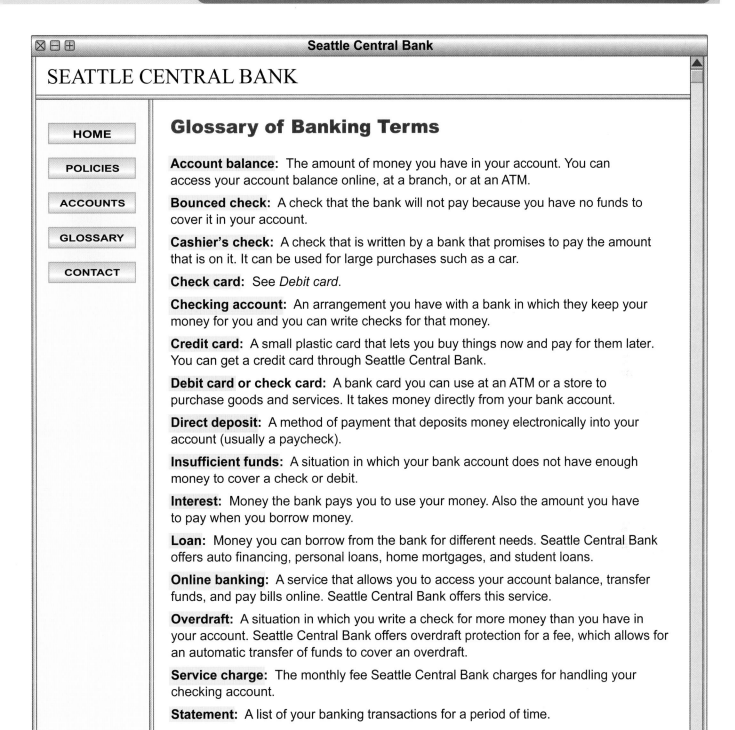

Seattle Central Bank

SEATTLE CENTRAL BANK

HOME

POLICIES

ACCOUNTS

GLOSSARY

CONTACT

Glossary of Banking Terms

Account balance: The amount of money you have in your account. You can access your account balance online, at a branch, or at an ATM.

Bounced check: A check that the bank will not pay because you have no funds to cover it in your account.

Cashier's check: A check that is written by a bank that promises to pay the amount that is on it. It can be used for large purchases such as a car.

Check card: See *Debit card*.

Checking account: An arrangement you have with a bank in which they keep your money for you and you can write checks for that money.

Credit card: A small plastic card that lets you buy things now and pay for them later. You can get a credit card through Seattle Central Bank.

Debit card or check card: A bank card you can use at an ATM or a store to purchase goods and services. It takes money directly from your bank account.

Direct deposit: A method of payment that deposits money electronically into your account (usually a paycheck).

Insufficient funds: A situation in which your bank account does not have enough money to cover a check or debit.

Interest: Money the bank pays you to use your money. Also the amount you have to pay when you borrow money.

Loan: Money you can borrow from the bank for different needs. Seattle Central Bank offers auto financing, personal loans, home mortgages, and student loans.

Online banking: A service that allows you to access your account balance, transfer funds, and pay bills online. Seattle Central Bank offers this service.

Overdraft: A situation in which you write a check for more money than you have in your account. Seattle Central Bank offers overdraft protection for a fee, which allows for an automatic transfer of funds to cover an overdraft.

Service charge: The monthly fee Seattle Central Bank charges for handling your checking account.

Statement: A list of your banking transactions for a period of time.

5
LESSON

He goes shopping a lot.

Gerunds

Gerunds end in -*ing* and are used in the following ways:

1. As the subject of a sentence
   Buying a car is hard work.
   Not paying your bills is a bad idea.

2. As objects of certain verbs
   You should avoid **bouncing** checks.

3. As objects of prepositions
   You can make a claim by **calling** customer service.

4. As complements (after *be*)
   His favorite job was **selling** cars.

5. In expressions with *go*
   She goes **shopping** a lot.

Tip

We often use gerunds after these verbs:

admit	keep
appreciate	mind
avoid	miss
consider	permit
discuss	postpone
dislike	practice
enjoy	quit
finish	suggest

1 Complete the Sentences

Complete the sentences with a gerund form of a verb in the box.

cash	borrow	pay	finance	buy
return	exchange	plan	look	talk

1. She dislikes _paying_ with a credit card.

2. If he keeps _____ money, he won't be able to pay it all back.

3. I don't mind _____ that check for you.

4. You can get a new CD player by _____ the broken one.

5. _____ a house takes a lot of money.

6. Salespeople can learn about customers' needs by _____ to them.

7. _____ can be a good way to buy something really expensive.

2 Share Your Ideas

Use a gerund to complete the sentences. Share your ideas with a partner.

1. _____ is good exercise.

2. You can save money by _____.

3. I try to avoid _____.

4. My teacher permits _____.

66

3 Answer the Questions

Answer the questions with a gerund.

1. What do you enjoy doing on weekends?

   I enjoy exercising and eating out.

2. What do you hate about shopping?

   _____

3. What is something you do now that you plan to keep doing?

   _____

4. What is your favorite job?

   _____

5. What is something you would like to quit?

   _____

6. What do you like to do with your friends or family?

   _____

4 Write

Write 3 sentences about the photo. Use gerunds.

1. _____

   _____

2. _____

   _____

3. _____

   _____

Teaching Children about Money

1 Warm Up

Check (✓) the box to indicate your level of knowledge.

	a little	a lot	want to know more
1. I can read price tags and labels.	☐	☐	☐
2. I can evaluate a product advertised on TV.	☐	☐	☐
3. I can make a budget and stick to it.	☐	☐	☐
4. I can read a pay stub.	☐	☐	☐
5. I know the difference between gross and net pay.	☐	☐	☐
6. I can read the stock pages.	☐	☐	☐
7. I know the positives and negatives of credit card use.	☐	☐	☐
8. I understand compound interest.	☐	☐	☐

2 Check Your Answers

Read the article on page 69. Then read the sentences below and check (✓) True or False.

	True	False
1. Giving children a certain amount of money each week can help them learn to budget.	☐	☐
2. It's okay to buy kids expensive things whenever they want them.	☐	☐
3. Net pay is usually more than gross pay.	☐	☐
4. Name brands are usually cheaper than generic brands.	☐	☐
5. Reading labels is a good way to comparison shop.	☐	☐
6. There aren't any disadvantages to using a credit card.	☐	☐
7. It's a good idea to save for long-term goals such as college.	☐	☐

3 Apply

Read the situations below and answer the questions.

1. Your child always asks for an expensive name-brand cereal. It is advertised on TV during children's television programs. You don't want to buy the cereal. What can you do to help your child understand your point of view?

2. Someone in your family really wants the latest model television. The price of this kind of television is very high. What advice would you give?

3. You want to go on a vacation next summer. You figure the trip will cost about $1,500. What can you do between now and then to make sure you can afford the trip?

Discuss your answers with one or more classmates.

Basic Money Lessons Grow with Your Kids

1   Here are steps to teach your children to become money savvy from Don Blandin, president of the American Savings Education Council in Washington.

Preschool Years

2   Stick with the concrete, such as telling the difference between a penny, a nickel, a dime, and a quarter. Show them a $1 bill, and start showing them how to use dollars to buy items. When your child asks for something in the store, explain you have to pay for the item and it is not free. Let your children pay for an item and receive the change.

5 to 7 Years Old

3   Ask your children to pick out the cereal and recognize that a name brand is usually more expensive than a **generic** brand. If you use coupons, have your children help clip them. This is also a good time to pay an **allowance,** so you can introduce the concept of saving for short-term and long-term goals and giving to charity.

4   Children can begin to read price tags and labels, which you can turn into lessons on how to comparison shop, how to evaluate a product advertised on TV, and even how to stick to a budget.

8 to 12 Years Old

5   As children get older, they become more aware of **status objects,** such as high-priced sneakers or clothing. Help your children write down financial goals if they want a big-ticket item such as video equipment.

Teenage Years

6   Continue the focus on saving for long-term goals, such as a car or college.

7   Many teens have jobs. Make sure your teen knows how to read his or her pay stub and understands the difference between **gross pay** and **net pay.** Net pay is the amount of money you get after taxes are taken out.

8   Discuss the positives and negatives of credit-card use. That's a biggie as your teen prepares to go off to college or move out of the house.

Source: Steve Rosen, Knight Ridder

WINDOW ON MATH
Computing Interest on Loans

 A Read the information.

5% interest = amount × 5% ⟶ 5% interest on $100 = $5.00 (total owed = $105)
10% interest = amount × 10% ⟶ 10% interest on $200 = $20 (total owed = $220)
20% interest = amount × 20% ⟶ 20% interest on $50 = $10 (total owed = $60)

 B Compute the total amount owed on the following loans.

$100 + 10% interest = _____ $200 + 8% interest = _____

$25 + 10% interest = _____ $500 + 15% interest = _____

7 LESSON

What do you know?

1 Listening Review 🎧

Listen to the questions and choose the best answer. Use the Answer Sheet.

1. A. 22 miles a gallon
   B. a 1999
   C. 11,000

2. A. a 2002
   B. 28 miles per gallon
   C. 7,500

3. A. 25 miles a gallon
   B. a 2005
   C. 35,000

4. A. 6 months
   B. parts
   C. defects

5. A. 5 years
   B. scratches and dents
   C. a receipt

ANSWER SHEET

1	Ⓐ	Ⓑ	Ⓒ
2	Ⓐ	Ⓑ	Ⓒ
3	Ⓐ	Ⓑ	Ⓒ
4	Ⓐ	Ⓑ	Ⓒ
5	Ⓐ	Ⓑ	Ⓒ
6	Ⓐ	Ⓑ	Ⓒ
7	Ⓐ	Ⓑ	Ⓒ
8	Ⓐ	Ⓑ	Ⓒ
9	Ⓐ	Ⓑ	Ⓒ
10	Ⓐ	Ⓑ	Ⓒ

Listen to the conversations and choose the best response. Use the Answer Sheet.

6. A. It's $49.95.
   B. Here's the receipt.
   C. It doesn't work.

7. A. A student loan?
   B. $500?
   C. Will that be cash or credit?

8. A. 30 miles per gallon.
   B. I need an oil change.
   C. I want to lease, I think.

Listen to the conversations and choose the best answer. Use the Answer Sheet.

9. A. She wants to pay with a check.
   B. She wants to get a loan.
   C. She wants to pay cash.

10. A. buy a coffeemaker
    B. exchange a coffeemaker
    C. get a refund

2 Vocabulary Review

Write the missing noun or adjective form.

Nouns	Verbs	Adjectives
covering	cover	-----
	damage	damaged
	finance	financial
origin	originate	
validity	validate	

Write 5 questions using the words from your chart. Then ask your classmates the questions.

EXAMPLE: Have you ever returned a damaged item to the store?

✔ LEARNING LOG

I know these words:

NOUNS
- ☐ account balance
- ☐ allowance
- ☐ bounced check
- ☐ cashier's check
- ☐ check card
- ☐ checking account
- ☐ credit card
- ☐ damage
- ☐ debit card
- ☐ defect
- ☐ direct deposit
- ☐ financing
- ☐ gas mileage
- ☐ gross pay
- ☐ insufficient funds

- ☐ interest
- ☐ loan
- ☐ mileage
- ☐ net pay
- ☐ online banking
- ☐ original receipt
- ☐ overdraft
- ☐ period (of coverage)
- ☐ refund
- ☐ replacement
- ☐ service charge
- ☐ statement
- ☐ status objects
- ☐ warranty
- ☐ workmanship

VERBS
- ☐ bounce a check
- ☐ make a claim

ADJECTIVES
- ☐ generic
- ☐ insufficient
- ☐ pre-owned
- ☐ valid
- ☐ void

OTHER
- ☐ no money down

I practiced these skills, strategies, and grammar points:

- ☐ asking specific questions
- ☐ relating readings to personal experience
- ☐ using vocabulary in a role-play
- ☐ taking notes
- ☐ noticing suffixes
- ☐ reading for specific information
- ☐ listening for specific information

- ☐ offering polite disagreement
- ☐ using context to guess the meaning of a word
- ☐ computing interest on loans
- ☐ evaluating knowledge of money issues
- ☐ applying personal knowledge to situations
- ☐ using gerunds

UNIT 4: Money and Consumer Issues

Spotlight: Reading Strategy

FINDING THE MAIN IDEA

The *topic* is what a reading is about. The *main idea* is the important idea the writer is expressing about the topic. The topic can be expressed as a word or phrase. The main idea can be expressed in 2 ways.

1. The main idea may be stated directly in a sentence.

> EXAMPLE:
>
> Families flock to Cape Cod, Massachusetts, in the summertime. There are many things to do: sail, kayak, bike, shop, play miniature golf, and whale watch. The beaches are clean and not very crowded. Many people visit Provincetown, a historic village that is a haven for artists and writers. Cape Cod is a terrific place for a vacation.
>
> Topic: Cape Cod
> Main Idea: Cape Cod is a terrific place for a vacation.

2. The main idea may be presented through the paragraph as a whole. To find the main idea you can:
   * ask "What is the writer telling me?".
   * notice if the ideas are related in some way.
   * think of a sentence that describes the reading's message.

A longer reading can have many paragraphs. The reading as a whole has a main idea, and each paragraph can have a main idea.

---

1 Read the article. What are the main ideas in paragraphs 1, 2, 3, and 4? Write the paragraph numbers next to the main ideas below.

Main ideas:

a. _____ Kim worked hard at school and at his jobs.

b. _____ Kim got financial help to start his business.

c. _____ Kim developed a very successful product.

d. _____ Kim sold his company and is financially successful.

A Success Story

1   Jeong Kim is a Korean-American businessman who is very successful. He started a communications company. The company did very well, and Kim just sold it for $1 billion. He ended up with $510 million, making him a very rich man.

2   Kim immigrated to the U.S. from Korea when he was 14. He worked very hard. He started his career by working nights at a 7-Eleven to earn money for college. He graduated from Johns Hopkins University in three years with a degree in electrical engineering. Kim returned to school and got an advanced degree in two years. Then he joined the U.S. Navy for seven years on a submarine.

U.S. Navy submarine

3   When Kim first started his company, he worked 120 hours a week. He got financing for the new company by taking out second mortgages on his house and using credit cards. He also received financial aid from the federal government.

4   Kim's company offered a new product in the computer field. This product was cheaper and faster than other products. It allowed more information to be sent over computer networks at the same time. Many businesses and even the government bought it. The company made many sales and earned a lot of money.

5   Jeong Kim is a good example to anyone who wants to succeed in business. He had some difficulties because he was an immigrant and spoke with an accent. But he showed that if people work very hard to reach their goals, they can be successful. Set high goals and never give up if you want to succeed like Jeong Kim.

Source: Adapted from *The Christian Science Monitor*

2 Read the paragraphs below. Write a sentence about each paragraph that expresses the main idea.

1.   Jeong Kim is a good example to anyone who wants to succeed in business. He had some difficulties because he was an immigrant and spoke with an accent. But he showed that if people work very hard to reach their goals, they can be successful. Set high goals and never give up if you want to succeed like Jeong Kim.

Main idea: _____

2.   Many families want to own homes. Before buying, families should consider several things. First, they should make sure they have enough money for the down payment and can still pay their other bills. Second, families may want to wait if the interest rates on mortgages are too high. Another thing to consider is the type of mortgage that may be best. Sometimes a mortgage that offers a low interest rate now may require a much higher interest rate in a few years.

Main idea: _____

3.   Do you keep your cash at home under the bed or in a box somewhere? It may be a better idea to use a bank or credit union. Both banks and credit unions offer checking accounts and savings accounts. These are generally safe places to keep your money. By using a bank or credit union, you can save time and avoid theft. Many credit unions make it easier for immigrants to open accounts.

Main idea: _____

Spotlight: Writing Strategy

OUTLINING

A good way to organize your paragraph is to use an outline. When you make an outline, you should write a main idea, and support it with details, examples, or reasons. You can sometimes create an outline from your cluster diagram.

| Main idea | Reasons, examples | Additional details |

1. **Main idea** (The best car for me is a pickup truck.)
   A. Reason 1: I live on a farm.
      Detail: I sometimes drive on rough ground and not on streets.
   B. Reason 2: I have to tow a trailer.
      Detail: I need a heavy car or truck to pull the trailer.
   C. Reason 3: I have a lot of stuff.
      Detail: Sometimes I need to transport wood, tools, or other things.

---

1 Look at the cluster diagram below. Create an outline.

1. Main idea: _____

   A. Reason 1: _____

      Detail: _____

   B. Reason 2: _____

      Detail: _____

   C. Reason 3: _____

      Detail: _____

2 Think about something you bought recently and the reasons why you bought it or why you like it. Create a cluster diagram below.

3 Create an outline from your cluster diagram.

1. Main idea: _____

   A. Reason 1: _____

      Detail: _____

   B. Reason 2: _____

      Detail: _____

   C. Reason 3: _____

      Detail: _____

4 Use your outline to write a paragraph about your purchase.

_____

_____

_____

_____

_____

_____

_____

_____

1 LESSON

It's a hazard!

THINGS TO DO

1 Warm Up

Work with your classmates to answer these questions.

1. Have you ever been hurt at work? What happened?
2. What do you see people doing in the picture?
3. How might someone get hurt while working at a **construction site**? In a restaurant?

2 Check *True* or *False*

Work with a partner. Study the picture and read the sentences below. Check (✓) *True* or *False*. Then write 2 more true sentences about the picture.

	True	False
1. All of the employees at the construction site are wearing hard hats.	☐	☐
2. At least one person is wearing safety glasses.	☐	☐
3. The men working on the road are not wearing any safety equipment.	☐	☐
4. Someone just got hurt at this workplace.	☐	☐
5. This looks like a safe place to work.	☐	☐

6. _____

7. _____

3 Analyze

A **hazard** is anything that can hurt you. Which of these hazards are at the construction site in the picture? Check (✓) your answers.

Hazards

1. ☐ a lot of noise
2. ☐ a **slippery** floor
3. ☐ poor lighting
4. ☐ poor air quality
5. ☐ a hot **surface**
6. ☐ not enough fire exits
7. ☐ machinery
8. ☐ heavy things to lift
9. ☐ **flammable** materials
10. ☐ chemicals

Compare ideas with your classmates.

> EXAMPLES: There is a lot of noise at this construction site.
> There are . . .

2
LESSON

This is an emergency!

THINGS TO DO

1 Use the Vocabulary 🎧

Work with a partner. Take turns asking the question above each picture. If your partner answers "yes," ask another question to get more information.

> A: Have you ever <u>injured your back?</u>
> B: Yes, I have.
> A: <u>How did it happen?</u> (When did it happen?/What happened?)
> B: <u>I tried to lift a big box.</u>

2 Interview

Write an emergency or accident in the blank below to complete the question. Then ask 5 classmates your question. Record their answers in the chart below.

Question: What should you do if someone _____?

> EXAMPLES: What should you do if someone injures their back?
> What should you do if someone is in intense pain?

Classmate's Name	Advice
1.	
2.	
3.	
4.	
5.	

TRY THIS STRATEGY

Learn Word Forms Expand your vocabulary by learning different forms of a new word. Make a chart like this for each of the highlighted words in this lesson.

Noun	Verb	Adjective
injury	injure	injured
intensity	-----	intense
robbery	rob	-----

---

1 **injured** your back?

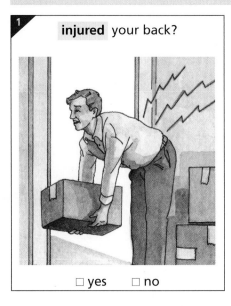

☐ yes   ☐ no

---

5 been exposed to **toxic** material?

☐ yes   ☐ no

---

9 been **robbed** ?

☐ yes   ☐ no

Have you ever . . .

2 been in **intense** pain?

□ yes   □ no

3 **fractured** a bone?

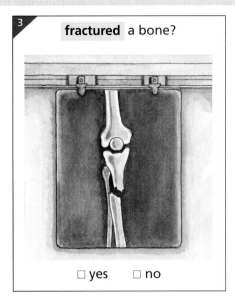

□ yes   □ no

4 had an eye **injury**?

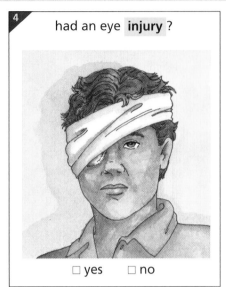

□ yes   □ no

6 had **heat exhaustion**?

□ yes   □ no

7 gotten a bad **shock**?

□ yes   □ no

8 lost **consciousness**?

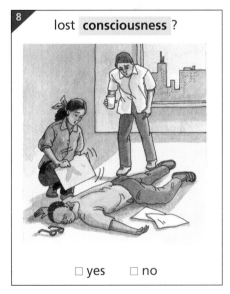

□ yes   □ no

10 had to **evacuate** your home?

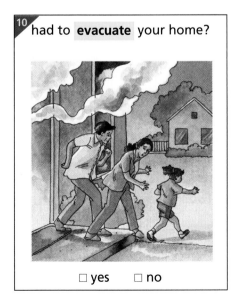

□ yes   □ no

11 been a **witness** to a crime?

□ yes   □ no

12 seen something **explode**?

□ yes   □ no

3 I won't do it again.

LESSON

THINGS TO DO

1 Warm Up

Work with your classmates to answer the questions below.

1. Look at the 3 pictures of people talking. What do you think their relationship is?
2. What do you think happened to each injured person?
3. Who do you think has the most serious injury? Why?

2 Listen and Take Notes 🎧

Listen to conversation #1 and identify the person's injury. Then listen again for the cause of the injury. Repeat with conversation #2 and #3.

Name	Injury	Cause of Injury
1. Sylvia	*got something in her eye*	
2. Sandra		
3. Joe		

Compare charts with your classmates. Then complete accident reports #1 and #2. Make your own accident report for #3.

3 Use the Communication Strategy 🎧

Work with a partner. Role-play a conversation between an employer and an employee. Replace the underlined words with your own ideas. Use the communication strategy in your conversation.

A: Why aren't you wearing your <u>hard hat</u>?

B: <u>I'm sorry. It won't happen again</u>.

A: Okay. I don't want any accidents around here.

B: No, of course not.

COMMUNICATION STRATEGY

Apologizing

You can apologize by expressing regret and reassuring the person that it won't happen again.

I'm sorry. It won't happen again.

Sorry. I'll be more careful in the future.

My mistake. I won't do it again.

Accident Report #1

1. Employee's name: _____ *Sylvia Hernandez* _____
2. Part of body affected: _____
   _____
3. Describe accident: _____
   _____
   _____
   _____
   _____
   _____
   _____

Accident Report #2

1. Employee's name: _____ *Sandra Rochev* _____
2. Part of body affected: _____
   _____
3. Describe accident: _____
   _____
   _____
   _____
   _____
   _____
   _____

4 LESSON

First Aid

THINGS TO DO

1 Warm Up

Work with your classmates to answer these questions.

1. What first aid equipment do you have at home?
2. What first aid equipment should you have at home?
3. Have you ever had to give someone first aid? Why? What did you do?

2 Read and Take Notes

Read the first aid instructions on page 83, and take notes in the chart below. Then compare charts with a partner.

Injury	Do	Don't
a serious burn	• *call 911 immediately*	• *use any medications* • *remove the person's clothing*
a minor burn		
a sharp object in the eye		
bleeding		
heat exhaustion		

First aid kit

Adhesive bandages

3 Evaluate

Work with several classmates to answer these questions. Then share your answers with the class.

1. Sam's 5-year-old daughter touched a hot iron and burned her hand slightly. There was a small red spot on her hand but no blisters. Sam immediately called 911. Did Sam do the right thing? What would you do in this situation?

2. Tom stepped on broken glass and got a deep cut in his foot. Tom's brother tried to get the glass out of Tom's foot before taking him to the hospital. Did Tom's brother do the right thing? What would you do?

3. Jasmine got a piece of a stick in her eye. Her friend Tonya covered both eyes with an ice bag and took her to the hospital. Did Tonya do the right thing? What would you do?

A roll of gauze

FIRST AID GUIDE
CALL 911 FOR ANY MEDICAL EMERGENCY!

BURNS

- If the burn is serious and the victim is in intense pain, call 911 immediately.
    - ✦ DO NOT apply medications.
    - ✦ DO NOT try to remove the victim's clothing.

- If the burn is **minor**, the skin will appear red and may have small blisters.
    - ✦ **Submerge** the injured area in cold water.
    - ✦ Do not break blisters.

EYE INJURIES

- If there is a sharp object in the eye, call 911 immediately.
    - ✦ DO NOT try to remove the object.
    - ✦ Cover both eyes with eye cups or gauze pads. Covering both eyes keeps the injured eye from moving.
    - ✦ DO NOT rub the injured eye or put ice on it.

- If there is something in the eye (not a sharp object), you should use an eye cup to flush the eye with water for 10 minutes.

BLEEDING

- Call 911 for medical assistance. Before providing care, put on protective gloves.
    - ✦ Keep victim lying down.
    - ✦ Apply direct **pressure** using a clean cloth or gauze directly on the wound.
    - ✦ DO NOT take out any object that is lodged in a wound; see a doctor for help in removal.
    - ✦ If there are no signs of a fracture in the injured area, carefully **elevate** the wound above the victim's heart.

HEAT EXHAUSTION

- Move the person to a cool place to rest. Remove as much clothing as possible. Give the person water. Don't allow the person to get chilled. Get medical help.

I wasn't paying attention.

The Past Continuous, Part 1

The past continuous describes an ongoing activity in the past.

EXAMPLES:

I **was standing** in the kitchen when the fire started.
She **was wearing** her seatbelt when her car went off the road.
They **weren't wearing** hard hats at the construction site yesterday.
I **wasn't paying attention** while I was washing the windows.
What **were** you **doing** when the alarm went off?

I		
She	**was sleeping** when the alarm went off.	
He	**wasn't working** when the bell rang.	
It		

We		
You	**were sleeping** when the alarm went off.	
They	**weren't working** when the bell rang.	

---

1 Complete the Sentences

Complete the sentences with the past continuous tense. Use the verbs in parentheses.

1. I hurt my back while I _____ *was lifting* _____ a heavy box. (lift)
2. Tom got hurt while he _____ a ladder. (climb)
3. Luckily, she _____ a harness when she fell off the scaffold. (wear)
4. The accident happened while we _____ to work. (drive)
5. Everyone _____ outside, so no one got hurt when the tank caught on fire. (stand)
6. While the boss _____ us directions, someone robbed his truck. (give)
7. I _____ anything unusual when I lost consciousness. (not/do)
8. They evacuated their home when they heard that a tornado _____. (come)

2 Write

Answer the questions with information about yourself.

1. What were you doing when the sun came up this morning?
   _I_____ *when the sun came up this morning.*

2. What were you thinking about on the way to class today?
   _____

3. Who were you talking to this morning while you were having breakfast?
   _____

> ## The Past Continuous, Part 2
>
> We often use the simple past and the past continuous in the same sentence. We use the simple past for a sudden action that interrupts the ongoing activity.
>
> | sudden action | | ongoing activity |
>
> EXAMPLE: He **fell** while he **was climbing up** the ladder.
>
> We often use the word *while* to introduce the ongoing activity. *While* means during the time that. We often use the word *when* to introduce the sudden action.
>
> EXAMPLES: The bell rang **while** I was sleeping.
> **When** the bell rang, I was sleeping.

3 Choose the Correct Verb

Circle the correct form of the verb to complete each conversation. Then practice with a partner.

1. A: What (happened/was happening) to your hand?
   B: I (broke/was breaking) my wrist.
   A: Really? How did you do that?
   B: I (slipped/was slipping) while I (climbed/was climbing) up a ladder at home.
   A: You're lucky you didn't get hurt worse.

2. A: What (happened/was happening) to Tom?
   B: He (hurt/was hurting) his back.
   A: How did he do that?
   B: He (pulled/was pulling) a muscle while he (lifted/was lifting) a box.
   A: That's too bad.

3. A: Did you know that Adnan (got/was getting) something in his eye?
   B: No, I didn't. How did he do that?
   A: He (cut/was cutting) some wood, but he (didn't wear/wasn't wearing) safety glasses.
   B: That's unfortunate.

4. A: How did Abe hurt his hand?
   B: I think he (cut/was cutting) it.
   A: How did he do that?
   B: I think he (used/was using) a saw and his hand (slipped/was slipping).
   A: Is it a bad cut?
   B: Not too bad.

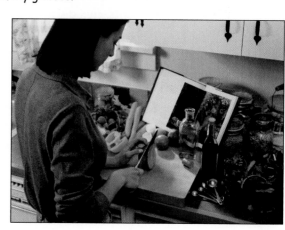

5. A: What did you do to your hand?
   B: Oh, I (burned/was burning) it.
   A: How did you burn it?
   B: Well, I (cooked/was cooking) and some grease (caught/was catching) on fire.

WORK

6

LESSON

Safety Procedures

1 Warm Up

Work with your classmates to answer these questions.

1. Have you ever had to evacuate your workplace? If yes, why?
2. What are some reasons why people might need to evacuate their workplace?

hurricane

chemical **spill**

flood

civil **disturbance**

2 Read and Respond

Read this information and answer the questions below.

EVACUATION PLANS

There are many different reasons why you might need to evacuate your workplace. These emergencies include fires, explosions, floods, earthquakes, hurricanes, tornadoes, toxic material releases, radiological and biological accidents, civil disturbances, and workplace violence.

How you respond will depend on the type of emergency. For some emergencies, your employer might want you to go to a special **assembly area** inside the workplace. For example, if there is a tornado warning or a chemical spill outside the workplace, your employer might ask you to go to the assembly area. For other emergencies, your employer might want you to evacuate the workplace and assemble outside the building. For example, if there is a fire in the building, you will probably be asked to leave the building.

Your employer should have an evacuation plan. This plan should identify when and how employees should respond to different emergencies.

Source: American Red Cross

1. How many reasons to evacuate does the article state? What are they?
2. For which emergencies would you probably stay inside the building?
3. For which emergencies would you probably leave the building?

3 Apply

Study the evacuation plan below. Tell how each person should get to the nearest exit.

> EXAMPLE: Sam should leave his room and turn left. He should then go straight ahead and turn right at the exit. From there he should walk out of the building.

Exit

WINDOW ON PRONUNCIATION 🎧
Intonation in Clauses

⭐A When a sentence has two clauses, each clause has an intonation pattern like a sentence, usually with rising-falling intonation. Listen to the sentences. Then listen and repeat.

1. I was standing in the kitchen / when the fire started.

2. She was wearing her seatbelt / when her car went off the road.

3. They weren't paying attention / while they were washing the windows.

4. You were working / when the bell rang.

5. He fell / while I was looking the other way.

⭐B Listen to the questions. Then listen and repeat. Listen a third time and mark the clauses for intonation. Use Activity A as a model.

1. What were you doing while the teacher was talking today?

2. What were you doing when class started?

⭐C Work with a classmate. Ask and answer the questions in Activity B.

87

7 LESSON

What do you know?

1 Listening Review 🎧

Listen to each conversation and the announcement. Choose the best answer to the question you hear. Use the Answer Sheet.

1. A. It's unsafe.
   B. It has poor lighting.
   C. It's very hot.

2. A. his eye
   B. his foot
   C. his back

3. A. her gloves
   B. her safety glasses
   C. her hard hat

4. A. He didn't have his hard hat.
   B. He had heat exhaustion.
   C. He was in intense pain.

5. A. There was a fire.
   B. There was a chemical spill.
   C. There was an explosion.

6. A. outside
   B. in the assembly area
   C. in the exit

7. A. a robbery
   B. a car accident
   C. an explosion

8. A. She put it in cold water.
   B. She elevated it.
   C. She rubbed it.

9. A. her leg
   B. her arm
   C. her head

10. A. He lost consciousness.
    B. He got an electric shock.
    C. He fell off a ladder.

ANSWER SHEET

	A	B	C
1	Ⓐ	Ⓑ	Ⓒ
2	Ⓐ	Ⓑ	Ⓒ
3	Ⓐ	Ⓑ	Ⓒ
4	Ⓐ	Ⓑ	Ⓒ
5	Ⓐ	Ⓑ	Ⓒ
6	Ⓐ	Ⓑ	Ⓒ
7	Ⓐ	Ⓑ	Ⓒ
8	Ⓐ	Ⓑ	Ⓒ
9	Ⓐ	Ⓑ	Ⓒ
10	Ⓐ	Ⓑ	Ⓒ

2 Vocabulary Review

Write the missing noun or verb form.

	NOUN	VERB
1.	evacuation	*evacuate*
2.	explosion	
3.		disturb
4.		assemble

	NOUN	VERB
5.	injury	
6.	robbery	
7.		spill
8.	fracture	

Choose 6 of the words from the chart and write 6 questions. Then ask your classmates your questions.

EXAMPLE: Have you ever fractured a bone?

✔ LEARNING LOG

I know these words:

NOUNS		**VERBS**	**ADJECTIVES**
☐ assembly	☐ heat exhaustion	☐ elevate	☐ civil
☐ chemical	☐ injury	☐ evacuate	☐ flammable
☐ consciousness	☐ pressure	☐ explode	☐ intense
☐ construction	☐ shock	☐ fracture	☐ minor
☐ disturbance	☐ site	☐ injure	☐ slippery
☐ flood	☐ spill	☐ rob	☐ toxic
☐ hazard	☐ surface	☐ submerge	
	☐ witness		

I practiced these skills, strategies, and grammar points:

☐ taking notes
☐ listening for specific information
☐ looking in a dictionary for word forms
☐ apologizing
☐ interviewing someone
☐ giving advice

☐ learning word forms
☐ predicting
☐ reading an evacuation map
☐ evaluating someone's actions
☐ using the past continuous
☐ using the simple past

Spotlight: Reading Strategy

THE SQ3R STRATEGY

SQ3R is a five-step strategy that helps you read and understand a piece of writing. SQ3R stands for Survey, Question, Read, Recite, and Review. Here's what you do at each step:

Step 1: Survey	Step 2: Question	Step 3: Read	Step 4: Recite	Step 5: Review
To survey or preview the material, first skim it to get a general understanding of the topic. Read the title and the first sentence of each paragraph and look at any illustrations and headings.	Write down 5 or more questions that you thought of while you were surveying the article.	Read the material and look for answers to your questions from Step 2. Underline or take notes on the important ideas in the text.	After reading the material, say out loud the most important points in the text. Try to use your own words.	Look back over your notes and text you underlined. Ask yourself if you understand the important points in the text.

1 Follow the steps below to practice the SQ3R strategy.

Step 1: Survey the article on page 91. What's the topic?

Step 2: Read the questions in the chart below, write 3 questions you thought of while you were surveying the article.

Questions	Answers
• *What should teens know about safety and health on the job?* • *Why do so many teens get hurt on the job?*	

Step 3: Read the article and look for answers to the questions in Step 2. Write the answers in the chart above.

Step 4: Say out loud the most important points in the article. Try to use your own words.

Step 5: Look back at your chart in Step 2. Do you understand the main points in the article?

What Working Teens Should Know about Safety and Health on the Job

Every year about 70 teens die from work injuries in the United States. Another 70,000 get hurt badly enough that they go to a hospital emergency room.

Here are the stories of three teens:

- 18-year-old Sylvia caught her hand in an electric cabbage shredder at a fast food restaurant. Her hand is permanently disfigured and she'll never have full use of it again.

- 17-year-old Joe lost his life while working as a construction helper. An electric shock killed him when he climbed a metal ladder to hand an electric drill to another worker.

- 16-year-old Donna was assaulted and robbed at gunpoint at a sandwich shop. She was working alone after 11 P.M.

Why do injuries like these occur? Teens are often injured on the job due to unsafe equipment and stressful conditions. Also, teens may not receive adequate safety training and supervision. Teens are also more likely to be injured when working on jobs they are not allowed by law to do.

What are my rights on the job?

By law, your employer must provide:

- a safe and healthful workplace.

- safety and health training, in many situations, including providing information on chemicals that could be harmful to your health.

- for many jobs, payment for medical care if you get hurt or sick because of your job. You may also be entitled to lost wages.

You also have a right to:

- report safety problems to OSHA (Occupational Safety and Health Administration).

- refuse to work if the job is immediately dangerous to your life or health.

- join or organize a union.

What Hazards Should I Watch Out For?

Type of Work	Examples of Hazards
Janitor/Clean-up	• Toxic chemicals in cleaning products • Blood on discarded needles
Food Service	• Slippery floors • Hot cooking equipment • Sharp objects
Retail/Sales	• Violent crimes • Heavy lifting
Office/Clerical	• Stress • Harassment • Poor computer work station design

Source: U.S. Department of Health and Human Services, Centers for Disease Control and Prevention

Spotlight: Writing Strategy

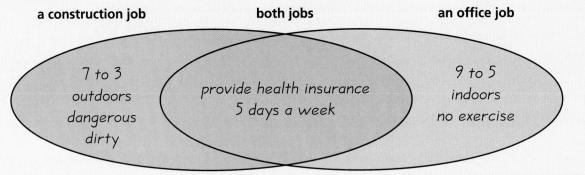

MAKING A VENN DIAGRAM

Making a Venn Diagram is a good way to organize your ideas when you need to compare two things. To make a Venn Diagram, draw 2 overlapping circles. In the center area, list the similarities. In the outer areas, list the differences.

a construction job   **both jobs**   **an office job**

7 to 3
outdoors
dangerous
dirty

provide health insurance
5 days a week

9 to 5
indoors
no exercise

1 Read the paragraph on page 93 and take notes in the Venn Diagram below.

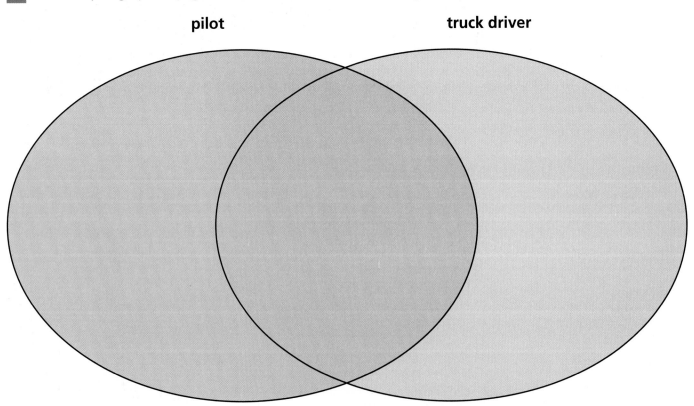

pilot   **truck driver**

A pilot or a truck driver?

Would you rather be a pilot or a truck driver? Both of these jobs are interesting and unpredictable. That is because both a pilot and a truck driver are always on the move. They never stay in the same place for very long. Both a pilot and a truck driver also need to know a lot about engines. One of the biggest differences between a pilot and a truck driver is the training. It takes a long time to learn to fly a plane—much longer than it takes to learn to drive a truck. Another big difference is that many truck drivers own their own truck but it's unusual for a pilot to own the plane that he or she flies.

2 Choose 2 jobs. Make a Venn Diagram comparing them. Then use your ideas to write a paragraph.

Job 1: _____ **both jobs** **Job 2:** _____

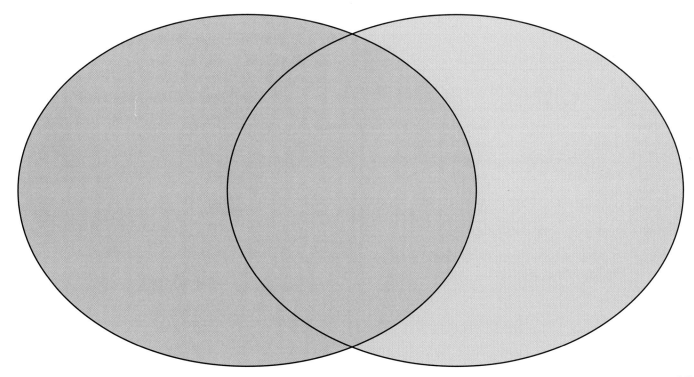

1 LESSON

What makes a community good?

THINGS TO DO

1 Warm Up

Work with your classmates to answer these questions.

1. What are the people in the picture doing?
2. What do you like about your town or city? What do you dislike about it?
3. What makes a community good? Make a list of 5 qualities. For example, good schools.

2 Identify

Study the picture and read the sentences below. Check (✓) the sentences that are true. Then compare ideas with a partner.

1. No one is entering the **courthouse** . ☐
2. The police officer is making a **traffic stop** . ☐
3. A garbage collector is collecting **trash** . ☐
4. The town hall is across from the **jail** . ☐
5. A woman is walking her pet on a **leash** . ☐
6. The girl on the bicycle is wearing a **helmet** . ☐
7. There are **speed bumps** in front of the school. ☐
8. A man is cleaning **graffiti** off the wall of the museum. ☐

3 Evaluate

Which of the things below should you do? Which shouldn't you do? Check (✓) the things you should do.

___ **litter**
___ draw graffiti
___ walk your child to school
___ ride a motorcycle
___ **demonstrate** about an issue

___ play on steps
___ wear a seat belt
___ keep a pet on a leash
___ pay **traffic tickets**
___ pick up trash

Compare ideas with your classmates.

EXAMPLE: I think people should ride motorcycles because motorcycles use less gas than cars.

2 LESSON

Littering is prohibited.

THINGS TO DO

1 Warm Up

Work with your classmates to answer these questions.

1. What public spaces do you use in your community?
2. Look at the prohibited activities on page 97. Which 3 are the most serious problems in your community?
3. What are 3 other problems in your community?

A library is an example of a public space.

2 Read and Respond

Work with a partner. Read the information about Mountain Glen on page 97. Take turns asking the questions. Write the answers.

1. What word means that something is not allowed? ___*prohibited*___
2. What is the word for leaving trash on the ground? _____
3. Who has to wear helmets when riding bicycles? _____
4. Where are you not allowed to park? _____
5. What is **vandalism**? _____
6. What do you need when you walk your dog? _____
7. Can you drink **alcoholic beverages**? _____
8. What do you need a **license** for? _____
9. If you drive too fast, what are you doing? _____

3 Analyze

Think about the rules at Mountain Glen. Write them in the appropriate place on the chart.

Safety	Protection of Property	Politeness to Others
no swimming in posted areas		

4 Discuss

Work with your classmates. List 3 rules in your community. Why are they good for the community?

TRY THIS STRATEGY

Learn Synonyms

Synonyms are words that are similar in meaning. For example, the words *a drink* and *a beverage* are synonyms. You can expand your vocabulary quickly by learning synonyms for words. Find a synonym in Lesson 1 for each of these words: *prison, garbage, go into, neighborhood, protest*.

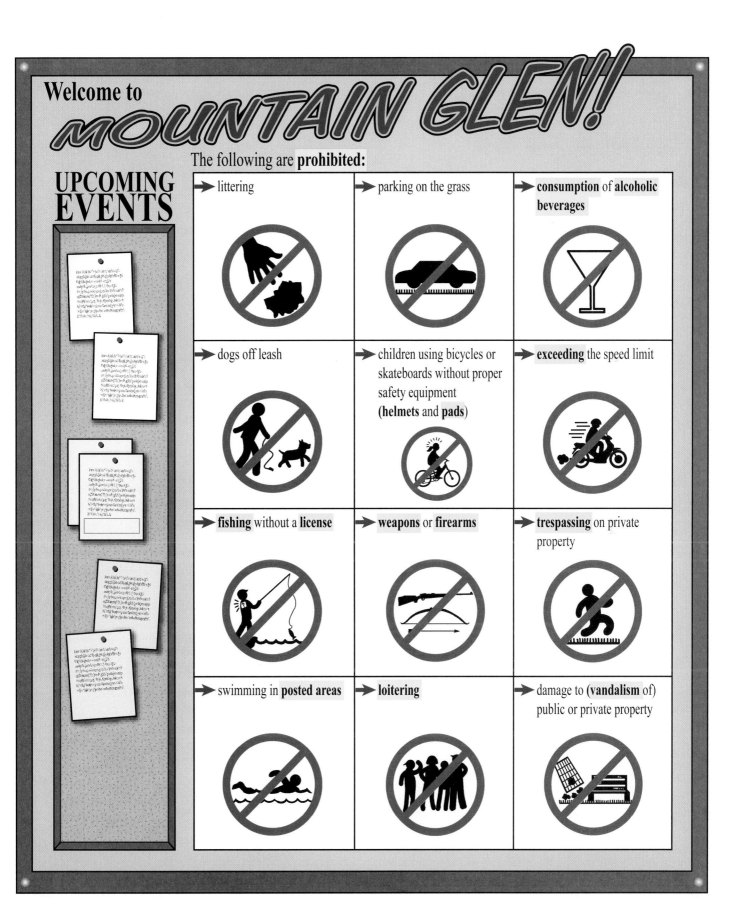

Welcome to
MOUNTAIN GLEN!

UPCOMING EVENTS

The following are **prohibited:**

- littering
- parking on the grass
- **consumption** of **alcoholic beverages**
- dogs off leash
- children using bicycles or skateboards without proper safety equipment (**helmets** and **pads**)
- **exceeding** the speed limit
- **fishing** without a **license**
- **weapons** or **firearms**
- **trespassing** on private property
- swimming in **posted areas**
- **loitering**
- damage to (**vandalism** of) public or private property

LESSON 3

I'm sorry, officer.

THINGS TO DO

1 Warm Up

Work with your classmates to answer these questions.

1. In pictures 1, 2, and 3 someone has done something wrong or caused a problem. What do you think the problem is?
2. Which problem is the most serious? Why?
3. Have you ever talked to a police officer in your community? When? What did you talk about?

2 Listen and Take Notes

Listen to each conversation and identify the problems. Then listen to the consequences. Complete the chart.

	Problems	Consequences
1.		
2.		
3.		

3 Use the Communication Strategy 🎧

Work with a partner. Role-play a conversation between a driver and a police officer. Replace the underlined words in the example with your own ideas. Try to use the communication strategy.

A: Did you know <u>you were speeding</u>?

B: No. I'm sorry.

A: I need to see your license and **registration**.

B: Of course. Right away.

A: Please <u>watch your speed</u> from now on.

B: I will. I'll be very careful.

In the U.S., police officers carry guns.

TRY THIS STRATEGY ◆◆◆◆◆◆◆◆◆◆◆◆◆◆◆◆

Compare and Contrast You can understand new information better if you compare and contrast it with what you already know. Discuss ways that the U.S. and another country you know differ regarding these issues: drinking alcohol, wearing seat belts, carrying guns, having loud parties. List 2 surprising differences.

◆◆◆◆◆◆◆◆◆◆◆◆◆◆◆◆◆◆◆◆◆◆◆◆◆◆

COMMUNICATION STRATEGY

Accepting Criticism

In some situations, especially if you have done something wrong, you will want to respond politely to criticism. Try these phrases:

I'm sorry.

I didn't realize that.

I apologize.

It won't happen again.

Please forgive me.

CALIFORNIA
DRIVER LICENSE
EXPIRES: 04-19-07   7805067644   CLASS: 2

ROBERT MANUEL GARZA
1521 MARKET STREET
SAN FRANCISCO, CA
94821

DOB: 03-02-75

HAIR: BRN   EYES: BRN
HT: 5'10"   WT: 160 LBS

Robert Garza

Department of Natural Resources Fishing License	**DNR**
Application	

Date	Official use only:
Feb. 16, 2006	License No. Issued

Name
Sammy Taylor

Street Address
1565 N. Broad St.

City	State	Zip
Lincoln	NE	68522

Date of Birth	Height	Sex (circle one)	Eye color
10/03/1972	5' 11"	(M) / F	Brown

Social Security No.	Driver's License No.	Telephone No. (include area code)
123-45-6789	U1200000	402-555-1000

I certify under penalty of law that the statements made herein are true.

Signature of Applicant:
Sammy Taylor

LESSON 4

An American Hero

THINGS TO DO

1 Warm Up

Work with your classmates to answer these questions. Look at the title, subtitles, and photos on pages 100 and 101.

1. What do you think the story is about?
2. What are 3 questions you have about the story?
3. Who do you think is a hero? Why?

2 Match

Read the story. Use context to guess the meanings of the highlighted words. Write the letter of the definition next to each word below.

1. _c_ migrant
2. ___ look down on
3. ___ unfair
4. ___ protest
5. ___ strike
6. ___ union
7. ___ struggle

a. think badly of
b. an agreement to stop working
c. moving from one place to another looking for work
d. effort to do something difficult
e. disagree with
f. an organization of workers who work together for better treatment
g. not right

3 Analyze

List 3 problems that Cesar Chavez noticed and 3 things he did to help solve the problems.

Problem	Solution
• low wages for migrant workers	• joined a strike

4 Discuss

Work with a small group. What are 4 things Cesar Chavez did that helped workers?

CESAR CHAVEZ
Fighting for La Causa* and Human Rights

A STRONG FAMILY

1   Cesario Estrada Chavez was born on March 31, 1927. He grew up on a ranch near the town of Yuma, Arizona. Cesario would later become known to the world as Cesar Chavez. Even as a child, Cesario had to work hard. But his family was strong and loving. As he later remembered, "I had more happy moments as a child than unhappy moments."

A HARD LIFE

2   The Great Depression made life difficult for the Chavez family. When they lost their land in 1939, they moved to California looking for farm work. Cesario's family became **migrant** workers, people who move from place to place picking crops in different farms. The Chavezes earned very little money. Sometimes farm owners didn't pay them at all. By the time Cesario was a teenager, he had moved all over the state, and attended more than 30 elementary schools. He was **looked down on** for speaking Spanish. One teacher even changed his name to Cesar so it sounded less Mexican. When Cesar was 15, his father was hurt in a car accident and couldn't work. Cesar dropped out of school to work full time and support his family. After work, Cesar was a regular teen. He liked hanging out with his friends, going to dances, and listening to music.

AN UNFAIR WORLD

3   Cesar had to be careful about where he went. Mexican Americans were not allowed in many places, like movie theaters and restaurants. Some stores even had signs that said, "No Dogs or Mexicans Allowed." Cesar grew tired of the **unfair** treatment. In 1948, 21-year-old Cesar was working in a field. Cars

drove by filled with people waving flags and telling the workers to walk off their jobs to **protest** the low wages. Cesar and his fellow workers joined the **strike.** Cesar believed he would be a good leader in this new movement. He started a **union,** a group of workers who stood together for higher pay and better treatment.

LA CAUSA

4   Cesar spent years organizing his fellow workers to fight for better pay and treatment from farm owners. But many farm owners, especially the grape growers, didn't treat migrant workers with respect. On September 17, 1965, the anniversary of Mexico's Independence Day, Cesar spoke to the members of his union. He told them that they should stop working for the California grape growers. Their **struggle** was named La Causa (the cause). One thousand two hundred workers joined in the movement.

Farm workers harvesting grapes

AMERICAN HERO

5   Cesar spoke to reporters, college students, and everyday people about the farm workers and about La Causa. People gave donations and worked as volunteers. Cesar Chavez became a household name. On July 30, 1970, the California grape growers signed a contract with the union that represented migrant workers. The workers got higher wages, health insurance, and more rights. Cesar spent the rest of his life working for the rights of farm workers, African Americans, women, and many others. When he died on April 23, 1993, he was the president of the United Farm Workers of America. In 1994, President Clinton awarded Cesar Chavez the Presidential Medal of Freedom. Cesar was the second Mexican American to receive the honor.

* *La Causa* is Spanish for "the cause." In this case, the cause is the effort to improve the lives of farm workers.

Source: Jeannette Del Valle, *Scholastic Action*

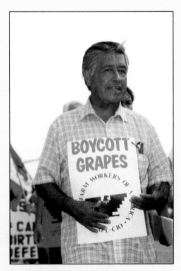

Cesar Chavez fought for migrant farm workers

LESSON 5

It's illegal to park on the lawn.

Infinitives

Infinitives are formed by putting *to* in front of the base form of a verb. Infinitives are used in the following ways:

1. After certain verbs
   Chavez wanted **to help** migrant workers.

2. After objects
   They told the workers **to walk off** their jobs.

3. To express purpose
   Cesar dropped out of school **to work** full time.

4. After adjectives in expressions beginning with *It*
   It's **illegal** **to park** on the lawn.

Tip

These are some verbs that infinitives often follow:

agree	need
ask	pay
begin	promise
decide	refuse
expect	want
learn	would like

1 Complete the Sentences

Complete the sentences with an infinitive of a verb in the box.

have	make	pick	protest	show	slow	smoke	take	vote	wear

1. It's wrong ____*to take*____ someone's money.

2. If you want _____ in the next election, you should register soon.

3. People who drive need _____ licenses.

4. The migrant workers refused _____ crops.

5. It's against the law _____ on many airplanes.

6. I told him _____ a helmet.

7. The officer warned her _____ down.

8. Many people went on strike _____ the poor working conditions.

9. Gandhi went on a hunger strike _____ the British leave India.

10. It's important _____ respect to police officers.

It's illegal to smoke here.

2 Rewrite

Rewrite these sentences using infinitives. Use *It* + *is* + an adjective + an infinitive.

1. Parking on the lawn is prohibited.

   It is prohibited to park on the lawn. _____.

2. Talking in the movie theater is rude.

   _____

3. Littering is irresponsible.

   _____

4. Fighting for human rights is sometimes necessary.

   _____

5. Telling stories is fun.

   _____

6. Getting a fishing license is important.

   _____

3 Complete the Sentences

Complete the sentences using your own ideas. Use an infinitive.

1. It's illegal _____ in this city.
2. It's wrong _____ your neighbors.
3. My teacher expects students _____.

4 Answer Questions

Answer the questions. Use an infinitive.

1. Why are you studying English?

   EXAMPLE: *I'm studying English to get a better job.*

   _____

2. Why do communities have laws about drinking and driving?

   _____

3. Why should children wear seat belts?

   _____

It's illegal to park here.

It's illegal to litter.

103

Report a Crime

1 Check *True* or *False*

Read the online form. Then read the statements below. Check (✓) *True* or *False*.

Report a Crime   ⊠ ⊟ ⊞

| HOME |
| CONTACT |
| SAFETY TIPS |
| BE INVOLVED |

Report a Crime
**If you have information regarding a crime,
please fill out this form or call (937) 555-4357.**

*Name Lee Trang

*Email Address Trang257@streetuse.net

*Phone Number 555-7234

Would you like us to contact you? ☐ Yes ◉ No

Location of offense East 15th St. and West Ave.

Please include detailed information about the crime here:

Some kids are loitering at Victory Park every night. They have damaged some park property and play their music really loud. They drink alcohol and bother the people who live near the park.

*You do not have to give your name or personal information.

SUBMIT

DO NOT USE THIS FORM TO REPORT AN EMERGENCY.
Please dial 9-1-1 if you believe someone or something is in danger of harm. Do not use this online form for any violent crime, theft of a firearm, or stolen vehicle.

This form has been developed to allow you to report certain problems such as noise violations, alcohol violations, property damage, loitering, property loss, trespassing, and suspicious activity. You may also telephone us at (937) 555-4357.

---

1. This form is available online.   ☐ True   ☐ False
2. You can use this form for emergencies.   ☐ True   ☐ False
3. You have to give your name.   ☐ True   ☐ False
4. A police officer will definitely contact you.   ☐ True   ☐ False

2 Identify

Check (✓) the crimes that you can report with this form.

☐ someone hurting another   ☐ loitering

☐ using a weapon or firearm   ☐ car theft

☐ someone's death   ☐ problems with noise

☐ damage to property   ☐ problems with alcohol

☐ trespassing   ☐ other emergencies

3 Interview

Work with a partner. Ask the questions. Write your partner's answers.

1. Have you ever seen someone commit a crime? If so, what was it?

_____

2. What problems do you have in your town or city?

_____

WINDOW ON PRONUNCIATION 🎧
Reductions with *To*

 Sometimes we say words quickly, and the pronunciation changes. Listen to the phrases. Then listen again and repeat.

have to (sounds like *hafta*)	used to (sounds like *usta*)
want to (sounds like *wanna*)	going to (sounds like *gonna*)
ought to (sounds like *otta*)	has to (sounds like *hasta*)

B Listen to the sentences. Write the missing words. Use the correct spelling.

1. I _____ renew my driver's license this month.

2. She's _____ take the dog for a walk.

3. Sam _____ pay a parking ticket.

4. They _____ live in New Mexico.

5. You _____ slow down. You're _____ get a ticket.

6. We _____ buy a house in that area.

 Work with a partner. Ask the questions below. Write your partner's answers. Then read the answers to the class.

1. What do you have to do to be a good community member?

_____

2. What do you want to do to help your community?

_____

LESSON 7

What do you know?

1 Listening Review 🎧

Listen to the sentences. Choose the best answer. Use the Answer Sheet.

1. A. People 12 and over need a fishing license to fish.
   B. People 16 and over need a driver's license.
   C. If you're at least 16, you need a fishing license to fish.

2. A. You can't drive for 5 years after the date of the ticket.
   B. Your license is good for a total of 5 years.
   C. You can get a license issued in 5 years.

3. A. You can pay your ticket in court.
   B. You can get a ticket in traffic.
   C. If you don't agree with the ticket, you can go to court to explain.

4. A. You can swim in the area.
   B. If the sign says "no swimming" you are not allowed to swim.
   C. You need a permit to swim.

5. A. You can't drink alcohol in the park.
   B. You can drink alcohol in the park.
   C. Alcohol is sold in the park.

6. A. Let your dog off the leash.
   B. It is not okay to let your dog off the leash.
   C. Leashes aren't necessary.

ANSWER SHEET			
1	A	B	C
2	A	B	C
3	A	B	C
4	A	B	C
5	A	B	C
6	A	B	C
7	A	B	C
8	A	B	C
9	A	B	C
10	A	B	C

Listen to the conversations. Choose the best answer to complete them. Use the Answer Sheet.

7. A. I'll go to court.
   B. That's too bad.
   C. I will. Again, I apologize.

8. A. I'll turn it down right away.
   B. Who is having the party?
   C. What kind of noise?

9. A. Do I need a license?
   B. Thank you. It won't happen again.
   C. I want to contest the ticket.

10. A. I didn't realize that.
    B. I apologize.
    C. Thank you. We will.

2 Vocabulary Review

Use the clues to complete the crossword puzzle.

Across

1 going on someone else's property
5 guns, knives
6 intentional damage to property
8 argue or demonstrate against
9 safety equipment that protects your knees and elbows

Down

2 places in the road that are higher to slow drivers down
3 drawing or writing on walls and public property
4 safety equipment that protects your head
7 leave trash on the ground

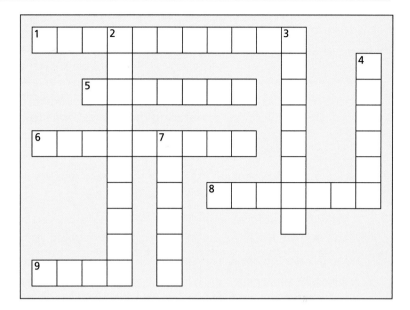

☑ LEARNING LOG

I know these words:

NOUNS
- alcoholic beverages
- consumption
- courthouse
- firearm
- graffiti
- helmet
- leash
- license
- migrant
- pad
- registration
- speed bump
- strike
- struggle
- traffic stop
- traffic ticket
- trash
- union
- vandalism
- weapon

VERBS
- demonstrate
- exceed
- fish
- litter
- loiter
- look down on
- protest
- trespass

ADJECTIVES
- illegal
- posted
- prohibited
- unfair

I practiced these skills, strategies, and grammar points:
- learning synonyms
- accepting criticism
- taking notes
- reading for specific information
- listening for specific information
- expressing an opinion
- evaluating actions
- using context to guess the meaning of a word
- using infinitives
- scanning
- skimming

Spotlight: Reading Strategy

PARAPHRASING	
Paraphrasing is saying or writing ideas in your own words. When you want to remember what you read, you should practice restating the information either out loud to yourself or to another person.	

How to Paraphrase	EXAMPLES
Use words that mean the same thing.	TEXT: Please dial 9-1-1 if you believe someone is in danger of harm. PARAPHRASE: If you think someone will get hurt, call 911.
Use ideas that have an opposite meaning.	TEXT: It is prohibited to let pets off the leash in this park. PARAPHRASE: In this park, you must keep your pets on a leash.
Combine ideas from different sentences.	TEXT: Cars drove by filled with people waving flags and telling the workers to walk off their jobs to protest the low wages. Cesar and his fellow workers joined the strike. PARAPHRASE: Cesar and his coworkers went on strike to protest low pay.

1 Read the sentences then paraphrase them.

1. The consumption of alcoholic beverages is prohibited.

   You are not allowed to drink alcohol.

2. It's a good idea to report a crime immediately.

3. The officer issued the driver a ticket because she was exceeding the speed limit.

4. If you don't want to bother your neighbors, you shouldn't play music late at night.

5. Park rules require that all children under the age of 12 wear a helmet when riding a bicycle.

2 Read the texts below. Choose the best paraphrases.

1. San Francisco has an ordinance allowing bicycle parking in all city-owned garages that rent automobile space to the public.

   A. In San Francisco, you can ride a bicycle.

   B. If a city-owned garage rents parking space for cars, it allows bicycle parking.

   C. If you own a bicycle in San Francisco, you must park it in a garage.

2. No dog is permitted to run loose off of its owner's property. The fine for failing to follow this rule is $150.

   A. You have to keep your dog on your property or on a leash. If you don't, you will have to pay a $150 fine.

   B. You can buy a dog for $150.

   C. It's okay to let your dog run loose when it's not on your property if you pay $150.

3. Marshville residents are upset about the increase in the number of people who are parking cars on their front lawns.

   A. Marshville residents think it's okay to park on lawns.

   B. A lot of people park their cars on lawns.

   C. More people are parking cars on front lawns and people living in Marshville are upset about it.

Bicycles parked in a garage

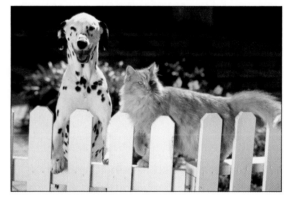

Furry friends behind a fence

3 Read the paragraph. Rewrite it in your own words.

Saltwater fishers could soon be required to have a license under a new law. The money earned by selling the licenses could be used to manage the fish, buy land for parks, and to maintain fishing areas. Lawmakers would also like to survey people who fish to find out how often they fish and what kind of fish they catch.

_____

_____

_____

_____

Spotlight: Writing Strategy

SUMMARIZING

When you summarize, you give a short account of the important information in a reading or about an event. Try these steps to write a summary of a reading:

- Identify the topic.
- Read it carefully and underline the important ideas.
- Find the main idea.
- Break the information down into smaller sections.
- Write a sentence that summarizes each section.

1 Read this article. Then answer the questions on page 111.

Mothers Against Drunk Driving (MADD)

One Mother Makes a Difference

On May 3, 1980 a 13-year-old girl named Cari Lightner was walking down the street when a car hit and killed her. The driver drank several alcoholic drinks before he got in the car. He was drunk. Cari's mother, Candy, decided to do something about this problem. She started Mother's Against Drunk Driving (MADD).

How MADD Grew

Candy Lightner traveled around the country. She talked to people everywhere about the dangers of drunk driving. Lightner was in charge of MADD for eight years. During that time every state in the country raised the legal age for drinking to 21. In 1980, 25,000 people were killed by drunk drivers. In 1992, that number fell to 17,700.

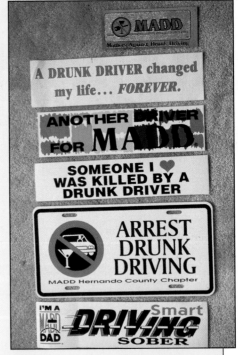

Bumper stickers against drunk driving

MADD Today

MADD is a national organization today with 3 million members. Its goals are to educate people about the dangers of drunk driving and prevent accidents. MADD works to change state and federal laws to make the consequences of drunk driving more severe.

Questions:

1. What is the topic? _____

2. What does the writer want to say about the topic (what is the main idea)?

   _____

3. What are the different sections in the article? Write them below.
   A. _____
   B. _____
   C. _____

2 Write a sentence that summarizes each section.
   A. _____
   B. _____
   C. _____

3 Write a summary of the article. Use the sentences from Activity 2. Add other important details if necessary.

   _____

   _____

   _____

   _____

4 Think about a story in the news, or a favorite story you have read. Write 5 sentences that summarize the story. Share your summary with a partner.

   _____

   _____

   _____

   _____

   _____

   _____

What makes a workplace good?

THINGS TO DO

1 Warm Up

Work with your classmates to answer these questions.

1. What jobs have you had? Which job did you like the best? Why?
2. Look at the picture. Talk about 3 things you see that make this a good or a bad workplace.
3. What qualities make a workplace good?

2 Match

Study the picture and read the sentences below.
Write the names next to the jobs.

1. The **news anchors** present the news on TV.
   Rick and Tonya

2. The **meteorologist** tells TV viewers what the weather will be like. _____

3. A **writer** writes the stories the anchors read. _____

4. The **traffic reporter** goes up in a helicopter to see where there are accidents or delays on the roads.
   _____

5. A **camera operator** uses a camera like a photographer, but makes a video instead of taking pictures.
   _____

6. The **sound engineer** makes sure the audio is good.
   _____

7. An **account executive** sells advertising space or time. _____

3 Evaluate

Work with a partner and evaluate the workplace in the picture. What would you like and dislike about working at a television station? Complete the chart with at least 10 ideas.

We would like . . .	We wouldn't like . . .
working with interesting people	

KMGH 7 WEATHER

72°

65°

88°

KMGH 7 NEWS

 TRY THIS STRATEGY **Set Goals** Think about your dream job. What are 3 short-term goals you can set to help you get that job?

KMGH 7 NEWS • Weather • Traffic • Enter

Does the job have good benefits?

THINGS TO DO

1 Complete the Chart

Read the article. Work with a partner to complete the chart.

Which benefit is most important to these people?	
1. a woman expecting a baby	
2. a person who wants to get a university degree	
3. an athlete	
4. a person who lives far from his or her office	
5. you	

Explain your answers to another pair of students.

2 Classify

Make a diagram like this. Work with a partner. Write 3 workplace benefits in each category. Use ideas from the reading and your own ideas.

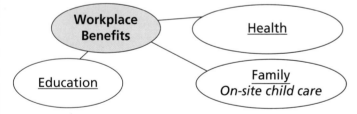

Workplace Benefits

Health

Education

Family
On-site child care

3 Evaluate

Put the benefits in order of their importance to you. Write 1 next to the most important benefit. Write 9 next to the least important benefit. Share your ideas with a classmate.

_____ health insurance

_____ dental insurance

_____ gym

_____ paid family leave

_____ on-site child care

_____ flex time

_____ tuition reimbursement

_____ telecommuting

_____ on-site training/ ABE classes

Health care: Look for a company that provides a good **medical insurance** plan. Things to look for:

• Choice of health care provider

• Low **co-pay**

Paid family leave: All employers must allow workers up to six weeks off to care for family members. Some companies provide longer family leave, and pay for it!

TRY THIS STRATEGY

Visualize Visualizing, or associating a picture with a new word or phrase, can help you remember it. For example, to remember *tuition reimbursement*, picture a classroom and a dollar sign. Choose 3 new words or phrases from this lesson and draw pictures to help you remember each one.

Finding the right job with good **benefits**

If you're in the market for a new job, find a workplace that meets your professional, personal, and family needs. Many employers offer excellent benefits to attract and retain good workers.

Tuition reimbursement: Look for a company that will pay for your classes.

Dental care: Ask about **dental insurance.** Many plans cover routine visits and **preventive care.**

Gym: Some companies provide an on-site gym or membership in a health club to improve the health of their employees.

On-site child care: If you're a parent, an on-site child care center is an important benefit. You can bring your child to a day care center at your workplace and pick him or her up right after work.

Flex time: You may want to work flexible hours instead of 9:00–5:00 each day. Some employers allow you to plan your work schedule to meet family and personal needs.

Telecommuting: For some positions, it's possible for you to work from home some or all of the time.

On-site basic skills courses: Some companies offer Adult Basic Education courses, or ABE, to help you with reading, writing, math, and communication skills.

3 **LESSON**

I'm calling about the ad for a photographer.

THINGS TO DO

1 Warm Up

Work with your classmates to answer these questions.

1. What are 3–5 things you can do to find a job?
2. How did you or someone you know find out about a job?
3. Read the job listings posted on the website. Which job is most interesting to you? Why?
4. Which job on the website seems the most difficult? Why?

2 Listen and Take Notes 🎧

Listen to each conversation and look at the job descriptions on page 117. Write 2 questions each applicant asks. Then write the answers.

Job	Questions	Answers
1. Writer	a. *Are you hiring for 1 writer position?*	a. *No, we're hiring for 2.*
	b.	b.
2. **Production assistant**	a.	a.
	b.	b.
3. **Account assistant**	a.	a.
	b.	b.

Dressed for an interview

3 Use the Communication Strategy 🎧

Work with a partner. Role-play a telephone conversation between a receptionist and a person looking for a job. Replace the underlined words in the example with your own ideas. Try to use the communication strategy.

A: Hi. I'm calling about the ad for a <u>photographer</u>.
B: Yes. How can I help you?
A: Can you tell me a little about the job?
B: Sure. We're looking for an experienced <u>portrait photographer</u>.
A: I've done a lot of <u>portrait photography</u>. <u>Is the job full time?</u>
B: <u>Yes, it is.</u>
A: What should I do if I'm interested in applying?
B: <u>Send 2 copies of your résumé and a cover letter.</u>

COMMUNICATION STRATEGY

Asking Polite Questions

Asking questions directly can sometimes be impolite. Using phrases with models such as *could, can, would,* and *may* to obtain information is more polite.

Could you tell me . . . ?

Can you tell me . . . ?

Would you know . . . ?

May I ask . . . ?

Broadcasting Job Bank ⊠ ⊟ ⊞

BROADCASTING JOB BANK

BJB

New Listings

Résumé Help

Apply

Announcements

What's New

New Listings:

WBNC, Trenton, NJ
WRITER

Duties: Write news stories, write live updates, contact sources by phone.

Qualifications: College degree preferred. News writing experience preferred. Excellent writing skills, attention to details, good computer skills, ability to gather information quickly, ability to work on a team and meet deadlines.

* * * * * * * * * * * *

KNRR, San Jose, CA
PRODUCTION ASSISTANT

Duties: Write, help producer, schedule guests for shows, research story ideas.

Qualifications: College degree, excellent writing skills, good organizational skills, creative, strong computer skills. Must have excellent communication skills and be able to deal with pressure.

* * * * * * * * * * * *

WQAP, Tallahassee, FL
ACCOUNT ASSISTANT

Duties: Sell advertising time to advertising agencies and retail businesses. Call on community contacts to develop new business. Develop and maintain business contacts.

Qualifications: Minimum three years sales experience preferred. Ability to meet goals. Excellent oral and written communication skills, strong mathematical ability, Florida driver's license and personal transportation required.

Other Listings:

Meteorologist (4/27)

Account executive (4/20)

Camera operator (4/14)

Sports announcer (4/10)

Résumés

LESSON 4

THINGS TO DO

1 Warm Up

Work with your classmates to answer these questions:

1. Look at the résumés on page 119. What does Peter Brodsky want to do?
2. What information is usually on a résumé?
3. What have you done to apply for jobs? Have you ever written a résumé?

2 Label

Read the article on page 118. Then look at the résumés on page 119. Write either *chronological* or *functional* above each résumé.

3 Analyze

Read the information. Answer the questions.

1. Marsha has just graduated from college. All her paying jobs have been in fast-food restaurants, but she had an internship with the state parks department. Now she is applying for a job with the city parks and recreation department. Should she use a chronological or functional résumé? Why?
2. Ed has worked for 20 years as a teacher in an elementary school. His degree is in education. Now he is moving to a different state. He is applying for a teaching job there. Should he use a chronological or functional résumé? Why?

4 Evaluate

Work with your classmates. Decide if Peter Brodsky should use a chronological or functional résumé. List 3 reasons for your answer.

1. _____
2. _____
3. _____

TRY THIS STRATEGY

Evaluate When you evaluate, you make a judgment about something and give your opinion. Always try to support your opinion with at least 3 reasons. Choose one of Peter Brodsky's résumés and evaluate it. Is it clear and well written? Why or why not?

TWO TYPES OF RÉSUMÉS: WHICH ONE IS RIGHT FOR YOU?

There are two types of résumés: **chronological résumés**, and **functional résumés**. The chronological format is more traditional, and employers can read it very easily. The information is presented in reverse chronological order with your most recent job at the top. The chronological résumé includes dates and names of employers. Functional résumés list experience according to the type of skill, and often **omit** dates and names.

Use a chronological résumé if:

- you have worked steadily in one field.
- you meet all the qualifications for a job and have significant experience.
- you don't have any **gaps** in your work history.
- you haven't changed jobs often.
- you plan to stay in the same **field**.

Use a functional résumé if:

- you have worked in a variety of positions in different fields.
- you don't have very much experience.
- you have stopped working for periods of time.
- you have changed jobs a lot.
- you want to change fields.

3 + 2

Résumé type: _____

Peter Brodsky

1321 Fourth St. • Oakland, CA 94601
(510) 555-9033 • pbrodsky99@global.com

JOB OBJECTIVE: To work as an account assistant in broadcast news

WORK EXPERIENCE

Oakland Temps
Office assistant, 2001–present
- Maintain computer information systems
- Manage supply inventory
- Communicate effectively with customers

Computer Globe
Sales associate, 1999–2000
- Sales leader in 2000, earning *Sales Associate of the Year*
- Demonstrated excellent communication skills with customers and coworkers

WBNC
Marketing/Advertising intern, 1997–1998
- Assisted account associate in all marketing campaigns for local news affiliate
- Solicited ads from local businesses
- Maintained long-term business contacts

---

7 - 3 = 4

Résumé type: _____

Peter Brodsky

1321 Fourth St. • Oakland, CA 94601
(510) 555-9033 • pbrodsky99@global.com

JOB OBJECTIVE: To work as an account assistant in broadcast news

WORK EXPERIENCE

Advertising/Marketing
- Assisted account associate in all marketing campaigns for local news affiliate
- Solicited ads from local businesses
- Maintained strong relationships with business contacts
- Demonstrated effective communications skills with business contacts

Sales/Customer Service
- Sales leader in 2000, earning *Sales Associate of the Year*
- Demonstrated excellent communication skills with customers and coworkers
- Handled customer requests and complaints

Office/Clerical
- Excellent computer skills, including maintenance of information systems
- Communicated by writing and phone with the public

LESSON 5

If the company closes, she'll go back to school.

Real Conditionals

Real conditionals are statements that say what *will* or *might* happen under certain conditions. We use the real conditional to talk about the present or the future.

Use the simple present in the *if* clause. Use the simple present, the future, or a modal (*might, may, should, could, must*) in the result clause.

Present conditions

If clause (condition)	Result clause
If you **have** a lot of experience,	you **should use** a chronological résumé. (advice)
If he **wants** to change careers,	he **could use** the functional résumé. (possibility)
If employees **want** to exercise,	they **go** to the on-site gym. (habitual action)

Future conditions

If clause (condition)	Result clause
If I **decide** to change jobs,	**I'll look for** one with at least six weeks of vacation time. (plan)
If the company **closes**,	**she'll go back** to school. (definite plan)
If they **offer** flex-time next year,	he **might go back** to school. (possibility)

---

1 Match

Match the condition clause with the result clause.

If clause (condition)

1. ___h___ If Ellen has gaps in her work experience,
2. _____ If Tom wants to telecommute,
3. _____ If José is a new parent,
4. _____ If the company wants to get good workers,
5. _____ If Alice needs a new job,
6. _____ If Linda saves enough money,
7. _____ If Lisa goes back to school,
8. _____ If there is bad weather,

Result clause

a. he should get a computer.
b. he can take family leave.
c. the company might close for the day.
d. she will update her résumé.
e. it should offer onsite training and tuition reimbursement.
f. she'll take some time off to travel.
g. she might have to quit her job.
h. she should use a functional résumé.

---

2 Complete the Sentences

Complete each sentence. Use the cues in parentheses or your own ideas when you see a question mark in parentheses (?).

1. If Mario has bad teeth, _he should look for a job with dental insurance._
   (look for/job/with dental insurance).

2. If the employer provides on-site day care, _____
   (you/not worry/about your children).

3. If I get a raise, _____
   (not need/a second job).

4. If her résumé is full of mistakes, _____
   (not get/an interview).

5. If we telecommute, _____
   (save money/on gas).

6. If they go to the gym every day, _____ (?).

7. If I don't hear from the employer soon, _____ (?).

8. If your son gets sick at the on-site child care center, _____ (?).

3 Answer

Answer the questions. Use *if* and result clauses in your answers.

1. What happens to your English class if it rains or snows a lot?
   If it rains a lot, the school ...
   _____

2. What will you do if you win a million dollars?
   _____
   _____

3. What will you do if someone in your family gets very sick?
   _____
   _____

4. What resources can people use if they want to find new jobs?
   _____
   _____

5. What will you look for in a workplace if you need to find a job?
   _____
   _____

6. What should job applicants ask if they call about a job opening?
   _____
   _____

Work with a classmate. Take turns asking and answering the questions.

Cover Letters

1 Read and Label

Read about the parts of a cover letter. Then label the parts of the letter below.

Parts of a cover letter	Where	What
1. Return address	in the upper right corner	the writer's address and date
2. Inside address	on the left side above the salutation	the name and address of the person receiving the letter
3. Salutation	below the address	title, or Mr., Ms., Mrs. and last name
4. Opening paragraph	below the salutation	why you are writing, what position you want, how you heard about it
5. Middle paragraph	between the opening and final paragraphs	your strengths and achievements; refer to your résumé here
6. Final paragraph	below the middle paragraph	restate interest in position; say you look forward to hearing from the person, express your appreciation
7. Closing	above the signature	*Sincerely, Yours Truly,* etc. + comma
8. Signature	below the closing	the writer's name in handwriting

42 West 34th Street ------------ *Return address*
New York, NY 10121
June 16, 2006

Howard Smith
Account Executive
WWNY News
26 West 49th Street
New York, NY 10006

Dear Mr. Smith: --

   I am writing in response to your ad for a production assistant in the *New York Gazette* on ------
June 15. I would enjoy the opportunity to meet you to speak with you about this position.

   As you can see in the enclosed résumé, I have worked as a research assistant for two
years at City University of New York while I pursued a graduate degree in media studies.
I have excellent writing and computer skills. I am also very organized, have excellent
communication skills, and am able to deal with pressure.

   I am truly interested in the position of production assistant at WWNY News and would
appreciate the opportunity to discuss my qualifications in person. I can be reached at your
convenience at the email address or telephone number at the top of my résumé.

Sincerely, --

May Kim --

2 Evaluate

Answer these questions. Share your answers with a partner.

1. Look at job listings in a newspaper or on a website to find a job you are interested in. Why are you interested in this job?

2. What are your strengths or achievements that would help you in the job you have selected?

3 Apply

Write a cover letter on a separate piece of paper. Use the cover letter format in Activity 1 and your answers from Activity 2.

WINDOW ON MATH
Understanding Payroll Deductions

 A Read the information.

Total Pay (or **Gross Pay**) = the amount earned per hour/week/year

Deductions = the amount subtracted from the gross pay before you get your paycheck. Deductions can include medical insurance, dental insurance, retirement plans, and taxes.

Net Pay = total pay minus deductions (the actual amount of the paycheck)

 B Look at the pay stub. Compute the gross pay, total deductions, and net pay for this pay period and for the year to date.

Employee name: **Eva Haslam**	Period beginning: **03/15/05**		Period ending: **03/31/05**
Earnings	Hours This Pay Period	Earnings This Pay Period	Earnings Year to Date
$16.00/hour	80	$1,280.00	$7,680.00
Federal taxes deducted		$230.40	$1,382.40
State taxes deducted		$140.80	$844.80
Medical insurance deducted		$40.00	$240.00
Dental insurance deducted		$15.00	$90.00

	Gross Pay	Total Deductions	Net Pay
1. This pay period:	_____	_____	_____
2. Year to date:	_____	_____	_____

123

LESSON 7

What do you know?

Listening Review 🎧

Listen to the sentences. Choose the best answer. Use the Answer Sheet.

1. A. $10 an hour

B. 40 hours a week

C. first shift

2. A. $1000 a month

B. a résumé

C. first and second shifts

3. A. Send a résumé and a cover letter.

B. I can come for an interview.

C. Full-time is 40 hours a week.

4. A. part time

B. medical and dental insurance

C. $12 an hour

ANSWER SHEET

1	Ⓐ	Ⓑ	Ⓒ
2	Ⓐ	Ⓑ	Ⓒ
3	Ⓐ	Ⓑ	Ⓒ
4	Ⓐ	Ⓑ	Ⓒ
5	Ⓐ	Ⓑ	Ⓒ
6	Ⓐ	Ⓑ	Ⓒ
7	Ⓐ	Ⓑ	Ⓒ
8	Ⓐ	Ⓑ	Ⓒ
9	Ⓐ	Ⓑ	Ⓒ
10	Ⓐ	Ⓑ	Ⓒ

5. A. three years in sales

B. Fill out this form.

C. Can you come for an interview at 3?

6. A. Have you been to the beach?

B. Have you read the newspaper?

C. Have you worked in news before?

7. A. ten weeks after the birth of a child

B. Yes, but it depends on the class.

C. Yes, it's downstairs on the first floor.

8. A. Monday

B. three weeks the first year

C. in June

Listen to the conversations. Choose the best response. Use the Answer sheet.

9. A. I could come at 10 on Friday.

B. Thanks a lot.

C. Sure. That sounds great.

10. A. How much is the salary?

B. the administrative assistant

C. I see you offer health benefits.

2 Vocabulary Review

Use the clues to complete the crossword puzzle.

Across

1 The person on TV who tells about the roads is a traffic _____.

4 Another word for area or subject is _____.

6 _____ are the amounts of money subtracted from your paycheck.

8 An _____ executive sells ads for the TV station.

9 The person who handles the camera is called a camera _____.

10 The person who forecasts the weather is usually a _____.

Down

2 When you work from home using a computer, telephone, and/or fax, you are _____.

3 Some companies help with employees' education by providing _____ reimbursement to pay for classes.

4 Companies that allow for flexible schedules offer _____.

5 _____ insurance pays for the care of your teeth.

7 An empty space between 2 things is a _____.

✔ LEARNING LOG

I know these words:

NOUNS
- □ account assistant
- □ account executive
- □ basic skills course
- □ benefits
- □ camera operator
- □ chronological résumé
- □ co-pay

- □ deductions
- □ dental insurance
- □ field
- □ flex time
- □ functional résumé
- □ gap
- □ gym
- □ health care

- □ medical insurance
- □ meteorologist
- □ news anchor
- □ on-site child care
- □ paid family leave
- □ preventive care
- □ production assistant
- □ sound engineer

- □ traffic reporter
- □ tuition reimbursement

VERBS
- □ omit
- □ telecommute

I practiced these skills, strategies, and grammar points:

- □ evaluating a workplace
- □ visualizing as a memory tool
- □ asking polite questions
- □ taking notes
- □ reading for specific information
- □ listening for specific information
- □ supporting an opinion

- □ classifying benefits
- □ using context to guess the meaning of a word
- □ brainstorming
- □ evaluating a résumé
- □ using real conditionals
- □ paraphrasing

Spotlight: Reading Strategy

MAKING INFERENCES

When you make an inference, you draw a logical conclusion from evidence or facts.

Evidence: *Maria has <u>lived</u> her whole life in <u>Spain</u>.*
Inference: *Maria speaks Spanish.*

Evidence: *David is a <u>computer programmer</u>.*
Inference: *David knows how to use a computer.*

Evidence: *For this position, you will need a valid <u>driver's license</u> and your own <u>car</u>.*
Inference: *You will have to drive in this job.*

1 Read the evidence. Circle the best inference.

1. Evidence: Lee was born in the United States.
   Inference:
   A. Lee is 20 years old.
   B. Lee is an American citizen.
   C. Lee lives in New York.

2. Evidence: Vera plays soccer every day.
   Inference:
   A. Vera doesn't have a broken leg.
   B. Vera likes to swim.
   C. Vera's parents like soccer.

3. Evidence: I graduated from the University of California in 1978.
   Inference:
   A. I am a doctor.
   B. I finished high school.
   C. I am married.

4. Evidence: Sales associate: 4 years experience needed.
   Inference:
   A. To apply for this job you need 4 years of work experience.
   B. To apply for this job you need 4 years of sales experience.
   C. You need to be 4 years old to apply for this job.

5. Evidence: You need excellent computer skills for this position.
   Inference:
   A. You will have to use a computer in the job.
   B. The supervisor likes computers.
   C. There are three computers in the office.

2 Read the article below. Then read the statements and check (✓) if they are *True* or *False*.
For each statement, write a piece of evidence from the reading that supports your answer.

International Reporter Goes Local

Evan Thompson took a job as a television reporter in 1996. It had always been his dream to work as an international reporter. He traveled around the world for five years covering the news. He thought that traveling to new countries was great. But then something happened one weekend when Evan was home. He was disciplining his teenaged son and his son said: "You can't tell me what to do. You don't even live here."

Evan knew his son was right. He talked with his wife and sons and decided to change jobs. He said, "I want to be home with you more. Our family should come first, not my job." Evan knew too many people in the news business who were on their second or third marriages. Many of these people also had poor relationships with their kids. Evan decided that being a good father was more important than traveling the world to cover the news. He left his job as an international reporter and started covering local news in his town.

A reporter at a crime scene

1. Evan didn't like his job in the news.   ☐ True   ☑ False

   Evidence: *He didn't quit reporting. He became a local reporter instead*
   of an international reporter.

2. People working in the television industry are busy.   ☐ True   ☐ False

   Evidence: _____

3. Evan thought his family was more important than his job.   ☐ True   ☐ False

   Evidence: _____

4. Evan's son was happy about his father's job in TV.   ☐ True   ☐ False

   Evidence: _____

5. A career in TV news can be hard on family.   ☐ True   ☐ False

   Evidence: _____

6. Evan wanted to spend more time with his family.   ☐ True   ☐ False

   Evidence: _____

Spotlight: Writing Strategy

REVISING AND PROOFREADING RÉSUMÉS

Revising: When you revise your résumé, you change the content to make the writing stronger. Ask yourself these questions when you revise your résumé:

1. Will my readers understand my strengths and see how I can fill their company's needs?
2. Is all of the information in my résumé relevant?
3. Have I included personal information like my marital status, age, or gender? This information <u>shouldn't</u> be included in a résumé.
4. Is my résumé well organized? Remember to group skills in a functional résumé. Start with the most recent job and work backwards in a chronological résumé.

Proofreading: When you proofread, make sure the spelling, grammar, and punctuation is correct. Ask yourself these questions:

1. Are all of the words spelled correctly?
2. Is all of the grammar correct?
3. Is all of my punctuation correct? Have I begun each sentence with a capital letter? Have I capitalized each proper noun? Are there periods at the end of all sentences?

1 Find the 10 spelling, grammar, and punctuation errors in this résumé.

Bruno p. Hudson
93 Oak Streete
El Paso, tx 80901

WORK EXPERIENCE

Value Discount Stoor, El Paso, TX
Salesclerk, (2004–present)
- Manage inventory
- Serve customers
- Handles complains

Martin Engineering company, Norfolk, VA
Head Engineer, (2001–2004)
- Managed ongoing engineering projects
- Supervised 10 other engineers
- administered project budgets

Topflight Construcion, St. Louis, MO
Engineering, (1999–2001)
- Worked as an engineer on highway construction projects
- acted as team leader
- Planned and implemented construction schedule

---

2 Write a résumé to accompany the cover letter you wrote in Activity 3 on page 123. Reread the 2 versions of Peter Brodsky's résumé below, and use either the chronological or functional résumé as a model.

Peter Brodsky

1321 Fourth St. • Oakland, CA 94601
(510) 555-9033 • pbrodsky99@global.com

JOB OBJECTIVE: To work as an account assistant in broadcast news

WORK EXPERIENCE

Oakland Temps
Office assistant, 2001–present
- Maintain computer information systems
- Manage supply inventory
- Communicate effectively with customers

Computer Globe
Sales associate, 1999–2000
- Sales leader in 2000, earning *Sales Associate of the Year*
- Demonstrated excellent communication skills with customers and coworkers

WBNC
Marketing/Advertising intern, 1997–1998
- Assisted account associate in all marketing campaigns for local news affiliate
- Solicited ads from local businesses
- Maintained long-term business contacts

Peter Brodsky

1321 Fourth St. • Oakland, CA 94601
(510) 555-9033 • pbrodsky99@global.com

JOB OBJECTIVE: To work as an account assistant in broadcast news

WORK EXPERIENCE

Advertising/Marketing
- Assisted account associate in all marketing campaigns for local news affiliate
- Solicited ads from local businesses
- Maintained strong relationships with business contacts
- Demonstrated effective communications skills with business contacts

Sales/Customer Service
- Sales leader in 2000, earning *Sales Associate of the Year*
- Demonstrated excellent communication skills with customers and coworkers
- Handled customer requests and complaints

Office/Clerical
- Excellent computer skills, including maintenance of information systems
- Communicated by writing and phone with the public

---

3 Revise and proofread your résumé following the guidelines on page 128.

UNIT 8: Communication

Are you talking to me?

THINGS TO DO

1 Warm Up

Work with your classmates to answer these questions.

1. What forms of communication did you use yesterday?
   - ☐ talked to someone in person
   - ☐ sent an email
   - ☐ left a message on an answering machine
   - ☐ wrote a letter
2. What are some other ways people communicate?
3. What forms of communication can you find in the picture? What are they?

2 Identify

Body language is one important way that people communicate. Which of these examples of body language can you find in the picture? Check (✓) them.

- ☐ waving to someone
- ☐ pointing at something
- ☐ rubbing his chin
- ☐ smiling
- ☐ frowning
- ☐ pointing at herself
- ☐ holding up a finger
- ☐ shaking hands
- ☐ yawning
- ☐ holding out both hands

3 Make Inferences

Look at the picture. Who is probably saying these things? Write each person's name.

1. "Put it over there, please."   _____Jon_____
2. "Nice to meet you."   _____
3. "Isn't this nice?"   _____
4. "Wait just a minute."   _____
5. "Are you talking to me?"   _____
6. "I'm tired."   _____
7. "I don't know."   _____
8. "Oh no!"   _____
9. "Come here."   _____
10. "I'm thinking about it."   _____

2 LESSON

Could you give me a hand?

THINGS TO DO

1 Match

Read the comments in boxes 1 to 12. Match each comment to a response below. Then say the comments and responses with a partner.

a. ___ Thanks.

b. ___ It looks good, but I think this can be bigger.

c. ___ You're welcome.

d. ___ I'm not sure. Could you repeat the last part?

e. ___ Sorry, but I can't. My sister's getting married on Sunday.

f. _1_ Sure. Go ahead.

g. ___ Sure. I'd be glad to. Those look heavy.

h. ___ I thought it was great.

i. ___ Yes. I'd like to fill this prescription.

j. ___ Oh, I'm sorry. Can you tell me how I can do better?

k. ___ That's a good idea.

l. ___ That's OK. Don't worry about it.

2 Use the Vocabulary

Write the missing word forms. Then complete the questions.

Noun	Verb
a. **interruption**	_interrupt_
b. _____	understand
c. **criticism**	_____
d. **expression**	_____
e. _____	**appreciate**
f. _____	suggest

a. Did anything ___*interrupt*___ your sleep last night?

b. Do you have a good _____ of U.S. history?

c. Who wouldn't you _____?

d. How do people _____ sadness?

e. When someone gives you a gift, how do you express your _____?

f. Do you have any _____ for improving this book?

Take turns asking and answering the questions with a partner.

1

interrupt

Could I interrupt for a minute?

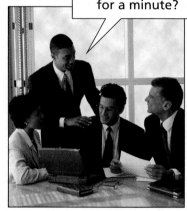

5

criticize

I'm a bit disappointed with your work.

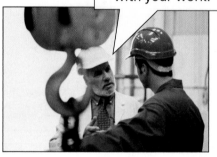

9

ask for help

Could you give me a hand?

Communicating at Work

2 compliment

You did a nice job on this!

3 make a **request**

Could you possibly cover my shift next weekend?

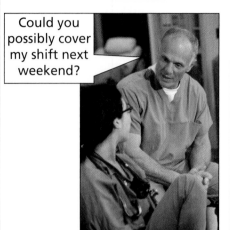

4 ask for an opinion

What did you think of the presentation?

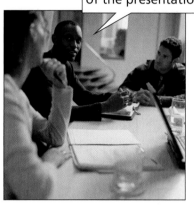

6 express appreciation

Thanks for your help.

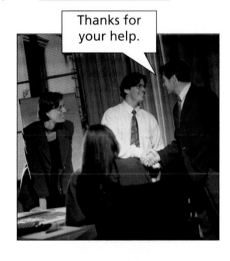

7 check for **understanding**

Is there anything you didn't understand?

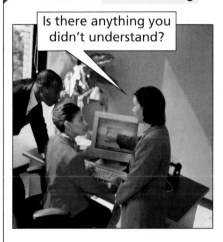

8 make **suggestions**

Why don't we put this whiteboard over there?

10 ask for **feedback**

Could you tell me what you think of this?

11 express **regret**

Sorry about that.

12 **offer** help

Can I help you?

3 LESSON

Can I help you?

THINGS TO DO

1 Warm Up

Who do you think the people are in pictures 1, 2, and 3? Write the number of each picture next to a pair of people below. Then compare ideas with your classmates.

_____ a parent and a child   _____ a doctor and a patient

_____ a supervisor and an employee _____ two friends

_____ two coworkers   _____ a salesperson and a customer

2 Listen for Specific Information 🎧

Listen to conversation #1. Who does each thing below—the man or the woman? Write *M* (the man) or *W* (the woman). Then repeat with conversations #2 and #3.

Conversation #1			
1. offers help	_M_	3. makes a request	____
2. asks for an opinion	____	4. expresses appreciation	____

Conversation #2			
1. compliments	_W_	4. makes a suggestion	____
2. offers help	____	5. asks for feedback	____
3. checks for understanding	____	6. expresses appreciation	____

Conversation #3			
1. criticizes	_W_	3. makes a suggestion	____
2. asks for feedback	____	4. offers help	____

3 Listen and Summarize 🎧

Listen to conversation #1 again and find 3 mistakes in the summary below.

> In the first conversation, a car salesman is talking to a customer. The salesman asks if the customer needs help, and she tells him she is looking for a big car. He shows her a car, but she says she only wants a car with air conditioning. She asks the salesman if she can drive the car home to show her father. Of course, the salesman says she can't do that, so the woman thanks him and leaves.

Now listen to conversations #2 and #3 again and take notes on a separate piece of paper. Then write a summary of each conversation. Compare your summaries with a partner's.

Coworkers:
People who work together

Synonyms for Supervisor:
administrator, boss, director, manager

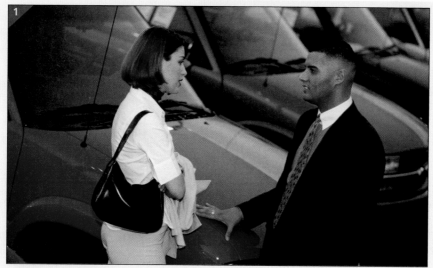

I'm looking for something small.

Let me try it.

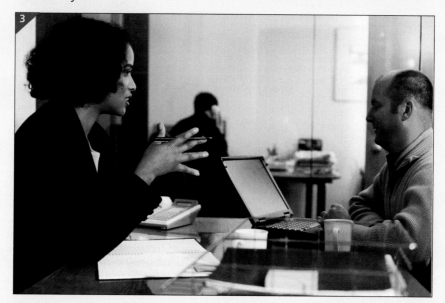

Could you tell me why?

LESSON 4

Being a Good Listener

THINGS TO DO

Friends at a coffee shop

1 Warm Up

Work with your classmates to answer these questions.

1. What are the people in the pictures doing that shows they are good or poor listeners?
2. Are you a good listener? What does a good listener do?
3. Do you know anyone who is a poor listener? What does a poor listener do?

2 Read and Respond

Use the reading strategies below as you read the article on page 137.

1. Preview the reading. Look at the title and read the first sentence in each paragraph. What do you think the topic is? What do you already know about this topic?
2. Write 3–5 questions you have about this topic. Then predict the answers.
3. Read the article and look for answers to your questions. Remember to use context to guess the meaning of unfamiliar words.

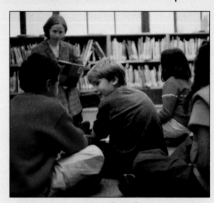
At school

3 Analyze

Work with a partner to answer these questions about the article.

1. According to the writer, what can you do to become a better listener?
2. What can you do to help someone who is listening to you?
3. Was there any useful advice for you in this article? What was it?

4 Summarize

Write a 1-paragraph summary of the article. Remember to include only the most important ideas in the article and to use your own words.

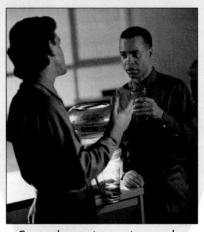
Coworkers at a water cooler

TRY THIS STRATEGY

◆◆◆◆◆◆◆◆◆◆◆◆◆◆◆◆◆◆◆◆◆◆◆◆◆

Use Prefixes Prefixes are word parts that come at the beginning of many words. Write 3 words that begin with each of these prefixes.

pre- (before)	*in- (not)*	*re- (again, back)*
preschool	ineffective	reconsider

◆◆◆◆◆◆◆◆◆◆◆◆◆◆◆◆◆◆◆◆◆◆◆◆◆

Speak, Listen, and Learn

By Jinny Hopp, Human Development Specialist

We spend 3/4 of our waking hours in some form of communication. And while listening is the skill we use the most, we are poor listeners. Why? Several factors contribute. One reason is that we think faster than someone else can speak. Most of us speak at about 125 words per minute, but we can understand someone speaking at 400 wpm. So, we use only 25% of our mental capacity and the other 75% wanders . We must listen carefully and concentrate to prevent mental wandering.

We are also inefficient listeners. We comprehend and retain only 1/4 of what we hear! Inefficient listening causes us many personal and professional problems.

Here are three things that you can do to become a better listener.

1. Anticipate the speaker's next point. If you are correct, learning has been reinforced. If you are wrong, you wonder why and this, too, helps to increase attention.

2. Identify the supporting ideas a speaker uses in building points. We use three ways to build points: we explain the point, we get emotional , or we illustrate the point with a factual illustration. Identifying point-supporting material is highly profitable in terms of listening efficiency.

3. Make mental summaries as you listen.

If you must communicate with a poor listener, how do you get your message across? Here are three things you can do to deliver you message effectively .

1. Pay attention to your body language. The way you hold your body, your tone of voice, and eye contact influence how the listener hears what you are saying.

2. Be specific and get to the point .

3. Probably the best way to be sure that you have been heard is to ask the person to repeat what they hear.

It's a challenge to be a good speaker as well as a good listener. But clear communication brings big rewards !

Source: Jinny Hopp, Human Development Specialist, University of Missouri Extension

137

★5 LESSON

What would you do?

Present Unreal Conditional Statements
We use the present unreal conditional to talk about unreal, unlikely, or impossible situations.

EXAMPLES:
    If I were president of the U.S., I would work for better health care. (I'm not the president.)
    If she had a million dollars, she would move to Italy. (She doesn't have a million dollars.)

To form the present unreal conditional, use the simple past in the *if* clause (the condition) and *would* + the simple form of the verb in the main clause (the result).

EXAMPLES: (Condition)   (Result)
    If my boss **got** angry with me for something, I **would** talk to her about it.
    If someone **asked** me to do something illegal, I **wouldn't do** it.

Note: In the *if* clause, we usually use *were* instead of *was*.

If I **were** you, I'd take the job.

1 Match

Match each condition with a result.

Condition

1. ___d___ If today were a holiday,
2. _____ If I had a lot of money,
3. _____ If my boss complimented my work,
4. _____ If she criticized him,
5. _____ If we didn't have telephones,
6. _____ If there weren't so many cars on the road,
7. _____ If I walked into someone,

Result

a. he would get angry.
b. we would write more letters.
c. I would say, "I'm sorry."
d̸. I would stay in bed until noon.
e. the air would be cleaner.
f. I would say, "Thank you."
g. I would quit my job.

2 Write

Complete these sentences with your own ideas.

1. If I could live anywhere, I _____

2. If the U.S. president called me on the telephone, _____

3. If someone stole my car, I _____

4. If my boss criticized me unfairly, I _____

5. If I got to work late, I _____

6. If I lost my job, _____

7. If I were the leader of my country, _____

8. If I didn't go home for dinner, my family _____

Tips on Using the Present Unreal Conditional

The *if* clause (the condition) can go at the beginning or the end of the sentence. When the *if* clause begins the sentence, use a comma after it.

EXAMPLES:
If I didn't have to work, I would go to China to visit my family.
I would go to China to visit my family **if I didn't have to work**.

We sometimes use the phrase "If I were you, I would . . ." to give advice.

EXAMPLES:
If I were you, I'd look for a new job.
I would finish college **if I were you**.

---

3 Rewrite

Rewrite each sentence by moving the *if* clause.

1. If I had email, I would write to my family every day.

   _____

2. I would feel embarrassed if my boss criticized me in front of my coworkers.

   _____

3. If a coworker gave me an expensive gift, I'd feel uncomfortable.

   _____

4 Give Advice

Respond to each question with your own advice. Then write 1 more conversation.

1. A: My boss is always criticizing my work. He's never said one nice thing to me. What do you think I should do?

   B: If I were you, _____

2. A: My brother is always asking me for money. In the past I've always given it to him, but I'm not sure I'm helping him by doing this. What do you think I should do?

   B: If I were you, _____

3. A: I think one of my coworkers is avoiding me. She used to be very friendly, but now she won't look at me or talk to me. What should I do?

   B: _____

4. A: _____

   B: _____

FAMILY

6
LESSON

Telephone Messages

1 Warm Up

Work with your classmates to answer these questions.

1. How often do you use the telephone?
2. When you call someone on the telephone and their answering machine picks up, do you usually leave a message?
3. Do you have an answering machine at home? What does your message say?
4. When you leave a message on an answering machine, what should you say? What shouldn't you say?

2 Read and Evaluate

Work with a partner. Read the answering machine messages and rate them from 1 (the best) to 5 (the worst). Write the numbers in the chart below and give reasons for your decisions.

A. You have reached 555-3945. You know what to do.

B. You have reached the home of Bob and Shirley, their children Amy, Ted, and Sam, and Bob's parents Irma and Frank at 555-3895. As usual we're either working in the yard, having a meal, or out doing errands. But we are glad you called and we would like to return your call when we return from wherever we are. So, please leave your name and phone number and the time you called, and we'll get back to you as soon as we can. Of course, if this is an emergency, you can call Bob on his cell phone which is 555-6232. Have a great day and thanks for calling.

C. You have reached 555-4949, but we aren't available right now. Please leave a message at the beep and we'll get back to you.

Please leave a message.

D. Hi. This is Ted and Barbara. We can't talk right now, so please leave your name and number. Thanks.

E. You've reached the Wang residence. Please leave a message.

Message	Rating	Reason
A		
B		
C		
D		
E		

3 Apply

Write 3 different outgoing messages for your home machine. Read your messages to your classmates and ask them to choose the best one.

1. _____
   _____
   _____

2. _____
   _____
   _____

3. _____
   _____
   _____

WINDOW ON PRONUNCIATION 🎧
Word Stress Patterns in Two-Syllable Words

 A Usually, two-syllable words are stressed in one of three ways. Listen to the two-syllable words. Then listen again and repeat.

1. request	4. feedback	7. message	10. wander
2. express	5. suggest	8. doctor	11. someone
3. regret	6. welcome	9. offer	12. salesclerk

 B Write the words from Activity A in the correct place in the chart.

• •	• •	• •
request	*feedback*	*welcome*

 C Sometimes two-syllable words receive different stress depending on if they are used as nouns or as verbs. Listen to the words. Then listen again and repeat.

NOUN	VERB		NOUN	VERB
1. progress	progress		5. conduct	conduct
2. present	present		6. protest	protest
3. record	record		7. permit	permit
4. increase	increase		8. contract	contract

Listen a third time. Draw dots above each word to indicate the stress pattern.

LESSON 7

What do you know?

1 Listening Review 🎧

Listen to the questions and choose the best response. Use the Answer Sheet.

1. A. Sure. I'd be glad to.
   B. No, thank you.
   C. You're welcome.

2. A. That's great.
   B. Sure. What is it?
   C. Sure. I'd be happy to.

3. A. Thank you.
   B. You're welcome.
   C. No, thank you.

4. A. Sorry about that.
   B. Don't worry about it.
   C. That's a good idea.

5. A. No, thanks. I'm just looking.
   B. Sure. I'd be glad to.
   C. I don't think I can.

6. A. Excuse me for interrupting.
   B. Sure. Go ahead.
   C. Sure. I think you're doing a great job.

ANSWER SHEET

1	Ⓐ	Ⓑ	Ⓒ
2	Ⓐ	Ⓑ	Ⓒ
3	Ⓐ	Ⓑ	Ⓒ
4	Ⓐ	Ⓑ	Ⓒ
5	Ⓐ	Ⓑ	Ⓒ
6	Ⓐ	Ⓑ	Ⓒ
7	Ⓐ	Ⓑ	Ⓒ
8	Ⓐ	Ⓑ	Ⓒ
9	Ⓐ	Ⓑ	Ⓒ
10	Ⓐ	Ⓑ	Ⓒ

Listen to each conversation and choose the best answer to the question you hear. Use the Answer Sheet.

7. A. go to Ann's class
   B. help Ann
   C. give Ann a book

8. A. asking the teacher
   B. reading the instructions
   C. working alone

9. A. feedback
   B. an opinion
   C. help

10. A. a report
    B. feedback
    C. any time this week

2 Vocabulary Review

Write the missing noun or verb form.

	NOUN	VERB
1.	*understanding*	understand
2.	criticism	
3.	anticipation	
4.	interruption	
5.	expression	
6.	appreciation	

	NOUN	VERB
7.	contribution	
8.	compliment	
9.	influence	
10.		challenge
11.		suggest

Choose 6 words from the chart and write 6 questions. Then ask your classmates your questions.

EXAMPLE: What would you like to contribute money to?

✔ LEARNING LOG

I know these words:

NOUNS
- ☐ appreciation
- ☐ capacity
- ☐ challenge
- ☐ criticism
- ☐ expression
- ☐ feedback
- ☐ interruption
- ☐ regret
- ☐ request

- ☐ reward
- ☐ suggestion
- ☐ understanding

VERBS
- ☐ anticipate
- ☐ appreciate
- ☐ compliment
- ☐ criticize
- ☐ express

- ☐ influence
- ☐ interrupt
- ☐ offer
- ☐ retain
- ☐ wander

ADJECTIVES
- ☐ emotional
- ☐ inefficient
- ☐ mental

ADVERB
- ☐ effectively

OTHER
- ☐ get to the point

I practiced these skills, strategies, and grammar points:

- ☐ previewing
- ☐ making inferences
- ☐ listening for specific information
- ☐ using context to guess the meaning of a word
- ☐ summarizing a text
- ☐ learning word forms

- ☐ checking for mistakes
- ☐ giving advice
- ☐ evaluating telephone messages
- ☐ interpreting body language
- ☐ using present unreal conditional statements

Spotlight: Reading Strategy

DISTINGUISHING FACT FROM OPINION	
Facts	**Opinions**
Facts are statements that we can prove.	Opinions express a person's feelings or beliefs.
EXAMPLES:	EXAMPLES:
Most people speak at about 125 words a minute.	My best friend is very beautiful.
He apologized for being late.	I think it's hard to be a good listener.

1 Read these opinions. Underline the words that help you know it's an opinion.

1. In my opinion, it's rude to criticize someone older than yourself.

2. I don't think that movie is very good.

3. Chinese food is delicious.

4. Many people believe the Earth is getting hotter.

5. I feel strongly that we need to save more money.

6. I think I spent about $2,000 on food last year, but that's just an estimate.

2 Identify each statement as a fact or an opinion. Write *fact* or *opinion*.

1. Switzerland has 3 official languages: German, French, and Italian. _____*fact*_____

2. The telephone was the most important invention in the 20th century. _____

3. When it is winter in London, it is summer in Australia. _____

4. I think Italian food tastes better than French food. _____

5. There are more computers in the world today than there were 50 years ago. _____

6. Nevada is between California and Utah. _____

7. Maine is farther from Florida than Virginia. _____

8. I feel that we should spend more money on education. _____

9. There are more than 5 billion people on Earth today. _____

10. There are too many people in the world. _____

3 Read the paragraphs below. Underline 1 fact in each paragraph. Write an opinion you have about each paragraph.

Speaking English

It is estimated that there are about 375 million native English speakers in the world and about 1 billion others who have learned to speak English in addition to their native language. More people may speak Mandarin Chinese than English, but the use of English is more widespread throughout the world. English is the language used worldwide in aviation, diplomacy, computing, science, and tourism.

Important Telephone Numbers

Sometimes a telephone call can solve a problem fast. In an emergency, you can get help in the U.S. by calling 911. If you have a particular problem, there might also be a hotline you can call for help. And don't worry about money. A telephone call to most hotlines costs nothing. You can find a list of important hotlines in the front of your telephone directory.

Lost Languages

In the 19th century there were more than 1,000 Indian languages in Brazil. Today there are only 200. Languages have always come and gone, but now they are disappearing quickly. Experts think that the world loses one language every two weeks. Some experts believe that half of the world's languages could disappear in the next 100 years. That would be roughly 3,000 languages lost forever.

Spotlight: Writing Strategy

SUPPORTING YOUR IDEAS

In a piece of persuasive writing, the writer expresses an opinion. The writer then provides facts, examples, and personal stories to convince the reader that this opinion is correct. We call these facts, examples, and stories the supporting ideas. It's these ideas the writer uses to persuade the reader.

1 Read each paragraph on page 147 and identify the writer's opinion. Then list the facts and examples the writer gives to support this opinion.

	The writer's opinion or main idea	The supporting ideas	How persuasive? Why?
1.			
2.			
3.			

2 How persuasive is each paragraph? Does it include facts, examples, or stories to support the ideas? Is each paragraph *very persuasive, somewhat persuasive,* or *not very persuasive*? Why? Write your answers in the chart above.

3 Choose a topic you have a strong opinion about. Then brainstorm a list of facts, examples, or personal stories to support your opinion. Use your ideas in a persuasive paragraph. Read your paragraph to the class and try to convince your classmates that your opinion is correct.

Sample topics: using cell phones and driving
public transportation
fast food

1

Divorce Your Car

If you want to improve your lifestyle, the best thing you can do is get rid of your car. Just think of it. You won't have any more car payments, car repair bills, or empty gas tanks. Without a car, you will also get more exercise, lose weight, and feel better. Within 3 months of selling my car, I lost 10 pounds. And don't forget that every year there are more than 26 million car accidents. Without a car, you probably won't be in one of them. That will definitely make your life better.

2

Stop Talking or Stop Driving

Driving and talking on a cell phone is a very bad combination. Every year many people die in car accidents caused by drivers on cell phones. It is especially bad to talk on a cell phone when you are driving on the highway. At that speed, you need to focus on the road and not on your friend on the phone. I hope every state makes it illegal to drive while you are talking on a cell phone.

Talking while driving

3

Get Moving

One of the best things you can do for your body is to get plenty of exercise. Studies have shown that people who exercise live longer. For older people, exercising can even improve memory and reasoning skills. Of course, one of the best reasons to get exercise is that it just makes you feel better. And who doesn't want to feel better?

Women exercising

A Adjectives

Comparative Adjectives	
Spelling Rules	**Examples**
Adjectives with One Syllable	
• Add -er to one-syllable adjectives.	• clean → cleaner than bright → brighter than
• If the adjective already ends in -e, add only -r.	• nice → nicer than safe → safer than
• For one-syllable adjectives that end in a single vowel and a single consonant, double the consonant. Then add -er.	• big → bigger than thin → thinner than
Adjectives with Two or More Syllables	
• For two-syllable adjectives that end in -y, change the -y to -i and add -er.	• sunny → sunnier than ugly → uglier than
• Use more with other adjectives that have two or more syllables.	• reasonable → more reasonable than comfortable → more comfortable than
Irregular Adjectives	
• Some adjectives are irregular.	• good → better than bad → worse than far → farther than

Superlative Adjectives	
Spelling Rules	**Examples**
Adjectives with One Syllable	
• Add -est to one-syllable adjectives.	• clean → the cleanest bright → the brightest
• If the adjective already ends in -e, add only -st.	• nice → the nicest safe → the safest
• For one-syllable adjectives that end in a single vowel and a single consonant, double the consonant. Then add -est.	• big → the biggest thin → the thinnest
Adjectives with Two or More Syllables	
• For two-syllable adjectives that end in -y, change the -y to -i and add -est.	• sunny → the sunniest ugly → the ugliest
• Use the most with other adjectives that have two or more syllables.	• reasonable → the most reasonable comfortable → the most comfortable
Irregular Adjectives	
• Some adjectives are irregular.	• good → the best bad → the worst far → the farthest

Comparisons with *As/Not As* + Adjective + *As*

Your bathroom is	as big as	my kitchen.
The deck is	not as high as	the back door.
The air conditioner is	as loud as	you said it was.
The water is	not as hot as	it should be.
Is your new house	as nice as	your old one?

B Present Tense of *Be*

Affirmative Statements

I	am	a student.
You	are	a student.
He	is	a student.
She	is	a student.
It	is	a book.
We	are	students.
You	are	students.
They	are	students.

Negative Statements

I	am not	a teacher.
You	are not	a teacher.
He	is not	a teacher.
She	is not	a teacher.
It	is not	a map.
We	are not	teachers.
You	are not	teachers.
They	are not	teachers.

Contractions

I am	→	I'm	I am not	→	I'm not
you are	→	you're	you are not	→	you aren't/you're not
he is	→	he's	he is not	→	he isn't/he's not
she is	→	she's	she is not	→	she isn't/she's not
it is	→	it's	it is not	→	it isn't/it's not
we are	→	we're	we are not	→	we aren't/we're not
you are	→	you're	you are not	→	you aren't/you're not
they are	→	they're	they are not	→	they aren't/they're not

C Simple Present Tense

Affirmative Statements		
I	like	
You	like	
He	likes	
She	likes	music.
It	likes	
We	like	
You	like	
They	like	

Negative Statements		
I	don't like	
You	don't like	
He	doesn't like	
She	doesn't like	tea.
It	doesn't like	
We	don't like	
You	don't like	
They	don't like	

D Present Continuous Tense

Affirmative Statements	
I	am working.
You	are working.
He	is working.
She	is working.
It	is working.
We	are working.
You	are working.
They	are working.

Negative Statements	
I	am not working.
You	aren't working.
He	isn't working.
She	isn't working.
It	isn't working.
We	aren't working.
You	aren't working.
They	aren't working.

E Simple Past Tense

Affirmative Statements		
I		
You		
He		
She	worked	yesterday.
It		
We		
You		
They		

Negative Statements		
I		
You		
He		
She	didn't work	yesterday.
It		
We		
You		
They		

Yes/No Questions and Short Answers

Did	I you he she it we you they	work yesterday?	Yes,	I you he she it we you they	did.	No,	I you he she it we you they	didn't.

Information Questions

Where	did	I you he she it we you they	work?	Who did you work with? Who did she talk to?	Why did you go? Why did she leave?
				Who worked yesterday? Who called?	How did you get here? How did she feel?
				When did you arrive? When did she call?	What did you do? What did she say?

Spelling Rules for Regular Verbs

Spelling Rules	**Examples**
Verbs with One Syllable • If the verb ends in a consonant-vowel-consonant pattern (*C-V-C*), double the final consonant and add -*ed*. • Don't double the consonants -*w*, -*x*, or -*y*.	• stop—stopped rub—rubbed • fix—fixed
Verbs with Two or More Syllables • For two-syllable verbs that end in *C-V-C*, double the final consonant only if the last syllable is stressed.	• refer—referred
Verbs Ending in -*y* • If the verb ends in a consonant + *y*, change the *y* to *i* and add -*ed*. • If the verb ends in a vowel + *y*, add -*ed*.	• study—studied • play—played

Past Time Clauses With *When*

Time Clause With *When*	Main Clause
When she got a poor grade on the test,	she talked to her teacher.

Main Clause	Time Clause With *When*
He checked the online job bank	when he went to the career center.

F Present Perfect Tense

Affirmative Statements

I	have	
You	have	
He	has	
She	has	been here for
It	has	3 hours.
We	have	
You	have	
They	have	

Negative Statements

I	have not	
You	have not	
He	has not	
She	has not	left yet.
It	has not	
We	have not	
You	have not	
They	have not	

Yes/No Questions and Short Answers

Have	I			I	have.		I	haven't.
Have	you			you	have.		you	haven't.
Has	he			he	has.		he	hasn't.
Has	she	eaten yet?	Yes,	she	has.	No,	she	hasn't.
Has	it			it	has.		it	hasn't.
Have	we			we	have.		we	haven't.
Have	you			you	have.		you	haven't.
Have	they			they	have.		they	haven't.

Information Questions

	have	I		Who have you worked for?	Why have you applied?
	have	you		Who has she talked to?	Why has she written?
	has	he			
Where	has	she	worked?	Who has lived here since 1999?	How have you saved money?
	has	it		Who has called already?	How has he done so far?
	have	we			
	have	you		When have you finished early?	What have you done?
	have	they		When has it ever come on time?	What has he told you?

Simple Past Versus Present Perfect

Use the simple past to tell about something that happened at a definite time in the past.

    Examples: He **exercised** for an hour <u>yesterday</u>.

                    I **had** a fever <u>last night</u>.

                    The doctor **gave** me a prescription (<u>when I was at his office</u>).

Use the present perfect to tell about something that happened some time before now, or that started in the past and continues to have importance in the present.

    Examples: I**'ve been** to the dentist <u>many times</u>. (That's why I'm not afraid to go today.)

                    I**'ve had** a toothache <u>since last Tuesday</u>. (I need to do something about it now.)

                    She **hasn't filled** the prescription <u>yet</u>. (She's thinking about doing it soon.)

Irregular Verbs

Base Form	Simple Past	Past Participle		Base Form	Simple Past	Past Participle
be	was/were	been		keep	kept	kept
become	became	become		know	knew	known
begin	began	begun		leave	left	left
bleed	bled	bled		lend	lent	lent
break	broke	broken		lose	lost	lost
bring	brought	brought		make	made	made
buy	bought	bought		meet	met	met
choose	chose	chosen		pay	paid	paid
come	came	come		put	put	put
cost	cost	cost		read	read	read
cut	cut	cut		ring	rang	rung
do	did	done		run	ran	run
drink	drank	drunk		see	saw	seen
drive	drove	driven		sell	sold	sold
eat	ate	eaten		send	sent	sent
fall	fell	fallen		set	set	set
feel	felt	felt		shake	shook	shaken
fight	fought	fought		shut	shut	shut
find	found	found		sleep	slept	slept
forget	forgot	forgot		speak	spoke	spoken
fry	fried	fried		speed	sped	sped
get	got	gotten		spend	spent	spent
give	gave	given		take	took	taken
go	went	gone		teach	taught	taught
grow	grew	grown		tell	told	told
have/has	had	had		think	thought	thought
hear	heard	heard		wear	wore	worn
hold	held	held		write	wrote	written
hurt	hurt	hurt				

G Future Tense

Future with *Going to*						
I	am going to			I	am not going to	
You	are going to			You	are not going to	
He	is going to			He	is not going to	
She	is going to	leave tomorrow.		She	is not going to	be here tomorrow.
It	is going to			It	is not going to	
We	are going to			We	are not going to	
You	are going to			You	are not going to	
They	are going to			They	are not going to	

Future with *Will*			
I		I	
You		You	
He		He	
She	will come back soon.	She	won't be away for long.
It		It	
We		We	
You		You	
They		They	won't = will not

Future Time Clauses With *When*	
Time Clause With *When*	**Main Clause**
When she comes,	we will leave.
Main Clause	**Time Clause With *When***
They will graduate	when they finish their courses.
Time Clause With *When*	**Main Clause**
When I get my dream job,	I'm going to celebrate.
Main Clause	**Time Clause With *When***
She's going to study	when she gets home.

H Past Continuous Tense

Affirmative Statements

I	was working when the storm started.
You	were working when the storm started.
He	was working when the storm started.
She	was working when the storm started.
It	was working when the storm started.
We	were working when the storm started.
You	were working when the storm started.
They	were working when the storm started.

Negative Statements

I	wasn't sleeping when the storm started.
You	weren't sleeping when the storm started.
He	wasn't sleeping when the storm started.
She	wasn't sleeping when the storm started.
It	wasn't sleeping when the storm started.
We	weren't sleeping when the storm started.
You	weren't sleeping when the storm started.
They	weren't sleeping when the storm started.

Yes/No Questions and Short Answers

Was	I	working when she called?	Yes,	I	was.	No,	I	was not.
Were	you			you	were.		you	were not.
Was	he			he	was.		he	was not.
Was	she			she	was.		she	was not.
Was	it			it	was.		it	was not.
Were	we			we	were.		we	were not.
Were	you			you	were.		you	were not.
Were	they			they	were.		they	were not.

Information Questions

What	was	I	doing when he got there?	Who were you talking to?	Why were you leaving?
	were	you		Who was she talking to?	Why was she leaving?
	was	he			
	was	she		Where were you working last year?	How were you feeling yesterday?
	was	it			
	were	we		Where was she working last year?	How was she feeling yesterday?
	were	you			
	were	they			

Spelling Rules for adding *-ing*	
Spelling Rules	**Examples**
Verbs Ending in Silent *-e* • If the verb ends in a silent *-e*, drop the final *-e* and add *-ing*.	• shake—shaking
One-Syllable Verbs Ending in *C-V-C* • In one-syllable verbs that end in a consonant-vowel-consonant pattern, double the final consonant and add *-ing*. • Don't double the consonants *-w, -x,* or *-y.*	• stop—stopping • fix—fixing
Two- or More-Syllable Adjectives • For two- or more-syllable adjectives that end in *C-V-C*, double the final consonant only if the last syllable is stressed.	• permit—permitting
Verbs Ending in *-ie* • For verbs ending in *-ie*, change the *-ie* to *y*, and add *-ing*.	• die—dying

Simple Past and Past Continuous

We often use the simple past and the past continuous in the same sentence. We use the simple past for a sudden action that interrupts the ongoing activity.

(sudden action)   (ongoing activity)

Example: He <u>fell</u> while he <u>was climbing up</u> the ladder.

We often use the word "while" to introduce the ongoing activity. While means "during the time that." We often use the word "when" to introduce the sudden action.

Examples: The bell rang <u>while</u> I was sleeping.

I was sleeping <u>when</u> the bell rang.

▌ Gerunds

Some Verbs Often Followed by a Gerund (*base form of verb + -ing*)					
admit	consider	explain	love*	practice	regret
appreciate	continue*	finish	mind	prefer*	remember*
avoid	delay	hate*	miss	prevent	report
begin*	dislike	keep	permit	prohibit	stop*
can't stand*	enjoy	like*	postpone	quit	suggest*
* *These verbs can also be followed by infinitives.*					

J Infinitives

Some Verbs Often Followed by an Infinitive (*to + base form of verb*)			
afford	continue*	need	request
agree	decide	offer	stop*
arrange	expect	pay	suggest*
ask	hate*	prefer*	want
begin*	learn	promise	would like
can't stand*	like*	refuse	
choose	love*	remember*	

* These verbs can also be followed by gerunds.

K Real Conditionals

If Clause (present)			Result Clause (present or future)	
If	I	get a better offer,	I	will quit.
If	you	don't slow down,	you	are going to get a ticket.
If	he	is sick,	he	stays home.
If	she	doesn't leave soon,	she	won't be on time.
If	it	rains again,	it will	cause a flood.
If	we	get home late,	we are	going to eat out.
If	they	walk quickly	they will	get there in 5 minutes.

L Present Unreal Conditionals

If Clause (simple past)			Result Clause (with *would, could*)	
If	I	got a better offer,	I	would quit.
If	you	were speeding,	you	could get a ticket.
If	he	were sick,	he	would stay home.
If	she	didn't leave at 8 every day,	she	wouldn't be on time.
If	you	turned it too hard,	it	would break.
If	we	had enough money,	we	could eat out.
If	they	didn't have a car,	they	would take the bus.

ALL-STAR STUDENT BOOK 3 AUDIO SCRIPT

Note: This audio script offers support for many of the activities in the Student Book. When the words on the Student Book page are identical to those on the audio program, the script is not provided here.

UNIT ONE
Lesson 3.
2. Listen and Take Notes, page 8
1. Listen to conversation #1 and write the person's long-term goal.

Client: I think I need some advice about my program.

Counselor: Sure. That's what academic counselors are here for. What do you need?

Client: Well, I want to become a medical technician.

Counselor: To get into a med tech program, you need a high school diploma or a GED and you'll need to take a placement test in math and English.

Client: I really have trouble with math. Fractions just kill me.

Counselor: Maybe you need a tutor to help you with math before you do anything else. You can go to the Academic Learning Center for help.

Client: Where can I go for help?

Counselor: The Academic Learning Center. You can get a tutor there.

Listen again and write the suggested short-term goal.

2. Listen to conversation #2 and write the person's long-term goal.

Counselor: What brought you to the Career Center today?

Client: I need help getting a job.

Counselor: Full or part time?

Client: Part time. I'm taking a full load.

Counselor: What are you studying?

Client: International business.

Counselor: Do you want to work in that field?

Client: It doesn't matter. I just need to make some money.

Counselor: I'll show you how to access an online job bank in a minute.

Client: How to access a what?

Counselor: An online job bank. Do you have a current résumé?

Client: Not really.

Counselor: That's what you need to do first. Let me show you some information on résumé writing.

Listen again and write the suggested short-term goal.

3. Listen to conversation #3 and write the person's long-term goal.

Bank officer: How can I help you?

Customer: My husband and I would like to buy a house, so I wanted to get some information about mortgages.

Bank officer: Sure. I can give you a mortgage packet.

Customer: You can give me what?

Bank officer: A mortgage packet. It will probably answer most of your questions.

Customer: Let me ask you this. How much of a down payment is usually required?

Bank officer: That really depends on your circumstances, but most people put down at least 5% to 10% of the cost of the house.

Listen again and write the suggested short-term goal.

4. Listen to conversation #4 and write the person's long-term goal.

Parent: Excuse me. I'm looking for the English coordinator.

Coordinator: That's me. What can I do for you?

Parent: My name is Hugo Vasquez. I'm Daniela's father.

Coordinator: Oh yes, Mr. Vasquez. It's nice to meet you. Daniela is a great kid.

Parent: Thank you. I want to talk to you about Daniela. She doesn't want to study. She would rather play with her friends. She doesn't pay attention to her work. How can I help her?

Coordinator: Support from parents can really help children succeed in school. The most important thing is to show your daughter that you value education.

Parent: I should show her what?

Coordinator: That you value education.

Parent: How can I do that?

Coordinator: Well, the first thing you can do is make sure she has a time and a place to do her homework. Children need to keep up with homework to do well in school.

Listen again and write the suggested short-term goal.

Lesson 7.
1. Listening Review, page 16
Listen to the questions and statements. Choose the best answer. Use the Answer Sheet.

1. I want to take classes at the community college. What should I do first?
2. How can she prepare for the citizenship interview?
3. Alex has trouble getting everything done.
4. Fill out this financial aid application.

Listen to the sentences. Which answer means the same? Use the Answer Sheet.

5. A new car is very expensive. You should pay off your debts before you buy it.
6. She is very good at prioritizing.
7. He's filling out a mortgage application.
8. I think you should find a tutor to help you learn history.

Listen to the conversations. Then listen to the questions. Choose the correct answer. Use the Answer Sheet.

9. A: May I help you?
   B: Yes, I want to apply for a loan.
   A: What kind of loan?
   B: A student loan, so I can go back to school.
   C: *What does he want?*

10. A: How can I be more involved at my child's school?
    B: Well, you can attend the PTA meetings and parent-teacher conferences.
    A: When are they?
    B: Here is a schedule for this semester.
    C: *What should he do?*

UNIT TWO
Lesson 3.
2. Listen and Take Notes, page 26
1. Listen to telephone conversation #1 and write the tenant's problem.

Mr. Webster: Hello?

Louise: Is this Mr. Webster?

Mr. Webster: Yes, it is.

Louise: Hi Mr. Webster, it's Louise Menard, your tenant in apartment 23.

Mr. Webster: Yes, hi Louise. What can I do for you?

Louise: Well, I'm calling about the air conditioner in our apartment—it's not working.

Mr. Webster: What seems to be the problem?

Louise: I'm not sure. It just stopped working sometime during the night.

Mr. Webster: It was working when you went to bed?

Louise: Yes, that's right.

Mr. Webster: Is the fan running?

Louise: No, nothing is working.

Mr. Webster: Okay. I'll send someone over.

Louise: Will that be today?

Mr. Webster: Yes, it will. Sometime before 5.

Louise: Great. Thanks.

Mr. Webster: You're welcome. Bye.

Louise: Bye.
Listen to telephone conversation #1 again and write the landlord's response.

2. Listen to telephone conversation #2 and write the tenant's problem.

Mrs. Wang: Hello?

Mr. Adams: Can I speak to Mrs. Wang, please?

Mrs. Wang: This is Mrs. Wang.

Mr. Adams: Mrs. Wang, it's Mr. Adams, your tenant in apartment 8G.

Mrs. Wang: Yes, hi Mr. Adams. What can I do for you?

Mr. Adams: My wife and I just got home and the elevator isn't working.

Mrs. Wang: The elevator isn't working?

Mr. Adams: Yes, that's right. We had to walk all the way up to the eighth floor.

Mrs. Wang: Hmm. You're the first person to call. Are your lights working?

Mr. Adams: Yes, they are. And the lights in the hallway are working too.

Mrs. Wang: Okay, so it's not the electricity. Hmm. I'll send someone over to look at it.

Mr. Adams: How soon will that be?

Mrs. Wang: I'll try to get someone there in the next hour.

Mr. Adams: Okay. Thank you.

Mrs. Wang: Thanks for reporting the problem.

Mr. Adams: Sure. Bye bye.

Mrs. Wang: Bye.
Listen to telephone conversation #2 again and write the landlord's response.

3. Listen to telephone conversation #3 and write the tenant's problem.

Mr. Jones: Hello?

Dan: Hello. Can I speak with Mr. Jones?

Mr. Jones: This is Mr. Jones.

Dan: Oh, hi. This is Dan Wright. I'm one of your tenants on Lake Avenue.

Mr. Jones: Oh yeah, sure. What can I do for you?

Dan: Well, there seems to be something wrong with the clothes dryer in the basement.

Mr. Jones: What's the matter with it?

Dan: When I put my money in, nothing happens. And it won't return my money either.

Mr. Jones: Are you sure the dryer door is closed? Sometimes it won't start if the door's open.

Dan: Yes, I checked that. And I put money in twice.

Mr. Jones: Okay. I'll get over there tomorrow.

Dan: Great. Can you give me a rough time?

Mr. Jones: Yeah. It'll probably be in the afternoon between 3:00 and 4:00.

Dan: Good and can I get my money back?

Mr. Jones: Yes, of course. What apartment are you in?

Dan: It's number 35.

Mr. Jones: Okay. I'll stop by tomorrow.

Dan: Thanks.

Mr. Jones: Sure. See you tomorrow.
Listen to telephone conversation #3 again and write the landlord's response.

Lesson 7.
1. Listening Review, page 34
Listen and choose the statement that is closest in meaning to the statement you hear. Use the Answer Sheet.

1. To rent the apartment you have to pay the first and last month's rent plus one month's rent for a security deposit.
2. The landlord cannot enter a tenant's apartment without giving the tenant 24-hour prior notice.
3. The term of the rental agreement is from January 1, 2007 until July 1, 2007.
4. The rent is due by the first of each month.
5. All utilities are included in the rent except for the electricity.
6. We rented the apartment on Lake Avenue because it's sunnier than the apartment on Belmont Street.

Now listen to each conversation and choose the best answer to the question you hear. Use the Answer Sheet.

7.
A: Hello. Sanborn Real Estate.
B: Hi. I'm calling about the house for rent.
A: Which house are you interested in?
B: It's the house on Lake Avenue.
A: Actually we have two houses available on Lake Avenue. Are you interested in the two-bedroom house or the three-bedroom house?
B: The three-bedroom house.
A: When would you like to see it?
B: Is there a time tomorrow?
A: Sure. What about noon?
B: That's fine. Where should I meet you?
A: Why don't you just meet me at the house. It's at 2366 Lake Avenue. Do you know where that is?
B: Yes, I do. I'll meet you at 2366 Lake Avenue at noon tomorrow.
A: That's right.
B: See you then.
A: Bye.
C: *What is the woman going to do tomorrow?*

8.
A: Hello. This is Harper's Rental Agency. Can I help you?
B: Yes, I'm calling about an apartment for rent.
A: Which apartment are you interested in?
B: It's the one-bedroom apartment for $650 a month.
A: The one on Belmont Street?
B: Yes. That's the one.
A: Would you like to see it today?
B: Could you tell me first—is there parking available?
A: Yes, there is. It's outside parking.
B: That's okay. Can I see it sometime this afternoon?

A: Sure. Can you meet me here at the rental agency around 3? We're at 422 State Street.
B: That sounds good. I'll be at your office at 3. Thanks.
A: Goodbye.
B: Goodbye.
C: *What does the man want to look at?*

9.
A: Good morning. This is Johnson Real Estate. Can I help you?
B: Hi. I'm calling about your ad for an apartment on Mason Street. Is it still available?
A: Yes, it is. Would you like to see it?
B: Could you tell me—does the rent include utilities?
A: Let me see. For that apartment, the rent includes heat, but it doesn't include hot water or electricity.
B: I see. Do you know about how much the electric bill is each month?
A: No, I'm sorry. I don't have that information. But you can ask the landlord when you look at the place.
B: Okay. Can I see it some time tomorrow?
A: Is 10 A.M. okay?
B: Yes, that works for me. Should I come to your office?
A: Yes. We're at 1153 River Street. That's downtown near the court house.
B: Okay. I'll be there at 10 tomorrow.
A: Bye.
B: Bye.
C: *What utilities are included in the rent?*

10.
A: Hello?
B: Can I speak to Mr. Lee, please?
A: This is Mr. Lee.
B: Hi, Mr. Lee. It's Mrs. Jones. I'm your tenant in Apartment 56.
A: Yes, hi, Mrs. Jones. What can I do for you?
B: I'm calling about the kitchen sink.
A: What exactly is the problem?
B: It's not draining.
A: Hmm.
B: I used the plunger but it's still stopped up.
A: Okay. I'll send maintenance over to check it for you.
B: Will that be this morning?
A: Yes. I'll try to get him there before noon.
B: Good. Thanks.
A: Bye now.
B: Bye.
C: *What is the tenant's problem?*

UNIT THREE
Lesson 3.
2. Listen and Take Notes, page 44
1. Listen to conversation #1 and write the person's reason for visiting the doctor.

Doctor: Well, everything looks just fine. The baby's heartbeat sounds good and the measurements are just right. Do you have any questions?

Woman: I was just wondering, I'm beginning to have some trouble sleeping.

Doctor: Unfortunately, that's not unusual.

Woman: Is it okay if I sleep on my back?

Doctor: Well, you can spend some time on your back, but you really should try to sleep on your left side as much as possible. That's best for the baby.

Woman: Okay, but that won't help me sleep.

Doctor: What about caffeine? Are you eating or drinking anything with caffeine in it?

Woman: Not much. I'm only drinking about two cups of coffee a day.

Doctor: Well, why don't you stop drinking coffee and see if that helps.

Woman: Okay, I'll try.

Doctor: Okay. Your next check up is on the 15th.

Woman: Right.

Doctor: See you then.

Listen again and write the doctor's advice.

2. Listen to conversation #2 and write the person's reason for visiting the doctor.

Doctor: Hi. I'm Doctor Lopez.

Patient: Hi, Doctor Lopez. Nice to meet you. I'm Janice Wile.

Doctor: Nice to meet you. It says here that you are having trouble with your ear.

Patient: Yes. It's my left ear.

Doctor: So what's the problem? Does it hurt?

Patient: No, it doesn't hurt, but it's very itchy.

Doctor: Is it both ears or just the left ear?

Patient: Just the left ear.

Doctor: Okay. Let me take a look. Yes, I see. It's quite inflamed.

Patient: Inflamed?

Doctor: Yes, it looks very red. Tell me, do you have any allergies?

Patient: Not that I know of.

Doctor: Well, it doesn't look like anything serious, but I'm going to give you a prescription for ear drops.

Patient: Okay.

Doctor: I want you to put three drops in your left ear twice a day.

Patient: Three drops?

Doctor: Yes. It should clear up in a few days but if it doesn't, you should make another appointment.

Patient: All right. Is it okay to go swimming?

Doctor: Yes, but you might want to wear ear plugs.

Patient: Ear plugs?

Doctor: Yes. They'll keep the water from getting in your ear.

Patient: Do I need a prescription for them?

Doctor: No. You can get them at any drugstore.

Patient: Okay. Thank you.

Listen again and write the doctor's advice.

Lesson 7.
1. Listening Review, page 52
Listen and choose the statement that is closest in meaning to the statement you hear. Use the Answer Sheet.

1. My sister eats a low fat diet.
2. Use three drops daily in each ear.
3. You can refill this prescription two more times.
4. She needs to have surgery soon.
5. He went to see the doctor a month ago for his annual check-up.

Listen to each conversation and choose the best answer to the question you hear. Use the Answer Sheet.

6.
   A: Do you have the name of a good doctor?
   B: Are you looking for a family doctor?
   A: Yes. A good family doctor.
   B: Well, you could try my doctor, but I don't know if he is taking new patients.
   C: *What is the man looking for?*

7.
   A: How's your sister?
   B: Pretty good. The operation went well, but she's still in the hospital.
   A: When will she get out?
   B: Probably in three or four days.
   A: That's good.
   C: *What happened to her sister?*

8.

Doctor: Are you taking any medications?

Patient: No, I'm not.

Doctor: I think you should start taking some calcium supplements for your bones.

Patient: Calcium supplements?

Doctor: Yes.

Patient: Do I need a prescription?

Doctor: No, you can get them at any pharmacy or drugstore.

C: What does the doctor want her to get?

9.

A: Do you want some milk for you coffee?

B: No, thanks. I drink it black.

A: Really? I can't drink black coffee. It gives me a stomachache.

B: Well, I'm allergic to milk, so I have to drink it black.

C: What is she allergic to?

10.

A: Are you getting enough exercise?

B: Yes, I think so. I play basketball with my friends every week.

A: How often?

B: I try to play two or three times a week.

A: That's pretty good.

C: How often does he exercise?

UNIT FOUR
Lesson 3.
2. Listen and Take Notes, page 62
Listen to the 2 conversations. Write the missing information in the chart below.

1.

A: Good morning. How can I help you today?

B: Well, I'm interested in looking at a minivan.

A: Are you interested in a new model or one of our pre-owned cars?

B: Do you have any pre-owned minivans available?

A: Well, there's this one. It's a beauty and it's been well maintained. In fact, it just had a tune-up. And it's a great price. Just $18,500.

B: How many miles are on it?

A: Just 25,000.

B: What year is it?

A: It's last year's model, so it has great features.

B: But 25,000 miles seems like a lot for a car that's only a year old.

A: But it has automatic doors and a DVD player, all for this great price. And, it gets 22 miles to the gallon.

B: But don't you think that's a lot to pay for a car with so many miles on it?

A: Maybe we can knock a thousand off that price.

Listen again and check your answers.

2.

A: How can I help you today, sir?

B: I'd like to take a look at your pickup trucks.

A: Very good. What kind of pickup are you interested in?

B: I'm not sure exactly. I need one that can seat 5 people and it needs to be heavy enough to pull a horse trailer.

A: New or pre-owned?

B: New, I think.

A: Well, here are our new models. We just got them in. This model has been selling very well. In fact, we only have these two left.

B: What kind of gas mileage do these trucks get?

A: Pretty good for a pickup truck. About 12 miles per gallon.

B: Wow. I'm sorry, but that doesn't seem like very good gas mileage to me. I'd be spending all my money on gas.

A: Well, we have this smaller pickup truck here. It gets about 18 miles to the gallon, but it is pre-owned, not new.

B: That sounds more like it. Is it still big enough to pull a trailer?

A: Yes sir. And it's a great price, just $15,500 for a 2001.

B: I'm afraid that's a little older than I wanted. How many miles are on it?

A: That's the great thing about this vehicle. Only 32,000.

B: That's not bad. What kind of condition is it in?

A: It just came in yesterday, so I'll have to check. But, we'll make sure it has a complete tune-up before we sell it. Also, it comes with a great service warranty.

B: Can I take it for a test drive?

A: Sure. Let me get the keys.

Listen again and check your answers.

Lesson 7.
1. Listening Review, page 70
Listen to the questions and choose the best answer. Use the Answer Sheet.

1. What kind of gas mileage does that car get?
2. What year is your car?
3. How many miles does the truck have on it?
4. What is the period of coverage?
5. What isn't covered under the warranty?

Listen to the conversations and choose the best response. Use the Answer Sheet.

6. A: Can I help you?
   B: Yes, I'd like to return this cell phone.
   A: Okay. What's wrong with it?

7. A: How can I help you?
   B: I'd like to complete an application for a loan.
   A: What kind of a loan?
   B: It's for school.

8. A: Hi. I'm interested in a new car.
   B: Great. What are you looking for?
   A: Something small and with good gas mileage.
   B: Okay. Do you want to lease or buy?

Listen to the conversations and choose the best answer. Use the Answer Sheet.

9. A: I'd like to buy this bedroom furniture.
   B: Sure. How do you want to pay for it?
   A: I think I need to finance it.
   B: Okay. Let's look at some options.
   C: How does the customer want to pay for the furniture?

10. A: I'd like to return this coffeemaker.
    B: Sure. What's wrong with it?
    A: It leaks.
    B: Do you want to exchange it or get a refund?
    A: I'd like a refund, please.
    B: Okay. I just need your receipt.
    C: What does he want to do?

UNIT FIVE
Lesson 3.
2. Listen and Take Notes, page 80
1. Listen to conversation #1 and identify the person's injury.

Employer: How's your eye?
Sylvia: It's much better. Thank you.
Employer: Can you tell me what you got in your eye?
Sylvia: It was some paint.
Employer: Paint? How did that happen?
Sylvia: Well, I got some paint on my hand and then I rubbed my eye.

Employer: Did you have your safety glasses on?
Sylvia: Uhm, no I didn't.
Employer: But why not? You know it's a rule here.
Sylvia: I know I should wear them, but the glasses I have are all scratched. I can't see very well with them.
Employer: Then you need to ask your supervisor for a new pair.
Sylvia: Yes, you're right. I will.
Listen again for the cause of the injury.

2. Listen to conversation #2 and identify the person's injury.

Employer: I just heard that you got hurt this morning. What happened?
Sandra: I burned my hand.
Employer: You burned your hand? How did you do that?
Sandra: I slipped on something on the kitchen floor.
Employer: You slipped?
Sandra: Yeah. And then I grabbed the stove as I fell, and my hand hit the hot grill.
Employer: Ouch.
Sandra: Yeah.
Employer: Is it a serious burn?
Sandra: It's not so bad. I should be able to come back to work tomorrow.
Listen again for the cause of the injury.

3. Listen to conversation #3 and identify the person's injury.

Boss: Is anything broken?
Joe: No. Nothing is broken.
Boss: That's good.
Joe: Yeah, the doctor said it looks like I tore a muscle in my shoulder.
Boss: Is it serious?
Joe: She said it depends. It should heal if I don't use it for a while. I fell pretty hard.
Boss: I know. I heard you were about fifteen feet in the air when you fell. Where were you?
Joe: I was working on that scaffolding over there.
Boss: Were you wearing a safety harness?
Joe: No, I wasn't.
Boss: Oh, no. You know that standard safety equipment is required when you're on scaffolding.
Joe: I know. I just didn't think I'd be up there very long.
Boss: Even if you're only up there for a few minutes, you should make sure you're safe.
Joe: I know. Believe me, it won't happen again.
Boss: Well, you're lucky you didn't get hurt worse.
Listen again for the cause of the injury.

Lesson 7.
1. Listening Review, page 88
Listen to each conversation and the announcement. Choose the best answer to the question you hear. Use the Answer Sheet.

1.

A: Bob, could I talk to you for a minute?

B: Sure. What's on your mind?

A: I'm concerned about the lighting in the back office.

B: What's the problem?

A: Well, I just don't think it's bright enough. A couple of people have already complained of headaches.

B: That's not good. Let's go take a look.

C: *What's wrong with the back office?*

2.

A: What happened to Jack yesterday?

B: He fell off the scaffolding.

A: No way! That's terrible. Is he okay?

B: Yeah, he's lucky. He has a sore back but that's all.

C: *What did Jack hurt?*

3.

A: How did Sheila get hurt?

B: She got something in her eye.

A: How did she do that?

B: I don't know.

A: Was she wearing her safety glasses?

B: No, I don't think so.

A: Oh boy. Her supervisor isn't going to be happy about that.

C: *What wasn't Sheila wearing?*

4.

A: Is Joe here today?

B: You haven't heard?

A: Heard what?

B: He had to go to the hospital.

A: What for?

B: No one knows yet, but he was feeling terrible pains in his chest.

A: That doesn't sound good.

C: *Why did Joe go to the hospital?*

5.

A: Hi, Sonia. It's Bill.

B: Hi, Bill. Aren't you supposed to be at work?

A: I am at work, but they just evacuated the building.

B: You're kidding. Is everything okay?

A: Yes. It's nothing serious. There was a fire in a trashcan in the basement, but they wanted us to leave the building anyway.

C: *Why did they evacuate the building?*

6.

A: This is not a drill. Please leave the building by the nearest exit. Wait outside for further instructions. This is not a drill. Please leave the building by the nearest exit. Wait outside for further instructions.

B: *Where should you wait?*

7.

A: What happened in Fremont today?

B: The radio said there was a small explosion.

A: Really? What caused it?

B: I don't know, but no one got hurt.

C: *What was the emergency in Fremont?*

8.

A: What did you do to your finger?

B: It's nothing serious. I just burned it on the stove.

A: Did you put anything on it?

B: No, I just put it in some cold water for awhile.

C: *What did she do for her finger?*

9.

A: Do you feel any pain in your leg?

B: No. It feels okay.

A: What about your arm?

B: Yes, it's very sore.

C: *What hurts?*

10.

A: I heard someone got hurt during the first shift.

B: Yes, it was Paul down in the mixing room.

A: What happened?

B: I think there was a chemical spill and he passed out.

A: He lost consciousness?

B: Yes. Can you believe it? But they got him to the hospital right away.

C: *What happened to Paul while he was working?*

UNIT SIX
Lesson 3.
2. Listen and Take Notes, page 98
1. Listen to conversation #1 and identify the problem.

Officer: Good afternoon. Did you know that you were exceeding the speed limit, sir?

Driver: No. I'm sorry, officer.

Officer: You were doing 55 in a 35 mile per hour zone. Let me see your license and registration please.

Driver: Of course. Here they are. I'm really sorry.

Officer: I'm going to have to give you a ticket.

Driver: Okay. Will I have to go to court?

Officer: Not if you pay within two weeks.

Driver: How do I pay it?

Officer: You can pay with a credit card online by going to the county's website, or you can send a check to the address on the ticket. If you want to contest the ticket, you should go to court on the date on the ticket.

Driver: I don't want to contest it. I think I'll just pay it. Thanks for the information. I'll take care of it right away.

Officer: And please watch your speed.

Driver: I will. I'll be very careful.

Listen again and write the consequence.

2. Listen to conversation #2 and identify the problems.

Woman: Yes, officer, what can I do for you?

Officer: Ma'am, there's been a complaint about your party.

Woman: Oh, I'm sorry. What's the complaint?

Officer: Your music is a little loud and your guests are parked on the lawn.

Woman: We'll turn the music down right now. Is it illegal to park on the lawn?

Officer: Yes, ma'am. It's against a city ordinance.

Woman: I am so sorry. I didn't know that. We'll have our guests move their cars.

Officer: Thank you. Please remind them not to block any of your neighbors' driveways.

Woman: Of course. Thank you. Again, we're sorry if we caused a problem.

Listen again and write the consequences.

3. Listen to conversation #3 and identify the problems.

Park officer: Excuse me, do you have a fishing license?

Man: No, I'm sorry I don't. Do I need one?

Park officer: Yes. You need a license to fish in any state park.

Man: Oh, I'm sorry. I didn't know that. Where can I get one?

Park officer: You can apply online or go to the Department of Fish and Game. There's an office on Central Avenue.

Man: Okay, I think I'll look online.

Park officer: You're also not allowed to drink alcoholic beverages in the park. I'm going to have to ask you to put those drinks away.

Man: But I'm not driving, my friend is.

Park officer: No alcoholic beverages. It's a park rule. By the way, all the park rules are posted on green signs. I have a copy of the rules here. You should read them and make sure you understand them.

Man: Thank you. We're new to the area, and I guess we didn't read the sign very carefully.

Listen again and write the consequences.

Lesson 6.
Window on Pronunciation
Reductions with *To,* page 105
B. Listen to the sentences. Write the missing words. Use the correct spelling.

1. I *have to* renew my driver's license this month.
2. She's *going to* take the dog for a walk.
3. Sam *has to* pay a parking ticket.
4. They *used to* live in New Mexico.
5. You *ought to* slow down. You're *going to* get a ticket.
6. We *want to* buy a house in that area.

Lesson 7.
1. Listening Review, page 106
Listen to the sentences. Choose the best answer. Use the Answer Sheet.

1. You need a fishing license to fish anywhere in the state of Washington if you are over 16 years of age.
2. Your driver's license is valid for 5 years from the date it was issued.
3. You can go to traffic court if you wish to contest a ticket.
4. Swimming is not permitted in posted areas.
5. Consumption of alcoholic beverages is not permitted in the park.
6. Letting your dog off the leash is prohibited within city limits.

Listen to the conversations. Choose the best answer to complete them. Use the Answer Sheet.

7. A: Did you know you were over the speed limit?
   B: No, I'm sorry. I didn't realize that.
   A: I need to see your license and registration.
   B: Of course. Here you go.
   A: Please watch your speed from now on.

8. A: Excuse me, but we've gotten a complaint about your party.
   B: I'm sorry officer. What's the problem?
   A: The music is too loud. Your neighbor complained about the noise.

9. A: Excuse me, can I see your fishing license?
   B: Oh, I'm sorry I don't have a license. Do I need one?
   A: Yes. You need a license to fish in any state park.
   B: Oh, I apologize. I didn't realize that.
   A: I won't give you a ticket this time, but you can't fish until you get a license.

10. A: Good afternoon. The consumption of alcoholic beverages is not permitted in the park.

B: I'm sorry, but I don't understand.

A: You can't drink alcohol in the park. I'm going to have to ask you to put those drinks away.

B: I apologize. We didn't realize there was a rule about alcohol.

A: Here's a list of all the park rules. You should read them and make sure you understand them. If you don't, just ask me or one of the other park rangers.

UNIT SEVEN
Lesson 3.
2. Listen and Take Notes, page 116
1. Listen to conversation #1 and look at the job description. Write 2 questions the applicant asks.

A: Hello, may I speak to Katie Ruiz?

B: Yes, this is Katie Ruiz.

A: This is Carl Vang in the Human Resources department at WBNC. We received your application for the writer position, and I wanted to schedule you for an interview.

B: That's great. When would it be?

A: Well, we're looking at Thursday and Friday of next week. What time would be good for you?

B: How about 10 o'clock on Friday?

A: Okay. I've got you down for 10 on Friday. Please bring some writing samples.

B: Of course. May I ask you a question?

A: Sure.

B: Are you hiring for just one writer position?

A: We're actually interviewing for two writers at this time.

B: Okay. And when is the start date?

A: We'd like both writers to start on April 1, but there's flexibility.

B: Sounds great. I'll see you on Friday at 10.

A: Very good. We'll see you then.
Listen again and write the answers.

2. Listen to conversation #2 and look at the job description. Write 2 questions the applicant asks.

A: Hello, my name is Michelle Lambert. I'm calling about the ad for a production assistant. May I ask you a few questions?

B: Sure. What did you want to know?

A: What kinds of qualifications are needed?

B: The successful applicant needs a college degree and excellent writing and computer skills. You can find a description of the duties and qualifications online.

A: Thank you. What should I do if I'm interested in applying?

B: Send your résumé and a cover letter.

A: Thank you very much.
Listen again and write the answers.

3. Listen to conversation #3 and look at the job description. Write 2 questions the applicant asks.

A: Hello. I'm calling about the account assistant position you advertised.

B: Yes. How can I help you?

A: I think it's something I might be interested in, but the ad doesn't mention any benefits. Could you tell me if you provide health and dental insurance?

B: We provide a very comprehensive health plan, and if you're interested you can enroll in a dental plan.

A: Great. And how much vacation leave do you offer?

B: Two weeks of vacation leave for the first year. After that, you earn an additional two days of leave for every year you work.

A: Okay. Thanks for the information. What should I do to apply?

B: You can send a résumé and cover letter in the mail or submit them electronically through the company website.
Listen again and write the answers.

Lesson 7.
1. Listening Review, page 124
Listen to the sentences. Choose the best answer. Use the Answer Sheet.

1. What is the salary?
2. What shifts are available?
3. What do I need to do to apply?
4. What benefits do you offer?
5. What experience do I need?
6. I'm interested in the weather reporter position.
7. Do you provide tuition reimbursement?
8. How many weeks of vacation do you provide?

Listen to the conversations. Choose the best response. Use the Answer Sheet.

9. A: I'd like to schedule you for an interview.

B: That's great. When would it be?

A: Well, we're looking at Thursday and Friday of next week. What time would be good for you?

10. A: How can I help you?

B: I'd like to ask a few questions about the position in the paper.

A: Sure. Which position?

UNIT EIGHT
Lesson 3.
2. Listen for Specific Information, page 134

1. Listen to conversation #1. Who does each thing below—the man or the woman? Write M (the man) or W (the woman).

Car Dealer: Can I help you?

Customer: Yes, I hope so. I'm looking for a used car—something small.

Car Dealer: Any price range?

Customer: Yeah, I can't spend more than $8,000.

Car Dealer: Eight thousand. Hmm. Did you see the little silver one out front?

Customer: No, I didn't.

Car Dealer: Well, let me show it to you. This beauty sells for $7,500. You can't beat the price. It's in great condition. It's an automatic and it has air conditioning. So what do you think of it?

Customer: What's the mileage?

Car Dealer: I think it has 120,000 miles, but let me check. Yep, it's 122,345 miles.

Customer: I was really hoping to find something with fewer miles.

Car Dealer: But it's in very good condition and it was mostly highway miles.

Customer: Are you sure of that?

Car Dealer: No, but I can check.

Customer: That's alright. Could I possibly drive the car for a day to test it?

Car Dealer: Oh, I'm sorry we can't do that. But you can take it for a short test drive.

Customer: No, that's Ok.

Car Dealer: Can I show you anything else?

Customer: No, I guess not. But thanks for your help.

2. Listen to conversation #2. Who does each thing below—the man or the woman? Write M (the man) or W (the woman).

Sylvia: Dan, you're really good at this.

Dan: Thank you, Sylvia. Would you like to see how I do it?

Sylvia: That would be wonderful.

Dan: Watch and I'll do it. Do you see what I'm doing?

Sylvia: I think so. Let me try it.

Dan: Okay. That's good. Why don't you straighten it out a little bit.

Sylvia: Like this?

Dan: Yes, that's good.

Sylvia: Is this right?

Dan: Yes. That's it.

Sylvia: Well, thanks, Dan. That was very helpful.

Dan: You're welcome, Sylvia. Anytime.

3. Listen to conversation #3. Who does each thing below—the man or the woman? Write M (the man) or W (the woman).

Supervisor: Have a seat, Joe.

Joe: Thanks.

Supervisor: I want to talk to you about your work.

Joe: Yes?

Supervisor: Joe, tell me, do you like working here?

Joe: Yes, very much.

Supervisor: Well, Joe, this is difficult to say, but I'm a little disappointed with your work.

Joe: Disappointed?

Supervisor: Yes.

Joe: Could you tell me why? I mean, what am I doing wrong?

Supervisor: Well, the main thing is that you need to work faster.

Joe: Faster? But I'm working as fast as I can.

Supervisor: Well, Joe, I've noticed that your work area is very disorganized and you often have trouble finding things.

Joe: True.

Supervisor: So, I was wondering – maybe you could work faster if you got a little more organized. I can show you a few things that might help.

Joe: That would be great.

Supervisor: And one other thing.

Joe: Yes.

Supervisor: I've noticed that you're on the phone a lot.

Joe: Well, yes, sometimes.

Supervisor: You know that you should only make personal calls during your break.

Joe: Yes, of course. I'll be more careful.

Supervisor: Okay. Joe. Now let's go look at your work area.

Lesson 7.
1. Listening Review, page 142
Listen to the questions and choose the best response. Use the Answer Sheet.

1. Could you give me a hand?
2. Could I interrupt for a minute?
3. That's a nice photograph of you.
4. Why don't we stay home today?
5. Can I help you?
6. Can you give me some feedback on my work?

Listen to each conversation and choose the best answer to the question you hear. Use the Answer Sheet.

7.

A: Hi, Nancy. Have you seen Ann today?

B: No, I haven't, but I'll probably see her this afternoon.

A: Really?

B: Yes. She's in my afternoon class.

A: Look, do you think you could give her this book?

B: Sure. I'd be happy to. What should I tell her?

A: Nothing. She'll know it's from me.

B: Okay.

A: Thanks. That's a big help.

C: *What did the man ask Nancy to do?*

8.

A: Do you know how to do this?

B: No, I don't.

A: Hmm. Why don't we ask the teacher for help?

B: But there are some instructions here. Why don't we read them and see if we can figure it out?

A: Okay.

C: *What does the woman suggest doing?*

9.

A: Can you give me a hand for a minute?

B: Sure. What do you want me to do?

A: Can you just hold the door open for a minute?

B: Sure. Can I close the door now?

A: Yes and thanks.

B: No problem.

C: *What does the man ask the woman for?*

10.

A: Excuse me, Gerry?

B: Yes, who is it?

A: It's Sandra. Can I bother you for a minute?

B: Sure. What can I do for you?

A: I was just wondering if you could give me some feedback on this report.

B: Sure, I'd be happy to. How soon do you need it?

A: Any time this week would be fine.

B: Okay.

A: Thanks.

B: You're welcome.

C: *What does the woman ask the man for?*

PRE-UNIT

UNIT ONE

accomplish
advance
athlete
bilingual
communicate
continuing education
cut back (on)
debt
delegate
down payment
expenses
financial aid
fluent
focus
in charge of
long-term goal
monitor
mortgage
online job bank
organize
outstanding
parent-teacher conference
pay off
pet
practice
prioritize
PTA meeting
reduce
routine
short-term goal
support system
tutor
volunteer
waste time

UNIT 2

air conditioning
assumption
attached
available
colonial
Congress
consent
default
disturb
due
duplex
electricity

elevator
expire
furnish
immediately
in full
lease
let
location
maintain
maintenance
manner
neighborhood
orderly
parking
premises
prior to
property
ranch
remodeled
removal
security deposit
a specific time
sublease
term (of an agreement)
utilities
washer and dryer hookup

UNIT 3

abuse (n)
addiction
alcohol
allergic
allergy
anonymous
appendectomy
asthma
bleed
blood transfusion
bloody
caffeine
calcium
cancer
cancerous
check-up
cholesterol
crisis
currently
diabetes
diabetic
diet
disease

domestic violence
drug abuse
firm
health care provider
hotline
illicit
infect
infection
life-threatening
narcotic
on average
penicillin
physical exam
post-op
prenatal
prescribe
prescription
progress
prohibit
provide
rash
routine
supplement (n)
supplement (v)
surgery
surgical
well baby visit
yet

UNIT 4

account balance
allowance
bounce a check
bounced check
cashiers check
check card
checking account
credit card
damage
debit card
defect
direct deposit
financing
gas mileage
generic
gross pay
insufficient
insufficient funds
interest
loan
make a claim

mileage
net pay
no money down
online banking
original receipt
overdraft
period (of coverage)
pre-owned
refund
replacement
service charge
statement
status objects
valid
void
warranty
workmanship

UNIT 5

assembly area
chemical
civil
consciousness
construction
disturbance
elevate
evacuate
explode
flammable
flood
fracture
hazard
heat exhaustion
injure
injury
intense
minor
pressure
rob
shock
site
slippery
spill
submerge
surface
toxic
witness

UNIT 6

alcoholic beverages
consumption
courthouse
demonstrate
exceed
firearm
fish
graffiti
helmet
illegal
leash
license
litter
loiter
look down on
migrant
pad
posted area
prohibited
protest
registration
speed bump
strike
struggle
traffic stop
traffic ticket
trash
trespass
unfair
union
vandalism
weapon

UNIT 7

account assistant
account executive
basic skills course
benefits
camera operator
chronological résumé
co-pay
deductions
dental insurance
field
flex time
functional résumé

gap
gym
health care
medical insurance
meteorologist
news anchor
omit
on-site child care
paid family leave
preventive care
production assistant
sound engineer
telecommute
traffic reporter
tuition reimbursement

UNIT 8

anticipate
appreciate
appreciation
capacity
challenge
compliment
criticism
criticize
effectively
emotional
express
expression
feedback
get to the point
inefficient
influence
interrupt
interruption
mental
offer
regret
request
retain
reward
suggestion
understanding
wander

A

abuse *n.* the action of treating someone else very badly and hurting them, especially by hitting them: *Child abuse is a serious problem.* **(3)**

accomplish *v.* to complete something important: *What do you hope to accomplish while you are on the committee?* **(1)**

account assistant *n.* someone whose job is to help an account executive sell time for advertisements to different companies: *Account assistants should have experience in sales.* **(7)**

account balance *n.* the amount of money you have in your bank account: *I try to keep my account balance above $300.* **(4)**

account executive *n.* someone whose job is to sell time for advertisements to different companies: *Mr. Kimball is an account executive at the local TV station.* **(7)**

addiction *n.* a strong need that someone's body has to take a drug or other substance: *Lora is getting treatment for her addiction to drugs.* **(3)**

advance *v.* to help something progress and become more successful: *Roger is studying hard to advance his career.* **(1)**

air conditioning *n.* a system for making the air in a building or vehicle colder: *The apartment doesn't have air conditioning, but it's not too hot here in the summer.* **(2)**

alcohol *n.* a substance in wine, beer, and other drinks that affects people's behavior: *I don't like to get drunk, so I don't drink alcohol.* **(3)**

alcoholic beverage *n.* a drink that has alcohol in it: *You can buy alcoholic beverages like wine or beer at the supermarket in some states.* **(6)**

allergic *adj.* having an allergy: *Anna is allergic to peanuts.* **(3)**

allergy *n.* a medical condition in which you become sick, you sneeze, your skin becomes red, you have problems breathing, etc. when you eat, touch, or breathe a particular thing: *My allergies are really bad in the spring.* **(3)**

allowance *n.* a regular amount of money that is given to children by their parents for a period of time: *Parents can help children understand money by giving them an allowance.* **(4)**

anonymous *adj.* without a name, unknown: *Police got an anonymous call about the robbers.* **(3)**

anticipate *v.* to guess what is going to happen: *Try to anticipate how your listeners will react to what you say.* **(8)**

appendectomy *n.* a medical operation in which the appendix is taken out: *My father was in the hospital for only one day after his appendectomy.* **(3)**

appreciate *v.* to feel thankful for something: *I really appreciate your help writing this letter.* **(8)**

appreciation *n.* thankfulness: *I want to express my appreciation for all your help.* **(8)**

assembly area *n.* a place where people gather together or meet: *Do you know the assembly area for our building in case of a fire?* **(5)**

assumption *n.* a belief that something is true without knowing for sure: *Be careful when you make assumptions because you can often be wrong.* **(2)**

asthma *n.* a medical condition that makes it difficult to breathe: *She can't run very far because she has asthma.* **(3)**

athlete *n.* someone who plays sports well: *Jose is a very good athlete—he plays soccer and baseball.* **(1)**

attached *adj.* connected: *The house has an attached garage.* **(2)**

available *adj.* ready to be rented or used: *When will the apartment be available?* **(2)**

B

basic skills course *n.* a class that teaches basic skills, such English or math: *The company offers basic skills courses to all immigrant employees.* **(7)**

benefits *n.* extra things like health insurance and vacation time that your employer gives you in addition to your pay: *I'm looking for a job with good health benefits and at least two weeks' vacation a year.* **(7)**

bilingual *adj.* able to speak two languages: *Wei is bilingual— she speaks Chinese and English.* **(1)**

bleed *v.* to have blood flow from your body: *You're bleeding. Did you cut yourself?* **(3)**

blood transfusion *n.* a medical procedure by which blood from one person is put in another person's body: *She needed a blood transfusion during the surgery.* **(3)**

bloody *adj.* covered with blood: *His arm was cut and his shirt was bloody.* **(3)**

bounced check *n.* a check that the bank will not pay because you have no funds to cover it in your account: *The bank charges $25 for every bounced check, so check your balance before you write a check.* **(4)**

C

caffeine *n.* a substance in coffee, tea, and cola (and some foods) that makes people feel more awake and alert: *If I drink too much caffeine in the evening, I can't sleep.* **(3)**

calcium *n.* a mineral found in bones and teeth: *Calcium is found in milk, cheese, sardines, and vegetables such as broccoli.* **(3)**

camera operator *n.* someone whose job is to control a camera and make the video for use on a TV show: *TV reporters always take at least one camera operator with them.* **(7)**

cancer *n.* a serious disease that is caused by cells in your body growing in an uncontrolled way: *Liver cancer is very difficult to treat.* **(3)**

cancerous *adj.* causing cancer: *Scientists say that the chemical is cancerous.* **(3)**

capacity *n.* ability to do something: *Children have a great capacity to learn.* **(8)**

cashier's check *n.* a check that is written by a bank that promises to pay the amount that is on it: *The landlord wants a cashier's check for the deposit, not a personal check.* **(4)**

challenge *n.* something difficult that you must deal with by using a lot of skill and energy: *Learning English is a challenge, but it is worth the effort.* **(8)**

check card *n.* a small plastic card which takes money directly from your bank account that you can use at an ATM or in a store to buy things: *Using a check card is easier than writing checks.* **(4)**

checking account *n.* an arrangement you have with a bank in which they keep your money for you and you can write checks for that money: *I always pay my rent from my checking account.* **(4)**

check-up *n.* a visit to a doctor so he or she can check to see if you have any medical problems: *I take the kids for a check-up once a year.* **(3)**

chemical *n.* a substance used in chemistry: *A lot of food we buy contains artificial chemicals to make it last longer.* **(5)**

cholesterol *n.* a substance in your food and blood that can cause heart disease if you have too much of it: *Barack has to take medicine to reduce his cholesterol.* **(3)**

chronological résumé *n.* a list of your work history that is organized according to when you did the work, starting with your most recent job and going backward: *Most employers like chronological résumés because they are easy to read.* **(7)**

civil *adj.* relating to the people who live in a country: *Civil rights are the rights we have as citizens of this country.* **(5)**

colonial *n.* a style of house with a pointed roof and columns in front: *The Singhs bought a three-bedroom colonial on State Street.* **(2)**

communicate *v.* to express your ideas to someone else: *It's important to be able to communicate well if you want a good job.* **(1)**

compliment *v.* to say something nice to someone about what they have done, how they look, etc.: *When someone does something well, you should compliment them.* **(8)**

Congress *n.* the part of the U.S. government that makes laws: *Congress will vote on the proposal next week.* **(1)**

consciousness *n.* the state of being awake and knowing what is happening around you: *Jim hit his head and lost consciousness for a few minutes.* **(5)**

consent *n.* formal agreement: *You can't paint the apartment without the written consent of your landlord.* **(2)**

construction *n.* the work or activity of building buildings: *Rafael is strong because he works in construction.* **(5)**

consumption *n.* the action of eating or drinking something: *The consumption of alcohol is not allowed in the park.* **(6)**

continuing education *n.* courses for adults that allow them to study a wide variety of subjects: *There are some good continuing education classes at the local community college.* **(1)**

co-pay *n.* the amount of money you have to pay for medical treatment in addition to what your insurance company pays: *I have a $25 co-pay for doctors visits and a $10 co-pay for prescription drugs.* **(7)**

courthouse *n.* a building that has a courtroom in it for legal trials: *Reporters waited outside the courthouse during the trial.* **(6)**

credit card *n.* a small plastic card that lets you buy things now and pay for them later: *I use my credit card so I don't have to carry around so much cash.* **(4)**

crisis *n.* a very dangerous situation with lots of problems: *Whenever I have a crisis, I call my best friend.* **(3)**

criticism *n.* something you say to show that you think someone or something is bad or wrong: *Mr. Smith's criticism of my work really upset me.* **(8)**

criticize *v.* to say that you think something is bad or wrong about someone or something: *My boss always criticizes my work, but he never compliments me.* **(8)**

currently *adv.* at the present time: *Laszlo currently works downtown, but he's changing jobs soon.* **(3)**

cut back on *phr. v.* to reduce the amount of something: *I'm cutting back on snacks to try to lose weight.* **(1)**

D

damage *n.* physical harm that is done to something: *The table only had a little damage—just a few scratches.* **(4)**

debit card *n.* a small plastic card which takes money directly from your bank account that you can use at an ATM or in a store to buy things: *You can pay with a credit card or a debit card.* **(4)**

debt *n.* an amount of money that is owed: *The only debt I have is the loan for my car.* **(1)**

deductions *n.* the amount of money that is subtracted from your gross pay before you get your paycheck: *Deductions include health insurance and taxes.* **(7)**

default *v.* to fail to pay an amount of money that you owe on time: *If you default on the loan, the bank can take your car.* **(2)**

defect *n.* a mistake, flaw, or fault in a product: *Check the clothing carefully before you buy it to make sure there are no defects.* **(4)**

delegate *v.* to ask other people to do part of a job for you: *A good manager has to learn to delegate.* **(1)**

demonstrate *v.* to carry signs, march in parades, shout, etc. in public in order to protest against something you disagree with: *Thousands of people marched to demonstrate against the war.* **(6)**

dental insurance *n.* an arrangement you have with an insurance company in which you pay money to it regularly and it agrees to pay all or a large part of the bills for treatment for your teeth: *We have good dental insurance at work, so I go to the dentist twice a year.* **(7)**

diabetes *n.* a serious disease that makes your body unable to control the amount of sugar in your blood: *Overweight people are more likely to get diabetes.* **(3)**

diabetic *adj.* having diabetes: *Matt is diabetic, so he's not supposed to eat a lot of sugar.* **(3)**

diet *n.* the type of foods that you usually eat: *A healthy diet includes a lot of fruits and vegetables.* **(3)**

direct deposit *n.* a method of payment that deposits money, usually your paycheck, electronically into your account: *At work we can either get direct deposit or a paper check for our paycheck.* **(4)**

disease *n.* a medical condition that makes you sick or that makes part of your body stop working correctly: *In the past, children got diseases like chicken pox, mumps, and measles more often than they do today.* **(3)**

disturb *v.* to interrupt a peaceful situation and annoy people: *Someone reported Reggie to the police for disturbing the peace.* **(2)**

disturbance *n.* a situation in which people behave in a noisy, violent way in public: *Police were called to deal with the disturbance.* **(5)**

domestic violence *n.* violent behavior between members of the same family, especially a husband and wife: *Her husband was arrested for domestic violence.* **(3)**

down payment *n.* the first amount of money that you give for something when you are going to pay the rest later: *Many people give a down payment of at least 10% when they buy a house.* **(1)**

drug abuse *n.* the use of illegal drugs or other drugs in a way that they are not supposed to be used: *His drug abuse kept him from getting a job.* **(3)**

due *adj.* needing to be paid at a specific time: *The rent is due on the first of the month.* **(2)**

duplex *n.* a building that contains two homes: *We live in a duplex with my wife's parents.* **(2)**

E

effectively *adv.* in a way that produces the result you want: *The letter asking for money was written very effectively.* **(8)**

electricity *n.* the service of electric power used to run electrical machines: *The landlord pays for water, but you have to pay for electricity and gas.* **(2)**

elevate *v.* to put something in a higher position: *Elevate your feet to reduce swelling.* **(5)**

elevator *n.* a machine that is like a small room that moves people from one floor of a building to another: *We can use the stairs, or we can take the elevator if you're tired.* **(2)**

emotional *adj.* feeling strong emotions that affect the way you think and behave: *He gets emotional when he talks about his mother's death.* **(8)**

evacuate *v.* to make all the people in a place leave, usually because danger is coming: *They evacuated the town because of the flood.* **(5)**

exceed *v.* to go higher than or beyond a limit: *Alberto was exceeding the speed limit by 10 miles per hour.* **(6)**

expenses *n.* money that you have to spend regularly on something: *My expenses are so high, maybe I should get another job.* **(1)**

expire *v.* to end and stop being legal or valid: *The contract expires on January 1.* **(2)**

explode *v.* to blow up: *The machine exploded and broke all the windows in the garage.* **(5)**

express *v.* to show or tell your feelings or ideas to someone else: *How can I know what you think if you don't express your opinions?* **(8)**

expression *n.* the action of showing or telling your feelings or ideas to someone else: *We were surprised by her sudden expression of anger.* **(8)**

F

feedback *n.* comments about how good or bad someone or something is that are intended to help make improvements: *Could you give me some feedback on the report I wrote?* **(8)**

KEY: *adj.* = adjective; *adv.* = adverb; *n.* = noun; *n. phr.* = noun phrase; *phr. v.* = phrasal verb; *v.* = verb; *v. phr.* = verb phrase

field *n.* a subject that you study or type of work that you do: *What field would you like to work in?* **(7)**

financial aid *n.* help to pay for education: *Sheila got financial aid while she was going to college.* **(1)**

financing *n.* money that you borrow for a particular purpose: *We got the financing for our car from the credit union.* **(4)**

firearm *n.* a gun: *Keep all firearms away from children.* **(6)**

firm *adj.* definite and not likely to change your mind: *Our boss is firm, but fair.* **(3)**

fish *v.* to try to catch fish in a river, a lake, or the ocean: *My brother likes to fish in the river near our house.* **(6)**

flammable *adj.* able or easy to burn: *Gas is extremely flammable.* **(5)**

flex time *n.* a system that allows workers to decide which hours they work each day as long as they work the required number of hours: *With flex time, I come in at 10 in the morning and stay until 7 or 8.* **(7)**

flood *n.* a large amount of water that covers land that is usually dry: *The flood ruined hundreds of houses in the area.* (5)

fluent *adj.* spoken or written well in a smooth way, with no difficulties: *After a couple of years, Tran could speak fluent English.* **(1)**

focus *v.* to center your attention on something: *I can't focus with all the noise and activity in my apartment.* **(1)**

fracture *v.* to break a bone: *Anya fractured her right arm when she fell.* **(5)**

functional résumé *n.* a list of someone's work history that is organized according to the type of work you have done, not by when you have done it: *A functional résumé is good if you have gaps in your work history.* **(7)**

furnish *v.* to provide the furniture for a house or apartment: *It will take a lot of money to furnish the whole house.* **(2)**

G

gap *n.* an empty space between two things, or a period of time in your work history during which you were not working and for which you do not have a good explanation: *The interviewer asked about the gaps in Lara's work history.* **(7)**

gas mileage *n.* the number of miles a vehicle can travel using a gallon of gasoline: *Gas mileage is usually higher in smaller cars.* **(4)**

generic *adj.* relating to a general product rather than a specific brand: *Generic food is a lot cheaper than name brand food.* **(4)**

get to the point *v. phr.* to stop talking or writing about unimportant things and start talking or writing about what is most important: *I don't have much time, so could you get to the point?* **(8)**

graffiti *n.* words or pictures that are illegally drawn or painted on walls in public places: *There was graffiti all over the bathroom wall.* **(6)**

gross pay *n.* the total amount of money that you earn before anything such as taxes has been taken out: *Manny's gross pay is $1,100 every two weeks.* **(4)**

gym *n.* a building or club where you can go to exercise: *Jiao goes to the gym three times a week.* **(7)**

H

hazard *n.* something that can hurt you: *The weak railing on the stairway is a real hazard.* **(5)**

health care *n.* medical services that take care of your health: *As we get older, good health care becomes more important.* **(7)**

health care provider *n.* a doctor or organization that you go to for medical treatment: *Have you been to your health care provider in the past year?* **(3)**

heat exhaustion *n.* a medical condition in which your body gets too hot and stops working properly: *On hot days, rest often and drink lots of water to avoid heat exhaustion.* **(5)**

helmet *n.* a hard hat that you wear to protect your head: *The kids always wear helmets when they ride their bikes.* **(6)**

hotline *n.* a telephone number that you can call for information, usually in an emergency situation: *Call the AIDS hotline to find out about getting an HIV test.* **(3)**

I

illegal *adj.* not legal: *Selling alcohol to anyone under 21 is illegal.* **(6)**

illicit *adj.* illegal: *If the police catch you with illicit drugs, you will be arrested.* **(3)**

immediately *adj.* right away; as soon as possible: *I'm looking for an apartment that I can move into immediately.* **(2)**

in charge of *prep. phr.* responsible for a process, organization, or person: *Ted, you're in charge of sending out the invitations.* **(1)**

in full *prep. phr.* completely: *You have to pay the first month's rent in full before moving in.* **(2)**

inefficient *adj.* not working in a good, efficient way: *Electric heaters are an inefficient and expensive way to heat a whole house.* **(8)**

infect *v.* to give someone a sickness or disease: *My daughter got the flu first, and within a week her whole class was infected by it.* **(3)**

infection *n.* a disease that is caused by bacteria or viruses: *The doctor gave him ear drops for his ear infection.* **(3)**

influence *v.* to have an effect on the way someone thinks or feels: *The advertisements may influence people to buy the product.* **(8)**

injure *v.* to hurt someone and cause damage to his or her body: *How did you injure your leg?* **(5)**

injury *n.* damage to your body: *Ivan got several injuries in the accident, including a broken leg.* **(5)**

insufficient *adj.* not enough: *The money will be insufficient to finish the work.* **(4)**

insufficient funds *n.* a situation in which your bank account does not have enough money to cover a check or withdrawal: *The check was returned because of insufficient funds.* **(4)**

intense *adj.* extremely strong: *She gets intense headaches and has to stop working.* **(5)**

interest *n.* money that the bank pays you to use your money, or money that you pay when you borrow money: *Interest on our savings accounts is currently 2.5%.* **(4)**

interrupt *v.* to say or do something that stops someone when they are saying or doing something else: *I'm sorry to interrupt you, but you have a phone call.* **(8)**

interruption *n.* something you say or do that stops someone when they are saying or doing something else: *I can't get any work done with all these interruptions.* **(8)**

L

lease *v.* to rent a piece of property or vehicle: *The company will lease us office space for six months.* **(2)**

leash *n.* a long piece of leather, chain, plastic, or other material that you attach to a dog's collar and hold onto when you take the dog in public: *All dogs in the park must be on leashes.* **(6)**

let *v.* to rent a piece of property: *The landlord agreed to let the property to us for one year without raising the rent.* **(2)**

license *n.* an official card or piece of paper that says you are allowed to do something: *You need a license to carry a gun in this state.* **(6)**

life-threatening *adj.* likely to make you very sick or kill you: *It's just a cold—not a life-threatening illness.* **(3)**

litter *v.* to throw paper or other garbage on the ground instead of a garbage container: *Hey, pick that up! Don't litter.* **(6)**

loan *n.* money that you borrow: *We had to take out a loan to buy the house.* **(4)**

location *n.* the place where something is: *The house is in an excellent location, near the school and the shopping center.* **(2)**

loiter *v.* to stand and wait in a public place without a clear reason: *The owner doesn't want anyone to loiter outside his store.* **(6)**

long-term goal *n.* something that you want to achieve after a long time: *His long-term goal is to buy a house, but first he's going to get a second job.* **(1)**

look down on *phr. v.* to consider someone else not as good or important as you: *I think he looks down on me because I didn't go to college.* **(6)**

M

maintain *v.* to keep a building or vehicle in good condition: *Renters must agree to maintain their apartments in good condition.* **(2)**

maintenance *n.* a service to keep things in good condition and fix things that break in a building or vehicle: *The apartment building offers 24-hour maintenance.* **(2)**

make a claim *v. phr.* to report a problem to a company and ask them to fix it, replace something, or give you your money back: *You can make a claim by calling this number: 1-800-555-7290.* **(4)**

manner *n.* a way of doing something: *We want to make the repairs in the cheapest manner possible.* **(2)**

medical insurance *n.* an arrangement you have with an insurance company in which you pay money to it regularly and it agrees to pay all or a large part of your health care: *Health care in the U.S. is expensive, so it's important to have good medical insurance.* **(7)**

mental *adj.* relating to your mind and your ability to think: *We'll need to use all our mental abilities to solve this problem.* **(8)**

meteorologist *n.* someone whose job is to tell what the weather will be like: *The meteorologist says it will rain tomorrow.* **(7)**

migrant *adj.* traveling from one place to another, usually looking for work: *Migrant workers pick oranges in Florida in the winter.* **(6)**

mileage *n.* the number of miles a vehicle has traveled: *What's the mileage on your car?* **(4)**

minor *adj.* small and not very important: *You can treat minor burns at home with ice and cold water.* **(5)**

monitor *v.* to observe a situation carefully and keep close watch over its progress: *The doctors have to monitor her daily—she's very sick.* **(1)**

mortgage *n.* a loan used to pay for a house: *We got our mortgage from First Bank.* **(1)**

KEY: *adj.* = adjective; *adv.* = adverb; *n.* = noun; *n. phr.* = noun phrase; *phr. v.* = phrasal verb; *v.* = verb; *v. phr.* = verb phrase

N

narcotic *n.* a drug that takes away pain and changes your mood and behavior: *Andrew was arrested for selling narcotics on the street.* (3)

neighborhood *n.* the area around a particular place: *We live in a nice neighborhood with lots of trees and pretty houses.* (2)

net pay *n.* the amount of money that you take home from your pay after everything such as taxes has been taken out: *I didn't know my net pay would be so much less than my gross pay.* (4)

news anchor *n.* the main person who presents the news on a TV news program: *Robert Lange has been a news anchor at the station for 20 years.* (7)

no money down *n. phr.* used to describe a situation in which you are going to pay for something over a period of time, but do not have to pay any money at the beginning: *Buy a refrigerator on credit with no money down!* (4)

O

offer *v.* to give someone the choice of accepting something if they want it: *Hyung is always quick to offer help.* (8)

omit *v.* to leave something or someone out: *You can omit your date of birth if you don't want to reveal your age.* (7)

on average *prep. phr.* used for saying how often something usually happens, although it may happen more or less often at different times: *I talk to my sister on average twice a week.* (3)

online banking *n.* a service that lets you look at your account balance, transfer money, and pay bills on the Internet: *I prefer online banking because I can do it 24 hours a day from home.* (4)

online job bank *n.* a list of available jobs that you can find on the Internet: *Check the online job bank to see if there are any interesting jobs.* (1)

on-site child care *n.* a service for taking care of workers' children which is in the same place that the parents work: *On-site child care is very convenient for me—now I just take my two-year-old to work with me.* (7)

orderly *adj.* correctly and neatly organized: *Please line up in an orderly fashion.* (2)

organize *v.* to put things in order: *Can you help me organize these papers?* (1)

original receipt *n.* the piece of paper that a store gives you when you buy something to prove that you have paid for it: *You have to have the original receipt to return products.* (4)

outstanding *adj.* extremely good: *Sook is an outstanding singer.* (1)

overdraft *n.* a situation in which you write a check for more money than you have in your account: *For a fee, the bank will transfer funds from another account to cover any overdrafts.* (4)

P

pad *n.* a thick piece of soft cloth, plastic, or other substance that you attach to your body to protect it: *Don't you wear knee pads when you go skating?* (6)

paid family leave *n.* time off from work to take care of a sick family member that your employer pays for: *Sheryl took a week of paid family leave when her mother was sick.* (7)

parent-teacher conference *n.* an individual meeting between parents and a teacher to talk about how their children are doing in school: *We have parent-teacher conferences about four times a year.* (1)

parking *n.* a specific place to park your car: *Does the apartment come with parking?* (2)

pay off *phr. v.* to completely pay back an amount of money that is owed: *It took us three years to pay off the loan.* (1)

penicillin *n.* a medicine used to treat certain infections or diseases: *Penicillin can cure many diseases.* (4)

period of coverage *n.* the amount of time that something is valid: *The period of coverage for the warranty is two years.* (4)

pet *n.* a dog, cat, or other animal that you keep at your home: *My mother wouldn't let us have a pet when we were kids.* (1)

physical exam *n.* an occasion on which a doctor checks your body to make sure there are no problems: *Students need a physical exam before they can play on school teams.* (3)

posted area *n.* an area where a sign says you can do or not do a particular thing: *Smoking is allowed in posted areas only.* (6)

post-op *adj.* happening after an operation: *The post-op visits will continue for a year.* (3)

practice *v.* to do something again and again in order to become good at it: *Mei can't come with us—she has to practice the piano.* (1)

premises *n.* the rooms, buildings, or land that are used by a particular person, organization, or business: *If you do not follow the rules, you will be asked to leave the premises.* (2)

prenatal *adj.* happening before a baby is born: *Marla is pregnant—she just had her first prenatal check-up.* (3)

pre-owned *adj.* owned by someone else before: *Pre-owned cars can be a good deal if they're in good condition.* (4)

prescribe *v.* to write an order for medicine: *The doctor prescribed a pain reliever for my headaches.* (3)

prescription *n.* medicine that you can only get when a doctor officially says you can get it, or the paper the doctor gives you that allows you to get this medicine: *Can you go to the store and get this prescription for me?* **(3)**

pressure *n.* force pushing on someone or something: *Pressure will help stop the bleeding.* **(5)**

preventive care *n.* medical treatment and visits to the doctor that you do in order to keep from getting sick, not because you already are sick: *Regular preventive care can help you avoid major health problems in the future.* **(7)**

prior to *prep.* before: *You have to inform the landlord 30 days prior to moving out.* **(2)**

prioritize *v.* to deal with things in their order of importance: *If you don't have enough time for everything, you need to prioritize.* **(1)**

production assistant *n.* someone whose job is to help a producer prepare a show for TV: *Production assistants are responsible for scheduling guests for the show.* **(7)**

progress *n.* the process of getting better or getting closer to finishing something: *The doctor wants to check my progress since the surgery.* **(3)**

prohibit *v.* to officially say that someone cannot do something: *Laws prohibit taking guns on airplanes.* **(3)**

prohibited *adj.* officially not allowed: *Do not try to bring prohibited items, such as weapons, into the courthouse.* **(6)**

property *n.* land or buildings that someone owns: *The Kims just bought some property downtown.* **(2)**

protest *v.* to formally complain about something you disagree with: *Students are protesting the rise in fees.* **(6)**

provide *v.* to supply or give something to someone: *Who will provide the money for the project?* **(3)**

PTA meeting *n.* a meeting for teachers and parents of students in a school to decide how things should be done in the school: *My wife and I go to PTA meetings once a month.* **(1)**

R

ranch *n.* a style of house that has only one floor: *We're looking for a ranch so my mother won't have to go up and down stairs.* **(2)**

rash *n.* red, rough, itchy skin: *Chen gets a rash when he eats strawberries.* **(3)**

reduce *v.* to lower the amount of something: *You should really reduce the amount of fat that you eat.* **(1)**

refund *n.* money that is returned to you when you return something you have bought to a store: *You can return the product within thirty days for a full refund.* **(4)**

registration *n.* a piece of paper that shows that you have given information about your car to the government and paid for the right to drive it: *The police officer asked to see my driver's license and vehicle registration.* **(6)**

regret *n.* a feeling of being sorry that you have done something or you have not done something: *I live my life without regrets—I learn something even from my mistakes.* **(8)**

remodeled *adj.* changed and improved in structure or appearance: *The kitchen is completely remodeled.* **(2)**

removal *n.* the action of removing something or taking it away: *Garbage removal happens every Tuesday.* **(2)**

replacement *n.* a new product that you get to replace another one that is broken or that you do not like: *If the lamp doesn't work, we'll be happy to give you a replacement.* **(4)**

request *n.* an asking for something: *Could I make a small request for some help on the project?* **(8)**

retain *v.* to keep and remember: *We only retain a small amount of what we hear each day.* **(8)**

reward *n.* something good that happens as a result of something else: *Helping other people may not always earn you money, but it brings its own rewards.* **(8)**

rob *v.* to illegally take something from a person or a place: *The Nevskys' house was robbed while they were on vacation.* **(5)**

routine *adj.* usual and not happening for a special reason: *The doctor found the cancer during a routine medical exam.* **(3)**

routine *n.* a regular, repeated way of doing things: *Drinking a cup of coffee is an important part of my morning routine.* **(1)**

S

security deposit *n.* an amount of money that you give to a landlord before moving into a house or apartment that you get back when you leave if you have not caused any damage: *The security deposit is equal to two months' rent.* **(2)**

service charge *n.* a fee that you have to pay for a particular service: *There is a monthly service charge for all checking accounts at this bank.* **(4)**

shock *n.* a sudden burst of electricity that goes through your body: *Unplug the lamp before you change the light bulb, or you might get a shock.* **(5)**

short-term goal *n.* something that you want to achieve after a short time: *My short-term goal is to get a second job so I can buy a house.* **(1)**

site *n.* a place where something happens: *There's a big construction site next to the building where I work.* **(5)**

slippery *adj.* smooth, wet, or covered in a slick substance such as oil, and therefore difficult to stand on or hold: *The janitor just mopped the floor so it's still slippery.* **(5)**

KEY: *adj.* = adjective; *adv.* = adverb; *n.* = noun; *n. phr.* = noun phrase; *phr. v.* = phrasal verb; *v.* = verb; *v. phr.* = verb phrase

sound engineer *n.* someone whose job is to make sure the sound in a recording is good: *Sound engineers wear headphones when they work.* **(7)**

a specific time *n.* a definite time that something will happen: *The electric company gave me a specific time of 3:30 to come and fix my heater.* **(2)**

speed bump *n.* a long, thin raised area on a street or in a parking lot that is there to make drivers drive more slowly: *People were always speeding on our street until they put in speed bumps.* **(6)**

spill *n.* something that has accidentally poured out of its container: *The oil spill took months to clean up.* **(5)**

statement *n.* a list of everything that has happened with your bank account during a particular period of time: *According to my bank statement, the check was cashed on August 12.* **(4)**

status object *n.* something that you have that makes people think you have a higher social position: *Teenagers want to have status objects like name brand sneakers.* **(4)**

strike *n.* an occasion on which a group of workers agree to not work to protest their pay or work conditions: *Workers went on strike when they were not given a raise.* **(6)**

struggle *n.* the action of trying very hard to do something difficult over a period of time: *The struggle for equal rights in the U.S. continues today.* **(6)**

sublease *v.* to rent a piece of property that you are already renting to someone else: *Did you sublease your apartment while you were traveling?* **(2)**

submerge *v.* to put something under water: *Submerge the entire burn in cold water.* **(5)**

suggestion *n.* an idea that you give to someone to think about: *I have a suggestion. Why don't we have a picnic?* **(8)**

supplement *n.* a pill or special food that you take or eat in addition to your normal food to make sure your body gets all that you need of a particular substance: *Many women take supplements while they are pregnant.* **(3)**

supplement *v.* to take pills or eat special food in addition to your normal food: *I supplement my diet with vitamins and protein shakes.* **(3)**

support system *n.* friends and family that support you: *I don't think I could work and take care of the kids without my support system.* **(1)**

surface *n.* the top layer or outside part of something: *Put the box down on any flat surface.* **(5)**

surgery *n.* a medical operation in which a doctor cuts into someone's body: *Ilya had surgery to remove his appendix.* **(3)**

surgical *adj.* relating to surgery: *Doctors are going to use a surgical procedure instead of drugs.* **(3)**

T

telecommute *v.* to work at home and send your work into your company by e-mail, phone, or fax: *I like telecommuting because now I don't have to drive during rush hour.* **(7)**

term *n.* the period of time for which an agreement is in effect: *The term of the contract is one year.* **(2)**

toxic *adj.* poisonous and able to make people sick or kill them: *There are toxic chemicals in the lake that are killing the fish.* **(5)**

traffic reporter *n.* someone who goes up in a helicopter to report on where there are accidents or delays on the road: *Traffic reporters do most of their work during rush hour.* **(7)**

traffic stop *n.* an occasion on which a police officer stops a driver for doing something wrong while he or she is driving: *Officer Lane made three traffic stops for speeding today.* **(6)**

trash *n.* something that we throw away: *There was a lot of trash after the party.* **(6)**

traffic ticket *n.* a piece of paper from a police officer that says you have to pay money for doing something wrong while you are driving: *If you don't pay your traffic tickets, you might lose your driver's license.* **(6)**

trespass *v.* to go on someone else's property without his or her permission: *If you trespass on our property, we will call the police.* **(6)**

tuition reimbursement *n.* an arrangement by which your employer pays you back money that you spend to take classes: *The tuition reimbursement from my company made it possible for me to get my degree.* **(7)**

tutor *n.* a teacher who helps students one-on-one: *I hired a tutor to help me with my math class.* **(1)**

U

understanding *n.* the state of knowing what someone or something means: *It's good to ask your listener a few questions to check for understanding.* **(8)**

unfair *adj.* not fair or equal: *It's unfair that some people have to pay a fee and others don't.* **(6)**

union *n.* an organization for workers that tries to get them better pay and work conditions: *The union represents all hourly workers at the company.* **(6)**

utilities *n.* basic services such as water, electricity, and gas that you use in your home: *Utilities are included in the rent.* **(2)**

V

valid *adj.* legally accepted: *My driver's license is valid for six more months.* **(4)**

vandalism *n.* the action of damaging other people's property on purpose: *The vandalism is such a problem in this neighborhood that people are afraid to leave their cars on the street.* **(6)**

void a*dj.* a contract or agreement that is no longer valid or legal: *The repairs Angelo made to the radio himself made the warranty void.* **(4)**

volunteer *v.* to do work without pay: *Sally volunteers at the library on Saturdays.* **(1)**

W

wander *v.* to stop concentrating on one thing and start thinking about something else: *When I'm bored, my mind wanders.* **(8)**

warranty *n.* a written promise from a company to fix or replace a product within a specific period after you have bought it: *The computer comes with a one-year warranty.* **(4)**

washer/dryer hookup *n.* a connection in a house or apartment for a clothes washer or dryer: *The washer/dryer hookup is in the downstairs bathroom.* **(2)**

waste time *v.* phr. to use time poorly: *He wastes a lot of time watching TV.* **(1)**

weapon *n.* an object that you can use to hurt other people or damage things: *He used the baseball bat as a weapon to beat back the other man.* **(6)**

well baby visit *n.* a routine check-up at the doctor's for babies and children: *My doctor recommended 6 well baby visits during my baby's first year of life.* **(3)**

witness *n.* someone who sees something happen: *Were there any witnesses to the accident?* **(5)**

workmanship *n.* the skill or work that goes into making a product: *The workmanship on the furniture is fine, but some of the wood is bad.* **(4)**

Y

yet *adv.* before now; used in negative sentences and in questions: *Have you finished your homework yet?* **(3)**

KEY: *adj.* = adjective; *adv.* = adverb; *n.* = noun; *n. phr.* = noun phrase; *phr. v.* = phrasal verb; *v.* = verb; *v. phr.* = verb phrase

SKILLS INDEX

Skills index

A Sample W-2 Form: Wage and Tax Statement

Form W-4 (2004)

Purpose. Complete Form W-4 so that your employer can withhold the correct Federal income tax from your pay. Because your tax situation may change, you may want to refigure your withholding each year.

Exemption from withholding. If you are exempt, complete only lines 1, 2, 3, 4, and 7 and sign the form to validate it. Your exemption for 2004 expires February 16, 2005. See **Pub. 505**, Tax Withholding and Estimated Tax.

Note: *You cannot claim exemption from withholding if: (a) your income exceeds $800 and includes more than $250 of unearned income (e.g., interest and dividends) and (b) another person can claim you as a dependent on their tax return.*

Basic instructions. If you are not exempt, complete the **Personal Allowances Worksheet** below. The worksheets on page 2 adjust your withholding allowances based on itemized

deductions, certain credits, adjustments to income, or two-earner/two-job situations. Complete all worksheets that apply. **However, you may claim fewer (or zero) allowances.**

Head of household. Generally, you may claim head of household filing status on your tax return only if you are unmarried and pay more than 50% of the costs of keeping up a home for yourself and your dependent(s) or other qualifying individuals. See line **E** below.

Tax credits. You can take projected tax credits into account in figuring your allowable number of withholding allowances. Credits for child or dependent care expenses and the child tax credit may be claimed using the **Personal Allowances Worksheet** below. See **Pub. 919**, How Do I Adjust My Tax Withholding? for information on converting your other credits into withholding allowances.

Nonwage income. If you have a large amount of nonwage income, such as interest or dividends, consider making estimated tax payments using

Form 1040-ES, Estimated Tax for Individuals. Otherwise, you may owe additional tax.

Two earners/two jobs. If you have a working spouse or more than one job, figure the total number of allowances you are entitled to claim on all jobs using worksheets from only one Form W-4. Your withholding usually will be most accurate when all allowances are claimed on the Form W-4 for the highest paying job and zero allowances are claimed on the others.

Nonresident alien. If you are a nonresident alien, see the **Instructions for Form 8233** before completing this Form W-4.

Check your withholding. After your Form W-4 takes effect, use Pub. 919 to see how the dollar amount you are having withheld compares to your projected total tax for 2004. See Pub. 919, especially if your earnings exceed $125,000 (Single) or $175,000 (Married).

Recent name change? If your name on line 1 differs from that shown on your social security card, call 1-800-772-1213 to initiate a name change and obtain a social security card showing your correct name.

Personal Allowances Worksheet (Keep for your records.)

A Enter "1" for **yourself** if no one else can claim you as a dependent . . . . **A** _____

B Enter "1" if: { • You are single and have only one job; or
• You are married, have only one job, and your spouse does not work; or
• Your wages from a second job or your spouse's wages (or the total of both) are $1,000 or less. } . . **B** _____

C Enter "1" for your **spouse**. But, you may choose to enter "-0-" if you are married and have either a working spouse or more than one job. (Entering "-0-" may help you avoid having too little tax withheld.) . . . . **C** _____

D Enter number of **dependents** (other than your spouse or yourself) you will claim on your tax return . . . **D** _____

E Enter "1" if you will file as **head of household** on your tax return (see conditions under **Head of household** above) . **E** _____

F Enter "1" if you have at least $1,500 of **child or dependent care expenses** for which you plan to claim a credit . . **F** _____

   (**Note:** *Do **not** include child support payments. See **Pub. 503**, Child and Dependent Care Expenses, for details.*)

G **Child Tax Credit** (including additional child tax credit):

   • If your total income will be less than $52,000 ($77,000 if married), enter "2" for each eligible child.

   • If your total income will be between $52,000 and $84,000 ($77,000 and $119,000 if married), enter "1" for each eligible child plus "1" **additional** if you have four or more eligible children. **G** _____

H Add lines A through G and enter total here. **Note:** *This may be different from the number of exemptions you claim on your tax return.* ▶ **H** _____

For accuracy, complete all worksheets that apply. { • If you plan to **itemize or claim adjustments to income** and want to reduce your withholding, see the **Deductions and Adjustments Worksheet** on page 2.
• If you have **more than one job** or are **married and you and your spouse both work** and the combined earnings from all jobs exceed $35,000 ($25,000 if married) see the **Two-Earner/Two-Job Worksheet** on page 2 to avoid having too little tax withheld.
• If **neither** of the above situations applies, **stop here** and enter the number from line H on line 5 of Form W-4 below. }

- - - - - - - - - - - - **Cut here and give Form W-4 to your employer. Keep the top part for your records.** - - - - - - - - - - - -

Form **W-4**	**Employee's Withholding Allowance Certificate**	OMB No. 1545-0010
Department of the Treasury Internal Revenue Service	▶ Your employer must send a copy of this form to the IRS if: (a) you claim more than 10 allowances or (b) you claim "Exempt" and your wages are normally more than $200 per week.	2004

1 Type or print your first name and middle initial	Last name	**2** Your social security number

Home address (number and street or rural route)	**3** ☐ Single ☐ Married ☐ Married, but withhold at higher Single rate. **Note:** *If married, but legally separated, or spouse is a nonresident alien, check the "Single" box.*
City or town, state, and ZIP code	**4** If your last name differs from that shown on your social security card, check here. You must call 1-800-772-1213 for a new card. ▶ ☐

5 Total number of allowances you are claiming (from line **H** above **or** from the applicable worksheet on page 2) . . . **5**

6 Additional amount, if any, you want withheld from each paycheck . . . . **6** $

7 I claim exemption from withholding for 2004, and I certify that I meet **both** of the following conditions for exemption:
• Last year I had a right to a refund of **all** Federal income tax withheld because I had **no** tax liability **and**
• This year I expect a refund of **all** Federal income tax withheld because I expect to have **no** tax liability.
   If you meet both conditions, write "Exempt" here . . . . ▶ **7**

Under penalties of perjury, I certify that I am entitled to the number of withholding allowances claimed on this certificate, or I am entitled to claim exempt status.
Employee's signature
(Form is not valid unless you sign it.) ▶ _____ Date ▶ _____

8 Employer's name and address (Employer: Complete lines 8 and 10 only if sending to the IRS.)	**9** Office code (optional)	**10** Employer identification number (EIN)

For Privacy Act and Paperwork Reduction Act Notice, see page 2.   Cat. No. 10220Q   Form **W-4** (2004)

B Sample W-4 Form: Federal Income Tax

a Control number	22222		OMB No. 1545-0008		
b Employer identification number			**1** Wages, tips, other compensation	**2** Federal income tax withheld	
c Employer's name, address, and ZIP code			**3** Social security wages	**4** Social security tax withheld	
			5 Medicare wages and tips	**6** Medicare tax withheld	
			7 Social security tips	**8** Allocated tips	
d Employee's social security number			**9** Advance EIC payment	**10** Dependent care benefits	
e Employee's first name and initial Last name			**11** Nonqualified plans	**12a** Code	
			13 Statutory employee Retirement plan Third-party sick pay	**12b** Code	
			14 Other	**12c** Code	
				12d Code	
f Employee's address and ZIP code					

15 State Employer's state ID number	**16** State wages, tips, etc.	**17** State income tax	**18** Local wages, tips, etc.	**19** Local income tax	**20** Locality name

Form **W-2** Wage and Tax Statement

2004

Department of the Treasury—Internal Revenue Service

Copy 1—For State, City, or Local Tax Department

C Sample Pay Stub

FASHION SOLUTIONS, INC.

Employee: Julia Smith

Check Number: **56499543**

Social Security Number: 123-45-6789

Pay Period Date: 10/01/05 to 10/15/05

Check Date: 10/20/05

EARNINGS	**Rate**	**Hours**	**This Period**	**Year-to-Date**
	15.00	80	1,200.00	22,800.00
GROSS PAY			1,200.00	22,800.00
DEDUCTIONS				
	Federal Income Tax		156.00	2,964.00
	Social Security		132.00	2,508.00
	Medicare		31.20	592.80
	CA Income Tax		36.13	684.47
	CA State Disability Ins.		16.80	319.20
Total Deductions			372.13	7,069.27
NET PAY			827.87	

D Sample Telephone Bill

NORTHEAST TELEPHONE COMPANY

Statement:	05/01/05–06/01/05	Date:	**06/01/05**
Name:	**John and Sylvie Hopkins**	Invoice Number:	**234567890**
Address:	**123 Southtown Rd.**	Member Number:	**23ABC**
	Miami, FL 33101	Billing Period:	**05/01/05–06/01/05**

ACCOUNT SUMMARY

Amount of Last Bill	$24.55
Payment(s) Thank You	$24.55
Balance	$0.00

CURRENT CHARGES

Local Monthly Charges	$36.45
Long Distance Service Charges	$9.93
Total Due by 06/15/05	**$46.38**

Important Information – You are responsible for payment of all charges on your bill. Your "dial tone" may be disconnected if you do not pay your essential charges such as your telephone line, surcharges and fees. If you do not pay for other charges, such as voice mail, wireless, and Internet, those particular services may be disconnected.

Call 1-888-555-3217 for Customer Service

E Sample Work-Related Accident Report

ABC CONSTRUCTION

Accident Report of Workers' Compensation Claim
Complete *all* sections *within* 24 hours of injury or illness *before* claim can be filed.

To be eligible for benefits under the Workers' Compensation Act, ABC Employee Health Services *must* receive *both* this *completed* claim form (P-100) *and* the Physician Selection Form (P-101) by hand delivery or by mail:
- *Deliver* to: ABC Employee Health Services, 1200 East Broad Street, West Hospital, West Wing, First Floor, Room 120
- *Mail* to: ABC Employee Health Services, P. O. Box 980134, Richmond, VA 23298-0134

EMPLOYEE SECTION – Complete, sign and give to supervisor.

☐S ☐W
Name: _____ DOB: _____ ☐M ☐F ☐M ☐D
(last, first, middle) *(Gender)* *(Marital Status)*

SSN: _____ ABC Hire Date: _____ Home Address: _____
(street, city, zip code)

Home Phone: ( ) _____ Department: _____ Dept. P.O. Box #: _____

Work Phone: ( ) _____ ☐Staff ☐Hourly ☐Other Hrs Worked: _____ _____ _____
(Employee Type) *Daily* *Weekly* *Shift*

Job Title: _____ Location Where Injury Occurred: _____
(e.g., Sanger Hall, R. 1-032)

Date of Injury: _____ Time of Injury: _____ AM/PM Day of Week: _____

Describe activity prior to accident *and* type of accident: *(Attach additional sheet if necessary.)*

Cause *and* object of injury *(Describe in detail how and why injury occurred.)*:

Injuries Sustained: _____

Have you filed a WC claim(s) in the past? ☐Yes ☐No If "yes," list date(s): _____

Name(s) of any witness(es): _____

I certify that the information provided above is true and complete. *(May be signed by person acting on employee's behalf.)*

Signature: _____ Date: _____

SUPERVISOR SECTION – Complete, sign and send to EHS. If you do not agree with the employee's report, please contact the ABC WC Office at 555-1533. For assistance in accident investigation/prevention, please contact the ABC Occupational Safety Office at 555-0040.

Was the employee doing something **other** than required duties at the time of the accident? ☐Yes ☐No If "yes," please explain:

When did you **first** learn of this accident? _____

Was the employee given medical treatment? ☐Yes ☐No If "yes," physician's name and address:

Was the place of the accident on ABC premises? ☐Yes ☐No If "no," please explain:

Based on your investigation, what was (were) the cause(s) of the accident? *(Give details and attach additional sheet if necessary.)*

How could this accident have been prevented? *(e.g., wear protective equipment, equipment should have been repaired, procedure changed, etc.)*

What steps were taken to prevent another accident? *(e.g., training provided, etc.)*

Supervisor's Name: _____ P.O. Box #: _____ Work Phone: _____
(please print)

Signature: _____ Date: _____

MEDICAL PERSONNEL SECTION – Complete, sign and forward to WC Office.

Date Seen: _____ Time Seen: _____ AM/PM By Whom? _____

Facility Address: _____

Diagnosis: _____

Was the diagnosis related causally to the accident? ☐Yes ☐No If "yes," please explain:

Lost Time? ☐Yes ☐No If "yes" – dates: _____ Probable Length of Disability: _____

Return to Duty? ☐Yes ☐No If "yes" – dates: _____ Regular Duty ☐ Light Duty ☐

Explain Duty Restrictions: _____

Referral? ☐Yes ☐No If "yes" – where: _____ When: _____

Follow-up? ☐Yes ☐No If "yes" – where: _____ When: _____

Completed by: _____ Date: _____ OSHA Case #: _____

ABC Human Resource Division FORM P-100 Rev 3/03

F Sample Job Application

APPLICATION FOR EMPLOYMENT

PERSONAL INFORMATION:

Date _____   Available Start Date _____

☐ Full Time   ☐ Part Time   ☐ Temporary   Referral Source _____

Name _____   Phone _____

Street Address _____

City/State/Zip _____   SSN _____

EDUCATION:

Schools Attended	# of Years	Year Grad	Degree

EMPLOYMENT/WORK EXPERIENCE:

Start with your present or most recent position. (Attach another sheet of paper for additional work experience.)

Employer	Job Title
Supervisor	Phone
Describe Duties/Responsibilities/Accomplishments	Reason for Leaving
Dates of Employment (Month/Year) From: To:	

Employer	Job Title
Supervisor	Phone
Describe Duties/Responsibilities/Accomplishments	Reason for Leaving
Dates of Employment (Month/Year) From: To:	

BUSINESS REFERENCE:

Please provide contact information for one or more business references. (Attach another sheet of paper for additional references.)

Name _____   Company _____

Position _____   Phone _____

SPECIAL SKILLS:

Describe any skills or qualifications you have for this work.

_____

_____

Map of the United States

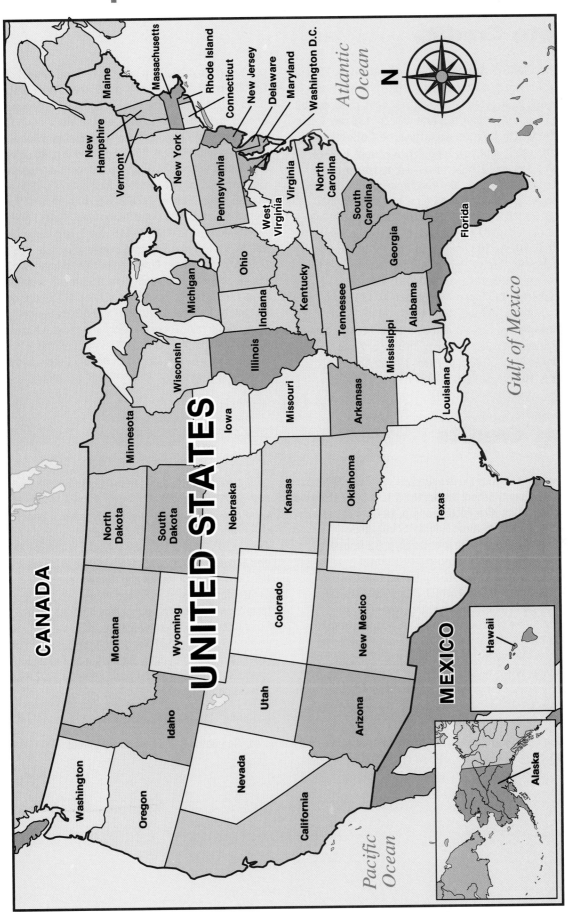

Photo Credits

From the CORBIS Royalty-Free Collection: p. 28 top; **p. 64** top, bottom; **p. 69** top left, right; **p. 73**; **p. 82** middle; **p. 86** far left; **p. 86** second from right, far right; **p. 98**; **p. 103** left; **p. 111**; **p. 114** bottom; **p. 117** middle; **p. 133** row 1, left; **From the Getty Images Royalty-Free Collection: p. 2** row 1, left; row 1, right; row 2, right; **p. 6** bottom; **p. 7** row 1, right; row 2, left; row 2, right; row 3, left; **p. 10** top; **p. 19**; **p. 24**, second from top; **p. 24** second from bottom; bottom; **p. 28** bottom; **p. 38**; **p. 42**; **p. 45** right; **p. 46** top, middle, bottom; **p. 50** top, middle; **p. 55** middle, bottom; **p. 64** middle; **p. 69** bottom left; **p. 82** top, bottom; **p. 85** top, bottom; **p. 91**; **p. 93** left; **p. 102**; **p. 103** right; **p. 114** top; **p. 115** row 2, left; row 2, right; row 1; row 4, left; **p. 117** top, bottom; **p. 119**; **p. 132** top, middle, bottom; **p. 133** row 1, middle; row 1, right; row 2, middle; **p. 135** top; **p. 135** bottom; **p. 136** middle, bottom; **p. 140**; **p. 147** top, bottom **Other Images: p. 2** row 2, left: Gen Nishin / Getty Images; **p. 6** top: Michael Cogliantry / Getty Images; **p. 7** row 1, left: Keith Dannemiller / CORBIS; **p. 7** row 3, right: Jutta Klee / CORBIS ; **p. 10** bottom: Peter Grumann / Getty Images;

p. 11 Homero Acevedo; **p. 24** top: Philippa Lewis; Edifice / CORBIS; **p. 37** Aslam Ahmed; **p. 39** Paul Taylor / Getty Images; **p. 45** left: Michael Keller / CORBIS; **p. 47** Ken Chernus / Getty Images; **p. 50** bottom: Tom & Dee Ann McCarthy / CORBIS; **p. 55** top: David McGlynn / Getty Images; **p. 67** Jose Luis Pelaez, Inc. / CORBIS; **p. 72** Robert Severi; **p. 86** second from left: Patrick Bennett / CORBIS ; **p. 93**, right: Adrian Weinbrecht / Getty Images; **p. 101** top: John Heseltine / CORBIS; **p. 101** bottom: Najlah Feanny / CORBIS; **p. 109** left: Whit Preston / Getty Images; **p. 109** right: Renee Lynn / Getty Images; **p. 110** Mark Peterson / CORBIS; **p. 115** row 3, left: James Levin / Getty Images; **p. 115** row 3, right: David Averbach; **p. 115** row 4, right: Steve McAlister Productions / Getty Images; **p. 127** Dennis Kitchen / Getty Images; **p. 133** row 2, left: Benelux Press / Getty Images; **p. 133** row 2, right: Robert Daly / Getty Images; **p. 133** row 3, left: Jon Riley / Getty Images; **p. 133** row 3, middle: Romilly Lockyer / Getty Images; **p. 133** row 3, right: Jeff Zaruba / Getty Images; **p. 135** middle: Walter Hodges / Getty Images; **p. 136** top: Jason Homa / Getty Images

Text Credits

p. 11 *Excerpt from Kids Explore America's Hispanic Heritage*, by Jefferson County School District No. R-1. © 1992. Used with permission of John Muir Publications. **p. 14** From Saint Paul Pioneer Press (MN), by Amy Lindgren, 1/9/02, Item: 2W70785762132. Used with permission. **p. 32** From U.S. Department of Housing and Urban Development. **p. 37** From *Consumer Hero: Aslam Ahmed*, Canadian Broadcasting Corporation, 1/21/03, (http://www.cbc.ca/consumers/market/files/home/housing_discrimination/aslam.html) Used with permission. **p. 55** Adapted from U.S. Food and Drug Administration, *FDA Consumer* Magazine, (http://www.fda.gov/fdac/default.html) **p. 69** Adapted from Knight Ridder article by Steve Rosen. *The Charlotte Observer* (NC), 4/20/04, **p. 2A**. (www.charlotteobserver.com) Used with

permission. **p. 72** Adapted from "Gold from the Melting Pot" 5/1/98 issue of *The Christian Science Monitor* www.csmonitor.com © 1998 The Christian Science Monitor. Used with permission. **p. 86** Adapted from The American Red Cross. **p. 91** Excerpt from *Are you a Working Teen? What You Should Know about Safety and Health on the Job.* U.S. Department of Health and Human Services, Centers for Disease Control and Prevention (CDC). (http://www.cdc.gov/niosh/adoldoc.html) **p. 101** From Scholastic Action article by Jeannette Del Valle. 10/1/2001, Vol. 25 Issue 3, p. 24. **p. 137** Reprinted from *Silver Threads*, "Speak, Listen, and Learn" by Jinny Hopp, Human Development Specialist, University of Missouri Extension. 9/02. Used with permission from author.

We apologize for any apparent infringement of copyright and if notified, the publisher will be pleased to rectify any errors or omissions at the earliest opportunity.